"Shinshu Roberts leads us into Dōgen's world as she models persistent care in listening to his heart pulsing through the words. Respecting him as a profound Dharma teacher, she fearlessly faces what appears to be impenetrable terrain in the landscape of his words, determined to mine their compassionate wisdom. Her success is our boon, enabling us to commune with Dōgen and the Dharma in our midst."

—PAULA ARAI, author of *Women Living Zen*,
Bringing Zen Home, and *Painting Enlightenment*

"Though it is inspiring, *Meeting the Myriad Things* is not an inspirational book; though it is enormously informative, its purpose is not to inform. With the blend of scholarship, painstaking attention to detail, and compassionate care for the actual condition of contemporary practitioners that characterizes her previous work, here Shinshu Roberts gives us a full and precise commentary to Dōgen's most famous essay, 'Genjokoan,' his most lofty work. This is an important book for anyone who wants to engage in serious Dōgen study."

—NORMAN FISCHER, Soto Zen priest and poet, author of
When You Greet Me I Bow and *Selected Poems 1980-2013*

"Shinshu Roberts brings Dōgen's 'Genjōkōan' into the contemporary spiritual culture. A wonderful book of American Zen for American practitioners."

—SHOHAKU OKUMURA, author of *Realizing Genjokoan:*
The Key to Dogen's Shobogenzo

"A unique treatment of one of the most celebrated works of Sōtō Zen, combining the author's close study of the text with a translation of the earliest Japanese commentary. A major contribution to the English-language literature on Dōgen."

—CARL BIELEFELDT, author of *Dōgen's Manuals of Meditation*

MEETING *the* MYRIAD THINGS

A Zen Practitioner's Guide to Dōgen's Genjōkōan

SHINSHU ROBERTS

Contributions by Shohaku Okumura and Zuiko Redding

SHAMBHALA

Shambhala Publications, Inc.
2129 13th Street
Boulder, Colorado 80302
www.shambhala.com

Cover art: "Fukui Bridge in Echizen Province," by Katsushika Hokusai. Metropolitan Museum of Art, Rogers Fund, 1922.
Cover design: Daniel Urban-Brown

9 8 7 6 5 4 3 2 1

First Edition
Printed in the United States of America

Shambhala Publications makes every effort to print on acid-free, recycled paper. Shambhala Publications is distributed worldwide by Penguin Random House, Inc., and its subsidiaries.

Library of Congress Cataloging-in-Publication Data
Names: Roberts, Shinshu, author. | Okumura, Shohaku, 1948- editor. | Redding, Zuiko Juliette, editor.
Title: Meeting the myriad things: a zen practitioner's guide to Dogen's genjōkōan/ Shinshu Roberts; contributions by Shohaku Okumura and Zuiko Redding.
Description: Boulder, Colorado: Shambhala, [2025] | Includes bibliographical references and index.
Identifiers: LCCN 2024041760 | ISBN 9781645472728 (trade paperback)
Subjects: LCSH: Dōgen, 1200-1253. Shōbo genzō. Genjō kōan. | Sōtōshū—Doctrines.
Classification: LCC BQ9449.D654 R64 2025 | DDC 294.3/444—dc23/eng/20241209
LC record available at https://lccn.loc.gov/2024041760

The authorized representative in the EU for product safety and compliance is eucomply OÜ, Pärnu mnt 139b-14, 11317 Tallinn, Estonia, hello@eucompliancepartner.com.

Contents

Preface v

Acknowledgments ix

Conventions xi

Genjōkōan (Actualization of Reality) translated by Shohaku
    Okumura xiii

Introduction 1

1 "Genjōkōan": The Realized Koan 23

2 Buddhist Study, Reality, and Human Experience 30

3 What Does Realization Look Like? 41

4 Perceptions and Verification 55

5 Dropping Body and Mind 63

6 Looking for the Path of the Authentic Self 74

7 Riding in a Boat 79

8 What Do I Experience as a Particular Self? 84

9 Who Dies, Who Lives? 90

10 Enlightenment: The Long and Short of It 96

11 There's Always Something 106

12 Fish, Birds, and Humans Practice 115

13 Walking the Walk 122

14 Encountering, Practicing, Permeating, and Realizing Each Moment 130

15 Knowing Is Not Knowing 139

16 Intimacy 145

17 The Student-Teacher Relationship 151

18 What Does It All Mean? 157

Appendix 1: Dharma Position: *Jū Hōi* 165

Appendix 2: Practice-Enlightenment or Practice-Verification? 183

Appendix 3: Introduction to *Okikigakishō* (御聴書抄) by Zuiko
    Redding 190

Appendix 4: Translation of *Okikigakishō* "Genjōkōan" by Shohaku
    Okumura 195

Notes 229

Bibliography 263

Credits 269

Index 271

Preface

When I first began studying Zen at San Francisco Zen Center, the liturgy included weekly recitations of "Genjōkōan." Being rather literal minded, parts of the fascicle made no sense to me. I felt stumped by sentences such as "If a bird departs from the sky . . . it immediately dies." At that time, I decided that I might never understand or be able to say anything intelligent about the text. Yet thirty-seven years later, I found myself writing a commentary on "Genjōkōan." What changed? In the interim, I had fallen in love with Dōgen's teachings, and in 2020 my students requested that I teach "Genjōkōan," which required me to go back and revisit the text.

The beauty of teaching is that we must study what we teach and figure out how to present the material in a way that is helpful for students. Hopefully the process leads to a deeper understanding. In my case, it did, and the teaching notes for that course served as the basis for this book. My thanks and appreciation to all the students at Ocean Gate Zen Center for giving me the opportunity to reacquaint myself with "Genjōkōan."

Another motivation for writing this book was my exposure to a copy of Shohaku Okumura's translation of a medieval Japanese commentary on "Genjōkōan" by two of Dōgen's students: Zen Masters Senne and Kyōgō. Their commentary is part of a larger work, the *Okikigakishō* (*Transcribed Comments and Notes*)—hereafter, the *Goshō*. This book includes a copy of Okumura's translation of the "Genjōkōan" *Goshō* commentary, edited by Rev. Zuiko Redding. To the best of my knowledge, this commentary has never

| v

been published in English. I am excited about being able to offer Okumura's translation of Senne and Kyōgō's commentary on "Genjōkōan."

To be able to read a commentary by two of Dōgen's students is an amazing gift to us—a rare opportunity for English readers to access the thoughts of practitioners who experienced Dōgen's teachings directly. Furthermore, when I read commentaries on "Genjōkōan" by Japanese Zen teachers, it is clear to me that they have used the *Goshō* as a guide for their understanding. Now we can read it as well. I hope in the future that more of Senne and Kyōgō's commentary, which covers all the fascicles in the seventy-five-chapter Shōbōgenzō, will become available in English.

I do not recall exactly how I came to have a copy of Okumura's draft of this text. He had been living at San Francisco Zen Center's city temple from 1999 to 2003, and it must have been during that time that I acquired a copy. When I later asked Okumura about the history of his translation of the *Goshō*, he wrote me an email saying that he first translated this text in the mid-1990s while teaching at the Minnesota Zen Meditation Center in Minneapolis. When he subsequently moved to San Francisco in 1997, he began a study group with some San Francisco Zen Center priests and presented a workshop on the *Goshō*. A copy of Okumura's translation was given out at the workshop. From this event, I eventually received a copy.

I am indebted to Okumura Roshi for permission to reprint his translation of the *Goshō*, as well as for his generosity in helping all American Zen students to understand Dōgen's teaching. Okumura has been a major translator, interpreter, and teacher of Dōgen for students in the United States, in addition to his work spreading the wisdom of his teacher, the twentieth-century Japanese Zen Master Kōshō Uchiyama Roshi.

When I asked Shohaku Okumura if I could include his draft of the text in my commentary, he said, "Yes, but you have to edit the text." Since my ability to edit this text would have been limited to making some grammatic changes, the task was beyond my skillset. I asked my colleague and friend Rev. Zuiko Redding—a Zen teacher, founder of the Cedar Rapids Zen Center, Dōgen scholar, and student of medieval Japanese—if she would do the editing. She agreed. I want to express my deepest gratitude to Zuiko for not only taking on this task but also writing the introduction to Okumura's "Genjōkōan" *Goshō* commentary translation. Sadly, Zuiko passed away in April 2024, as this book was being edited.

Over the years, the English "Genjōkōan" commentarial texts have mainly fallen into three major categories: (1) translations of Japanese commentaries, or commentaries by Japanese priests who have immigrated to the United States; (2) comparisons with a sundry of philosophies such as Western psychology or Chinese Daoism; and (3) scholarly articles that include commentaries on a line or paragraph of the text.

Perhaps because modern translations of Shōbōgenzō are divided into paragraphs, most commentaries examine each paragraph individually. Dōgen did not, however, write in paragraphs—his texts are continuous, without breaks. Because Dōgen's train of thought was uninterrupted by paragraph breaks, I pay particular attention to the transitions from one paragraph to another.

When looking at the structural transitions in "Genjōkōan," I asked myself, "What question is Dōgen addressing?" and "Why does he make certain transitions from one idea to another?" In my study of this text, as both a teacher and student, there were leaps of logic between sections that initially did not make sense to me.

For example, in translation, one paragraph ends with "It is clear that all things have no [fixed] self," followed immediately in the next paragraph with "Firewood becomes ash. Ash cannot become firewood again." Most commentaries address the meaning of the two paragraphs separately. Knowing that there is in fact no paragraph break between these sentences in the original text, I wanted to consider the two sentences as one continuous thought and explore Dōgen's logic as he transitioned from one sentence to the next.

In this case, Dōgen is explaining how it is that we experience the self as singular and separate by using the examples of firewood and ash as stand-ins for the self. I believe Dōgen was answering the question, "If there is no existing self, then what is it that we experience as the self?"

I am also interested in exploring other questions and misunderstandings Dōgen was trying to answer and clarify for his readers in "Genjōkōan" because I have found that contemporary Zen students encounter the very same problems.

While writing this book, I posted a handwritten note on my computer screen to remind me of my writing goal.

- How does one paragraph flow into the next?
- What did Senne and Kyōgō say in their commentary, and did it need further clarification?
- What did Dōgen say in other parts of Shōbōgenzō or other writings that will clarify his teaching in "Genjōkōan"?
- How does this teaching apply to our practice and life?

Although I do not read or speak Japanese, I have included the kanji for many of Dōgen's concepts relating to practice. Without the generosity of Dr. Carl Bielefeldt, who gave me access to the Sōtō Zen Text Project's Shōbōgenzō, which has both the Japanese characters and English translation, I could not have confidently cross-referenced words and terms used by Dōgen. Dr. Paula Arai, who is fluent in Japanese, also helped me with difficult passages and characters.

Because "Genjōkōan" is one of Dōgen's most-commented on fascicles, there is much commentarial work available in English. Such commentaries help inform our practice of the Dharma, and they serve as a continuous dialogue, thus providing ongoing insights into Dōgen's understanding of Buddhist teachings. It is my hope that this book will join the conversation we have had with ourselves and Dōgen over the centuries. I am deeply grateful that I am part of this never-ending discussion. I hope that you will find my observations on the meaning of "Genjōkōan" and practice helpful in your studies.

Acknowledgments

I would like to acknowledge and thank the Ocean Gate Zen Center students who were the catalyst for my deeper study of "Genjōkōan" for their questions and insights during our work together. Thanks to Rev. Kōun Franz, who was instrumental in bringing this commentary to the attention of Shambhala, and to Matt Zepelin, who was the editor of this book. As mentioned above, my gratitude to Dr. Carl Bielefeldt, who generously allowed me access to a draft of the new translation of Shōbōgenzō by the Sōtōshu's Sōtō Zen Text Project.

Dr. Paula Arai, a Buddhist studies scholar, helped me from time to time to decipher and translate Japanese phrases and words. As expressed in the preface, my deep gratitude to Revs. Shohaku Okumura and Zuiko Redding. Without them, we would not have access to Senne and Kyōgō's insights. A deep *gassho* to David Thompson at the Dōgen Institute, who freely gave me permission to publish the *Goshō* commentary. The Dōgen Institute is the educational department of Okumura Roshi's Sanshin Zen Community, and it is an amazing repository of his translations, commentaries, and talks on Dōgen.

Wisdom Publications gave me permission to use Okumura's translation of "Genjōkōan," which was originally published in *Realizing Genjokoan: The Key to Dogen's Shobogenzo*. Thanks to all the folks at Wisdom who helped facilitate permissions for this translation.

My deepest gratitude to everyone behind the scenes at Shambhala who worked on final edits, cover art, layout, indexing, and all the other careful work that must happen to bring a book to our hands. In particular, I would like to thank editors Matt Zepelin, Peter Schumacher, Dianna Able, and Emily Wichland, who meticulously copyedited my book.

Thank you to Shunryu Suzuki Roshi, who founded my lineage of Sōtō Zen in the United States, and to my late teacher and Honshi, Sojun Weitsman Roshi. Finally, my deepest love and appreciation for the wisdom and support of my partner in Zen and in life, Rev. Daijaku Kinst.

Conventions

Citations and Notes

Citations for the *Treasury of the True Dharma Eye: Dōgen's Shōbōgenzō; An Annotated Translation by the Sōtō Zen Text Project* include a volume number and bracketed numbers—for example, vol. 1, [20:16], referring to volume 1, fascicle 20, paragraph 16. Since the original eight-volume English translation of this edition of Shōbōgenzō is not readily available, I did not want to give page citations. There will be another printing of this text available in 2025 by the University of Hawai'i Press, which will use the same bracket locators.

In the citations, Shōbōgenzō is also given as SBGZ.

Okikigakishō is abbreviated as *Goshō*.

Goshō citations in the footnotes are cited as, for example, *Okikigakishō* "Genjōkōan," followed by the section number in *Goshō* and the name of the commentator, either Senne or Kyōgō.

I have omitted diacritic marks on common spellings, such as nirvana.

Unless noted, all foreign words and characters are Japanese.

Genjōkōan
(Actualization of Reality)

When all dharmas are the Buddha Dharma, there is delusion and realization, practice, life and death, buddhas and living beings.

When the ten thousand dharmas are without [fixed] self, there is no delusion and no realization, no buddhas and no living beings, no birth and no death.

Since the Buddha Way by nature goes beyond [the dichotomy of] abundance and deficiency, there is arising and perishing, delusion and realization, living beings and buddhas.

Therefore flowers fall even though we love them; weeds grow even though we dislike them. Conveying oneself toward all things to carry out practice-enlightenment is delusion. All things coming and carrying out practice-enlightenment through the self is realization. Those who greatly realize delusion are buddhas. Those who are greatly deluded in realization are living beings. Furthermore, there are those who attain realization beyond realization and those who are deluded within delusion.

When buddhas are truly buddhas they don't need to perceive they are buddhas; however, they are enlightened buddhas and they continue actualizing buddha. In seeing color and hearing sound with body and mind, although we perceive them intimately, [the perception] is not like reflections in a mirror or the moon in water. When one side is illuminated, the other is dark.

To study the Buddha Way is to study the self. To study the self is to forget the self. To forget the self is to be verified by all things. To be verified by all things is to let the body and mind of the self and the body and mind of others drop off. There is a trace of realization that cannot be grasped. We endlessly express this ungraspable trace of realization.

When one first seeks the Dharma, one strays far from the boundary of the Dharma. When the Dharma is correctly transmitted to the self, one is immediately an original person.

If one riding in a boat watches the coast, one mistakenly perceives the coast as moving. If one watches the boat [in relation to the surface of the water], then one notices that the boat is moving. Similarly, when we perceive the body and mind in a confused way and grasp all things with a discriminating mind, we mistakenly think that the self-nature of the mind is permanent. When we intimately practice and return right here, it is clear that all things have no [fixed] self.

Firewood becomes ash. Ash cannot become firewood again. However, we should not view ash as after and firewood as before. We should know that firewood dwells in the dharma position of firewood and has its own before and after. Although before and after exist, past and future are cut off. Ash stays in the position of ash, with its own before and after. As firewood never becomes firewood again after it has burned to ash, there is no return to living after a person dies. However, in Buddha Dharma it is an unchanged tradition not to say that life becomes death. Therefore, we call it no-arising. It is the established way of buddhas' turning the Dharma wheel not to say that death becomes life. Therefore, we call it no-perishing. Life is a position in time; death is also a position in time. This is like winter and spring. We don't think that winter becomes spring, and we don't say that spring becomes summer.

When a person attains realization, it is like the moon's reflection in water. The moon never becomes wet; the water is never disturbed. Although the moon is a vast and great light, it is reflected in a drop of water. The whole moon and even the whole sky are reflected in a drop of dew on a blade of grass. Realization does not destroy the person, as the moon does not make a hole in the water. The person does not obstruct realization, as a drop of dew does not obstruct the moon in the sky. The depth is the same as the height. [To investigate the significance of] the length and brevity of time, we should consider whether the water is great or small and understand the size of the moon in the sky.

When the Dharma has not yet fully penetrated body and mind, one thinks one is already filled with it. When the Dharma fills body and mind, one thinks something is [still] lacking. For example, when we sail a boat into the ocean beyond sight of land and our eyes scan [the horizon in] the four directions, it simply looks like a circle. No other shape appears. This great ocean, however, is neither round nor square. It has inexhaustible characteristics. [To a fish] it looks like a palace; [to a heavenly being] a jeweled necklace. [To us] as far as our eyes can see, it looks like a circle. All the myriad things are like this. Within the dusty world and beyond, there are innumerable aspects and characteristics; we only see or grasp as far as the power of our eye of study and practice can see. When we listen to the reality of myriad things, we must know that there are inexhaustible characteristics in both ocean and mountains, and there are many other worlds in the four directions. This is true not only in the external world, but also right under our feet or within a single drop of water.

When a fish swims, no matter how far it swims, it doesn't reach the end of the water. When a bird flies, no matter how high it flies, it cannot reach the end of the sky. Therefore, since ancient times, no fish has ever left water and no bird has ever left the sky. When the bird's need or the fish's need is great, the range is large. When the need is small, the range is small. In this way, each fish and each bird uses the whole of space and vigorously acts in every place. However, if a bird departs from the sky, or a fish leaves the water, it immediately dies. We should know that [for a fish] water is life, [for a bird] sky is life. A bird is life; a fish is life. Life is a bird; life is a fish. And we should go beyond this. There is practice-enlightenment—this is the way of living beings.

Therefore, if there are fish that would swim or birds that would fly only after investigating the entire ocean or sky, they would find neither path nor place. When we make this very place our own, our practice becomes the actualization of reality [*genjōkōan*]. When we make this path our own, our activity naturally becomes actualized reality [*genjōkōan*]. This path, this place, is neither big nor small, neither self nor others. It has not existed before this moment nor has it come into existence now. Therefore [the reality of all things] is thus.

In the same way, when a person engages in practice-enlightenment in the Buddha Way, as the person realizes one dharma, the person permeates that dharma; as the person encounters one practice, the person [fully] practices that practice. [For this] there is a place and a path. The boundary of the known is not clear; this is because the known [which appears limited] is born and practiced simultaneously with the complete penetration of the Buddha Dharma. We should not think that what we have attained is conceived by ourselves and known by our discriminating mind. Although complete enlightenment is immediately actualized, its intimacy is such that it does not necessarily form as a view. [In fact] viewing is not something fixed.

[The] Zen Master of Mt. Magu was waving a fan. A monk approached him and asked, "The nature of wind is ever present and permeates everywhere. Why are you waving a fan?"

The master said, "You know only that the wind's nature is ever present—you don't know that it permeates everywhere." The monk said, "How does wind permeate everywhere?" The master just continued waving the fan. The monk bowed deeply.

The genuine experience of Buddha Dharma and the vital path that has been correctly transmitted are like this. To say we should not wave a fan because the nature of wind is ever present, and that we should feel the wind even when we don't wave a fan, is to know neither ever-presence nor the wind's nature. Since the wind's nature is ever present, the wind of the Buddha's family enables us to realize the gold of the great earth and to transform the [water of] the long river into cream.

The First Chapter of Shōbōgenzō (The True Dharma Eye Treasury)

Genjōkōan (Actualization of Reality)

This was written in mid-autumn of the first year of Tenpuku era [1233] and given to my lay disciple, Yō Kōshū, who lived in Chinzei (Kyūshū).

Compiled in the fourth year of Kenchō [1252]

Translated by Shohaku Okumura

MEETING THE MYRIAD THINGS

Introduction

For Sōtō Zen practitioners, "Genjōkōan" has become one of Dōgen's most beloved and chanted texts because of its poetic language and deep reflection on the nature of actualizing the Buddha Dharma. It is one of a handful of essays by Dōgen that most Sōtō Zen practitioners are familiar with. "Genjōkōan" is part of a larger work, Shōbōgenzō (Treasury of the True Dharma Eye), a collection of essays that he wrote and continued to revise throughout his life. Shōbōgenzō is considered his masterwork.

There are multiple compilations of Shōbōgenzō, but Dōgen personally arranged the chapters in three of them: the 60-chapter, 75-chapter, and 12-chapter versions. In both the 60- and 75-chapter compilations, "Genjōkōan" is placed first.[1] Later versions of Shōbōgenzō, compiled by others, arrange Dōgen's essays in chronological order of composition, resulting in "Genjōkōan" usually occupying the third position.[2]

Since Dōgen always placed "Genjōkōan" as the opening chapter in the Treasury of the True Dharma Eye, we must assume that he felt it to be a crucial and comprehensive introduction to his teachings. Dōgen's disciple, Senne, writes, "The word genjōkōan can be used together with any term. . . . [Therefore] the title of each of the seventy-five chapters of this writing can be called genjō-kōan."[3] Senne explains why this is so in his definition of the word genjō. He defines gen as "manifestation"; and jō, he explains as "this jō of genjō (成, to become) as jō in jōbutsu (to become a buddha)."[4] In other words, every fascicle of the Treasury of the True Dharma Eye is a primer on manifesting buddha-nature through bodhisattva practice.

In this introduction, I want to offer biographical context for Dōgen's teachings in "Genjōkōan," followed by analysis and reflections on a couple of core concepts found throughout his writing. In order to keep this introduction more succinct and clearly focused on "Genjōkōan," I have added two appendices to this commentary: (1) a discussion of abiding in a dharma position (*jū hōi*, 住法位), and (2) an exploration of the translation of the term *shushō* (修證) as "practice-realization" or "practice-verification."

The Place of "Genjōkōan" in the Chronology of Dōgen's Writing

Dōgen only began to write extensively about the Dharma after returning from China, where he awakened under the tutelage of his master Rujing.[5] In 1227, immediately upon his return to Japan, Dōgen wrote "Fukanzazengi" (Recommending Zazen to All People).[6] In 1231, he wrote "Bendōwa" (On the Endeavor of the Way), which is clearly intended to introduce his understanding of Sōtō Zen to an audience of Japanese readers whom he knew would be unfamiliar with the tenets of Sōtō Zen (C. Caodong). "Fukanzazengi" is a meditation instruction, and "Bendōwa" presents very specific observations on the importance of zazen, as well as answers questions Dōgen believed represented common misunderstandings among his contemporaries about Buddhism.

Two years later, he wrote "Maka Hannya Haramitsu" (Manifestation of Great Prajñā), a commentary on the Heart Sutra. Perhaps initially presented as an oral teaching, this text was written at Dōgen's temple Kōshōji, near Kyoto, during the first summer *ango* (extended practice period) held there.[7] As a Zen teacher, I am not surprised that he began his first ango with a teaching on the Heart Sutra, as it is central to Zen and considered a primary text for almost all Mahayana schools of Buddhism.

Dōgen wrote the earliest version of "Genjōkōan" in the autumn of 1233 for a lay supporter named Yō Kōshū (also read as Yanagi Mitsuhide), although he may have continued to edit it until 1252, the year before his death.[8] Dōgen scholar Steven Heine speculates that Yō Kōshū may have been "the boatman who guided Dōgen's ship to and from China."[9] It has also been suggested that Yō Kōshū was an official in a government office in present-day Kyushu.[10] I can imagine that if Yō Kōshū was one of the crew on Dōgen's return voyage from China, he and Dōgen may have had extensive conversations about the nature of the Dharma and awakening as they sailed across the sea toward Japan. Perhaps they sat together under the night sky exchanging ideas. These talks were compelling enough to motivate Dōgen to write an essay explaining his understanding. Lucky for us, the result, "Genjōkōan," has endured as a guide to Sōtō practitioners, as well as other Buddhists, over the hundreds of years since its composition.

In the few years after composing "Genjōkōan," Dōgen did not produce a text he considered appropriate for inclusion in Shōbō-genzō, although he did write a separate practice commentary called *Gakudō Yōjinshū (Points to Watch in Practicing the Way)* in 1234. In the interim, his primary disciple, Ejō, compiled *Shōbōgenzō Zui-monki (Treasury of the True Dharma Eye: Record of Things Heard)*,[11] a collection of Dōgen's oral teachings, while Dōgen worked on *Shinji Shōbōgenzō* (Chinese-Language *Treasury of the True Dharma Eye*), a compilation of three hundred kōans in Chinese. In 1236, he also wrote "Tenzo Kyōkun" (Instructions for the Cook), a set of practice instructions for the monastery's head cook, which was included in a posthumous collection of essays titled *Eihei Shingi (Pure Standards for the Zen Community)*.

Dōgen continued to write essays and compile versions of Shōbō-genzō for the rest of his life.[12]

Dogen's Encounter with the Tenzo: Practice-Realization in Everyday Life

Before moving more deeply into some observations about the text of "Genjōkōan," I want to consider the question that propelled Dōgen's journey to China and to dwell on the transformative encounter he had with an older monk during the early part of his time there. I believe doing so will shed light on why Dōgen ultimately gave "Genjōkōan" pride of place as the first fascicle in Shōbōgenzō.

It is a common tenet in the Sōtō school that Dōgen went to China to answer a question that had plagued him. This question was recorded in *The Record of Kenzei*,[13] published in 1422: "If all sentient beings possess the buddha-nature and Tathagata exists without change [as enunciated in the Nirvana Sutra], then why must people develop the aspiration for awakening and vigorously engage in austerities in order to realize this truth?"[14]

As Heine points out, Dōgen posits the same question in the opening lines of "Fukanzazengi":

> Fundamentally, the basis of the Way is thoroughly pervasive, so how could it be contingent on practice and realization? The vehicle of the ancestors is naturally unrestricted, then why should we expend sustained effort?[15]

Thomas Kasulis, a scholar of Japanese religion, asserts that this transformative query became the basis of Dōgen's mature understanding.[16] How Kenzei phrased this question may not be historically accurate, but its presentation in "Fukanzazengi" indicates that Dōgen believed the basis of this question needed answering.

Dōgen was about twenty-three years old when he went to China. I imagine Dōgen, at that time, to be a person who tended to distill his religious experiences into intellectual paradigms. Perhaps he was a little arrogant but nonetheless a sincere and curious practitioner. He clearly trusted his own gut about what constituted authentic practice and realization. This is not surprising because he had been practicing Buddhism since he was ordained at thirteen, and by the time he went to China in 1223, he had been practicing continuously for ten years. Yet Dōgen clearly had not found what he felt was authentically Buddha's Way and was searching for answers in China.

In "Tenzo Kyōkun" (Instructions for the Cook), Dōgen relates that his first Dharma encounter upon arriving in China was with the sixty-one-year-old *tenzo* of Mount Ayuwang monastery, who visited Dōgen's ship harbored in Qingyuan. When the tenzo prepares to leave after their visit, Dōgen encourages him to stay and talk more about the Dharma rather than returning to his duties at the monastery. The tenzo declines, saying that it is his responsibility to oversee the meals. Puzzled, Dōgen asks why a person of his rank could not leave the preparation of the meals to his staff. When the tenzo replies that it is his practice to be there and his responsibility to be accountable, Dōgen is still reluctant to accept this as a valid reason for not staying to continue their conversation about the Dharma. After all, talking about the Dharma is surely more interesting and important than returning to the mundane task of preparing meals for the monastics.

As their discussion continues, Dōgen asks,

> "Venerable tenzo, in your advanced years, why do you not wholeheartedly engage the Way through zazen or penetrate the words and stories of the ancient masters, instead of troubling yourself by being tenzo and just working? What is that good for?"
>
> The tenzo laughed loudly and said, "Oh, good fellow from a foreign country, you have not yet understood wholeheartedly engaging in the Way, and you do not yet know what words and phrases are."
>
> Hearing this, I suddenly felt ashamed and stunned, and then asked him, "What are words and phrases? What is wholeheartedly engaging the Way?"
>
> The tenzo said, "If you do not stumble over this question, you are really a true person." [Dōgen comments], I could not understand at the time.[17]

Reading Dōgen's version of this initial encounter with the older monk, whom he would meet again later, we can glean a few things about his understanding and personality at that time. It underscores the young Dōgen's attachment to studying ancestral practice and his belief in zazen as the singular activity of practice. It also clearly indicates his curiosity and humility, for he was not defensive when the older monk laughed at him.

Most importantly, this encounter sparked within Dōgen a curiosity about the true nature of practice as presented by the tenzo. The monk's admonitions that "you do not yet know what words and phrases are" and "you have not yet understood wholeheartedly engaging in the Way" point out Dōgen's basic misunderstanding. At that time, Dōgen put more credence in studying the words of the buddhas and ancestors and in engaging in formal sitting than he did in actualizing practice through his daily activity. He thought intellectual study, formal zazen, and talking about practice were sufficient. According to Kasulis, Dōgen's previous practice as a Tendai monk would have mostly involved formal debates, "complex esoteric Buddhist ritual(s)" consisting of a "plethora of mantras, mudras, mandalas" as well as sutra chanting and hours of "Tendai-style tranquil meditation."[18] None of these activities are grounded in enacting practice in daily life. The tenzo's comments were an attempt to bring forth this deficiency in Dōgen's understanding.

When I was a senior student at San Francisco Zen Center, a student who was leaving City Center came to me informally for advice. He asked how he could continue his practice without the formal trappings of temple life. How, he wondered, could he practice in daily life without a zendo for sitting, group chanting service, and the daily schedule of a residential Zen center? I understood that for him, practice was only the formal training regime of Sōtō Zen, and those practices did not extend to the day-to-day tasks of daily life. This appears to have been Dōgen's understanding as well, at the time of his conversation with the tenzo.

Indeed, many of us come to practice thinking that our daily life is inferior to Buddhist practice. We understand that nirvana is something outside of our life, some place pure and without problems. If we study Dōgen with this model, we will have a hard time grasping his understanding. Studying the Buddha's Way and applying those teachings to our mundane life are not different. We are not trying to transcend our life.[19]

When Dōgen continued his dialogue with the monk a few months later, he asked about "words and phrases" and practice.

Dōgen relays the dialogue:

> [The (now retired) tenzo said], "People who study words and phrases should know the significance of words and phrases. People dedicated to wholehearted practice need to affirm the significance of engaging the Way."
>
> I asked him, "What are words and phrases?"
> The tenzo said, "One, two, three, four, five."
> Also I asked him, "What is wholeheartedly engaging the Way?"
> The tenzo said, "In the whole world it is never hidden."[20]

This fateful encounter with the tenzo opened Dōgen's eyes to engaging with the totality of his life as practice. These "words and phrases" are not empty platitudes, intellectual instructions, or puzzles but rather Dharma gates to seeing the Buddha Dharma as our daily life. One might reword the tenzo's final teaching in that exchange as, "In the whole world practice-realization is never hidden."[21] It is right where we are.

Dōgen praises this conversation with the tenzo as transformative. Then he continues his analysis of the tenzo's teaching with the following insight:

> What I previously saw of words and phrases is one, two, three, four, five. Today what I see of words and phrases is also six, seven, eight, nine, ten. My junior fellow-practitioners, completely see this [concrete particular phenomena] in that [universal interdependence], completely see that [universal interdependence] in this [concrete particular phenomena]. Making such an effort you can totally grasp one-flavor Zen through words and phrases.[22]

In other words, we cannot separate the day-to-day activities and encounters of our life from what we may perceive as something beyond daily life. They are intertwined, interdependent, and cannot be separated.

If we look back at Dōgen's dilemma as presented in *The Record of Kenzei*—"If all sentient beings possess the buddha-nature . . . then why must people develop the aspiration for awakening and vigorously engage in austerities in order to realize this truth?"—we can see that his conversations with the tenzo were a pivotal event in his development. The opening lines of "Fukanzazengi," which Dōgen presents as a question, can now be read as a statement:

> Fundamentally, the basis of the Way is thoroughly pervasive, enacting it [*genjōkōan* "manifesting suchness"] . . . is contingent on practice-realization [verification]. The vehicle of the ancestors is naturally unrestricted, [therefore] we should expend sustained effort.

Dōgen realized that practicing the Dharma is manifesting and verifying reality's functioning. Such manifestation only comes forth when practice is grounded in and reflective of all of our activity— not just formal practice. Our concrete and particular lives are not different from what is universal and codependent.

Although Dōgen's "Fukanzazengi" encourages and instructs practitioners to make seated meditation a primary focus of practice, he comments, "If you concentrate your effort single-mindedly, you are thereby negotiating the Way with your practice-realization undefiled. As you proceed along the Way, you will attain a state of everydayness."[23] In other words, this zazen mind must be carried over into one's daily life.

In Shōbōgenzō "Jinzū" (Mystical Power), Dōgen quotes the often-repeated phrase of Layman Pang (a.k.a. Layman Ho-on): "The mystical power and wondrous function, carrying water and lugging firewood."[24]

About this verse, Dōgen comments,

We must investigate this truth thoroughly. "Carrying water" means loading water and fetching it. There being our own work and the self-motivation, and there being the work of others and the motivation of others, water is caused to be carried. This is just the state of [a] mystically powerful buddha. . . . Even in a person's not knowing, that state of Dharma does not fade and that state of Dharma does not die. Although the person does not know it, [that] state of Dharma is the Dharma itself. Although [the person] does not know that carrying water is the mystical power, the state of carrying water as mystical power does not regress.[25]

This "carry water" and "lugging wood" is an apt metaphor for the work of the tenzo specifically, but also for all the activities of our daily life. These daily tasks, as Dōgen points out, are motivated not just by the self's needs but also through one's inter-being with others. This is the fundamental meaning of the bodhisattva path.

If formal zazen is the most important message of Dōgen's teaching, as many Sōtō Zen practitioners in the United States now believe, then why did Dōgen place "Genjōkōan," which does not specifically mention zazen at any point, as the first teaching in *Treasury of the True Dharma Eye*, instead of "Fukanzazengi"?[26] Dōgen never stopped advocating for the importance of zazen as an expression of our realization and as a practice that manifests and supports awakening. But he also taught that the whole of our activity should be a field of awakening.[27] This was the heart of the tenzo's teaching: our awakened life is manifest in daily life. From this perspective, "Genjōkōan" describes how a mature practitioner manifests reality's function in all their actions and interactions with others. Genjōkōan is the ground, the path, and the mature enactment of the bodhisattva vow.

The Locus of Practice-Realization or Practice-Verification

Dōgen's encounter with the tenzo in China helped to clarify one of his key teachings: practice-realization or practice-verification.

Practice-realization refers to effort in practice as actualizing the Buddha Dharma (in all aspects of our life). It is the "how" of enacting the Buddha Dharma. By conflating practice and realization, walking the path and actualizing the path become one.

The Japanese term Dōgen uses is *shushō ittō* (修證 一等), which translates literally as "practice-realization-one-equal" or "practice-verification-one-equal." Practice-verification, probably the most correct translation, is practice that verifies the Buddha Dharma as the Buddha Dharma verifies practice. Taken together, this verification of practice and practice of verification is manifest as actualizing the Buddha Dharma, or practice-realization. [28]

Practice-realization as one word means that we do not practice Buddhism to become enlightened but as an expression of buddha-nature. Practice holds the same importance as realization; they are not two sequential stages. Rather, they function together. Practice itself reflects our buddha mind/nature. As mentioned before, Dōgen went to China with the idea that practicing the Dharma centered around formal monastic training. I believe he returned with the much broader vision of the boundlessness of Buddhist practice and manifestation of the Buddha Dharma.

Dōgen offers a radical understanding that all being(s)—the whole world of things, persons, processes, and so on—are one event, as manifest by individual and specific times, beings, and persons. From this inter-beingness arises his vision of practice-realization. In "Uji" (Being-Time), he describes this process as "entirely worlding the entire world with the whole world."[29] His understanding is a kind of Buddhist theory of everything developed from the doctrines and teachings that preceded him.

This "theory of everything" manifests as our everyday life—nothing special, nothing hidden. In Shōbōgenzō "Shōji" (Birth and Death), he writes, "To seek Buddha apart from birth-and-death is like pointing . . . northward . . .when you want to go south. . . . Just understand that birth-and-death itself is nirvana, and you will neither hate one as being birth-and-death, nor cherish the other as being nirvana."[30] Furthermore, manifesting practice as realization happens in the particularity of what is unfolding in our life in the presencing moment. In "Genjōkōan," Dōgen states this clearly:

> When we make this very place our own, our practice becomes the actualization of reality [*genjōkōan*]. When we make this path our own, our activity naturally becomes actualized reality [*genjōkōan*]. This path, this place, is neither big nor small, neither self nor others. It has not existed before this moment nor has it come into existence now. Therefore [the reality of all things] is thus.

"This very place," "our activity," "this path" is the locus of "the actualization of reality [*genjōkōan*]." "[N]either self nor other" indicates our practice is in concert with others; and this very place, activity, path is complete actualization of particularity while eternally abiding in the suchness of now. This is where the rubber meets the road and we practice-realize, or when practice verifies or manifests Buddha Dharma. This point is essential to our understanding because it is only within the context of a particular encounter in our life that we may respond skillfully, unskillfully, or perhaps somewhere in between. This is not something that can happen in the abstract.

In Shōbōgenzō "Yuibutsu Yobutsu" (Only a Buddha and a Buddha), Dōgen observes,

> "The entire universe is the gate of liberation" means that you are not at all entangled or captivated. What is called "the entire universe" is undivided from the moment. . . . Even if you seek to enter or go through this gate of liberation, it cannot be done. How is this so? Reflect on the question raised. If you intend to seek outside what it is, nothing will be attained.[31]

There is no "outside" or "inside" the gate, so we cannot enter where we already are. What we need is already here. All aspects of practice-verification are presencing within each moment. Dōgen connects bringing forth the mind (of bodhi), practice, enlightenment, and nirvana as already available to us because of reality's suchness or buddha-nature's accessibility. We may not be manifesting our buddha-nature, but that doesn't mean that it isn't already presencing as "just this," reality's essential nature. These "stages" are in play simultaneously. Therefore,

- We are always capable of realization right now at this place.
- We do not need to wait for the right time to respond.

In "Uji," Dōgen writes, "The sixteen-foot Buddha-body also makes a passage as my being-time. Although it might seem as if it were somewhere else over there, it is the time right now."[32] We might not think that our self, our current life with others, is buddha. Nevertheless, according to this teaching, we are already the nature of bodhi-mind. Because it is the time right now, practice-realization (or verification) is a kind of turning toward: turning toward our buddha mind, turning toward the Dharma. Thus, integrating with all being(s) can be immediately accessed and manifested as skillful means from any dharma position. That is the elegant function of practice-realization as an expression of true nature or verification of the Buddha Dharma. To employ another of Dōgen's key terms, this is total exertion (gūjin, 究盡) in practice.

Our individual effort is of utmost importance. As Dōgen expresses in "Uji," "One must learn in practice that unless it is one's self exerting itself right now, not a single dharma or thing can either immediately manifest itself or make passage."[33] If we want to manifest the Buddha Dharma, we have to make an effort at this place and time. Without that effort, reality cannot come forth and meet us. We will be caught by our myopic self-centeredness and not be able to see that our exertion in practice is interdependent. Practice-realization is the work of self and others, those seen and unseen by us. The "self-exerting itself" is the particularity of all beings practicing together. This is a group activity requiring the help of all beings to bring forth our practice and theirs—to make the world, or embody the Buddha Dharma.

Immediately preceding the quotation above, Dogen writes,

> The deva kings and deva multitudes actually presencing to the left and right are even now being-time that puts forth my [and/or their] total exertion. And everywhere else in the universe the hosts of being-times in water and on earth are now immediately manifesting themselves in the full power that I [and they] exert.[34]

In this way, we are liberated to fully incorporate all aspects of our current life's activity. We see our life in all of its aspects: universal, fluid, impermanent, particular, spacious, and intimate with all of reality, fully engaged and incorporated. This, as Dōgen instructs in "Tenzo Kyōkun," is revealed in the everyday activity of cooking for the monastic community, which can also be applied to any aspect of daily life. Dōgen admonishes the cook (and us) to make every effort to apply the Buddha Dharma to all activities:

> Handle even a single leaf of a green in such a way that it manifests the body of the Buddha. This in turn allows the Buddha to manifest through the leaf. This is a power which you cannot grasp with your rational mind. It operates freely, according to the situation, in a most natural way. At the same time, this power functions in our lives to clarify and settle activities and is beneficial to all living things.[35]

This practice of recognizing the intrinsic value of all the ingredients of the food we prepare or the people we meet is practice-realization in action. Throughout "Tenzo Kyōkun," Dōgen encourages the practitioner to take up their life with the tenzo's mind of attention to detail, joy, and equanimity. These are all aspects of practice-realization.

Realization Is Perception

"Genjōkōan," like "Tenzo Kyōkun" and really all of Dōgen's teachings, is tactile—pertaining to the very stuff of our life. Practice manifests as we engage with people, things, weather, the earth, and so on through our senses. Realization itself manifests through form.

When we study the meaning of no-self, or no-inherently-existing-self, we may think that the goal of this practice is to annihilate the self. In perhaps a subtler way, we imagine that practice-realization (or verification) happens outside the self or outside the self that experiences itself. Or it is not the self of our ordinary life. Not our bodily self. We assume that our ordinary mind is delusional and that a mind unclouded by delusion is outside of our ordinary state. We think practice is enacted by a special person who is without personality or problems. Perhaps we think that the problem is that we think or experience our life through the self. Of course, this begs the question: Who else would practice and respond skillfully other than this particular person—this self?

Hee-Jin Kim writes, "If the cause for the arising of our predicament lies within discrimination, then the cause for the eradication of such a predicament also lies within that discrimination itself, not outside."[36] Discrimination or perceptions happen within the purview of each person's mind and senses. Kim comments a few sentences later,

> Yet, discriminative activities, once freed of substantialist, ego-centric obsessions, can function compassionately and creatively. Thus there are two kinds of discriminative thinking at an existential level, delusive and enlightened. To Dōgen, whether or not we use discrimination in the Zen salvific project is not the issue; rather, how we use it is.[37]

Our mental discriminations are based upon the activity of our five senses: sight, hearing, smell, taste, and touch. Our mental-emotional understanding, which is based upon our interpretation of incoming sensory awareness, can either selfishly override the totality of our experience with other beings or we can align ourselves with others and, in concert with self and other, respond skillfully, thus manifesting our buddha-nature.

Perhaps Dōgen's most famous statement on this topic comes in "Genjōkōan":

> To study the Buddha Way is to study the self. To study the self is to forget the self. To forget the self is to be verified by all things. To be verified by all things is to let the body and mind of the self and the body and mind of others drop off. There is a trace of realization that cannot be grasped. We endlessly express this ungraspable trace of realization.

Although you may have read or heard this teaching many times, let's pause and consider the question of "self" as the locus of awakening. Who is it that "studies the self"? Who is it that "forgets the self"? Who or what is "verified by all things"? And what is "dropped off"?[38] Furthermore, who or what "express[es] this ungraspable trace of realization"? Earlier in "Genjōkōan," Dōgen writes, "All things coming and carrying out practice-enlightenment through the self is realization." "Through the self" indicates that our practice is manifest by this body and mind—not another. It is the self's activity, in concert with all being(s)' activity throughout time and space, in this body, with this mind, that engages practice-realization.

Throughout "Genjōkōan," Dōgen directly or metaphorically refers to our experiential sensations and perceptions. He writes about seeing flowers fall and weeds grow. He observes how we carry ourselves toward things or we meet the other. When we see color and hear sounds, we may awaken. And we experience darkness and illumination. All the senses are activated: touch, perception, hearing, seeing, and even smell and taste—if we use our imagination.

We study the self and try to grasp realization. We experience riding in a boat and have the misconception of the shore moving when it is the boat that moves. We watch the shore, the water, and the self. We turn the Dharma wheel; we perceive the seasons and discern their qualities. We see the moon, feel dew, and gaze at the sky. We know depth and breadth, and we experience the Dharma filling our body and mind. We see land and feel the undulation of ocean waves and smell the salt water; our eyes scan the horizon. Fish swim, birds fly, and the world is dusty. We listen to our environment and we know. We walk the path of the Dharma and we realize that this is the place: solid and alive beneath our feet. We experience the intimacy of practice-realization, verifying the Buddha Dharma in this body and with this mind.

Yet, we have doubts about whether this very body and mind is buddha even as Dōgen writes in Shōbōgenzō "Hotsu Bodai Shin" (Bringing Forth the Mind of Bodhi), "The real marks are the real marks of suchness; suchness is the present body and mind. We should bring forth the [buddha] mind with this body and mind."[39] These doubts arise because of the limitations of our ability to perceive reality's presencing as codependent and cooperative function, yet salvation can only be achieved through our senses, not despite them. This is "bring[ing] forth the [buddha] mind with this body and mind," and this too is part of Dōgen's message in "Genjōkōan."

Because it is this body and this mind, we can study and see reality's functioning in our own life through examining both our delusions and realizations. We may struggle with the impermanence of flowers and the pervasive nature of weeds, yet we can, through our intimate "seeing" and "hearing," be liberated from our selfishness and suffering. How else can you be enlightened by this world except by living your particular life as a human discovering harmony with self, other, and all being(s)?

This self (with all of its difficulties) is, for each of us, the fulcrum point of awakening. This waking up is opening to all of our experience (both delusion and realization) and using this body and mind to express an enlightened response. We cannot jettison one to attain the other.

Dōgen's writing is about how this body and mind perceive and thereby awaken with the samsaric world, which is both delusional and amazingly vibrant and beautiful as bodhi mind. We walk with blue mountains, and we and our teachers are like twining vines supporting each other and learning together. We are bodhisattvas sitting in the fire of the blue lotus. Samsara becomes a crucible for awakened response. All this is sensual and intimate. It is the how and the is-ness of our senses. Our perceptions are Dharma gates to realization. They are the place and the way unfolding as genjōkōan.

Studying Dōgen

Dōgen's writings, especially in Shōbōgenzō, are often difficult to understand—but not impossible. He was clearly a brilliant scholar of Buddhism and, more importantly, a great practitioner, thinker, and transmitter of the teachings of Buddhism. Dōgen considered what he taught to be "just Buddha's Way," not a school called Sōtō Zen. He referred to many stories, koans, doctrines, and examples of past practitioners of the Dharma in his effort to articulate and argue with the Buddhist tradition as he received it.

Dōgen offers pointers and koans. Here's a good one from "Uji": "Just reflect: right now, is there an entire being or an entire world missing from your present time, or not?"[40] As a Zen student, you know the answer is probably no, but if you are honest as a human being, you must say yes. If you can't say yes and you can't say no, how can you find the answer?

Imagine your current teacher saying, "Quickly answer, right now is there anything missing or not?" What do you say? How do you reach this place of knowing? You could respond with an intellectual answer about the nonduality of our experience. But "the answer" is not intellectual; in fact, the answer is right in front of you. To use a baseball metaphor, it is being in the ballpark of your own life. You must roll around in the infield, smelling the grass, hearing the fans, feeling the dirt, acknowledging everything presencing, and then—quick, here comes the ball. Can you catch it?

The point is: don't skip over the questions Dōgen poses to you as a reader. These questions are koans. They are Dōgen's challenge to us to stop, contemplate, and absorb the teaching. Taking the time to reflect upon and apply these questions to your own life changes Dōgen's writing from intellectual study into a transformative and enlightening dialogue with a teacher.

A common pitfall in reading Dōgen is to translate what you do not understand into something you do understand. To return to an example from "Genjōkōan" used earlier in this introduction, Dōgen talks about going out in a boat and thinking that the shore is moving when it is the boat that is moving. He ends this section with ". . . it is clear that all things have no [fixed] self." Then he moves on to a famous passage about firewood and ash: "Firewood becomes ash. Ash cannot become firewood again."

Since, as mentioned above, Dōgen did not write with paragraph delineations—those are added by the translator—there is no break here between "it will be clear that all things have no [fixed] self" and the next line, "Firewood becomes ash. Ash cannot become firewood again."

Why does he throw in the observation that nothing has an unchanging or fixed self and then start talking about firewood? If you say at this point, "Well, it's because the self is empty of inherent existence," you might miss why Dōgen starts talking about firewood.

A more fruitful question we might ask at this juncture in the text is, "If nothing has an unchanging self, then what do I experience as the self?" And "What does this have to do with firewood and ash?" From that we may realize that Dōgen is using the states of firewood and ash as examples of how the self exists as the self we experience.

If we don't realize that Dōgen's original thought was continuous, we may not see the connection. Or if we think, "I know what no-self is," and just go on, we will probably miss Dōgen's teaching on how we experience the self. Then we don't realize that firewood and ash *are* the self.

This is illustrative of the problem of only focusing on each paragraph's meaning and not the flow of Dōgen's thesis. We do this in part because there is a paragraph break and in part because we are so focused on trying to figure out what each paragraph means that we do not follow the flow of his argument. Furthermore, commentarial literature tends to explain a text paragraph by paragraph. Consequently, knowing something about how Dōgen composed his work and being willing to go beyond the obvious, we can more clearly understand the meaning of his teaching.

In "Uji," Dōgen instructs us as to the best way to investigate practice: "Even though you do not have doubts about them, that is not to say you know them. Since a sentient being's doubtings of the many and various things unknown to them are naturally vague and indefinite, the course their doubtings take will probably not bring them to coincide with this present doubt."[41] Although Dōgen is talking about understanding being-time, we can also apply the sentiment he conveys in "Uji" to reading and learning Dōgen himself. You think you know what he is saying because it seems to correspond with something you already know. Consequently, you define it in the ways you know. But since you don't know what he is really talking about, although you think you do, you will not have the experience of being enlightened by your experience of not knowing.

When we study Dōgen, we should go beyond familiarities and received definitions and try to figure out what he is truly saying. For Dōgen, dualistic concepts, like form and emptiness, are never the full story. Form and emptiness are like two sides of a coin that can be juxtaposed by looking at one and then the other. But Dōgen asks us to take a very close look at the coin itself. Birth-death-nirvana-samsara is the whole coin. And bodhisattva practice is how we spend the coin—how we practice-realize our life.

In the end, we want to find out what *he meant*, not what we think he might have meant. It is helpful in this effort to study a trusted source about Dōgen's thought, which will give us a general idea of Dōgen's vision of reality's functioning. In this way, we begin to learn the rules of his game, to use a sports analogy. Without this, if you guess what he means, you may be very far afield of his intention.

One important thing to know about Dōgen's teaching style is that often, when he touches upon something briefly in a given fascicle, he will have written a complete essay on that topic elsewhere. For example, in "Genjōkōan" he briefly mentions the dharma positions of firewood and ash. In "Uji" he dedicates the whole text to the importance of understanding dharma positions. Or a phrase such as "radiant light," which appears just once in "Genjōkōan," is fully discussed in Shōbōgenzō "Kōmyō" (Radiant Light). Or he may talk about the meaning of a koan such as "The Hands and Eye of Great Compassion"—again, mentioned just briefly in "Genjōkōan"—in Shōbōgenzō "Kannon" (Avalokiteśvara).[42] If you have access to a translation with good footnotes, you can often cross-reference the Japanese words Dōgen is using and start tracing these connections across fascicles yourself.

Sometimes a translation of a word Dōgen uses, while technically accurate, is misleading. This is another reason to read different translations and, for those works that have them, to consult the footnotes explaining the Japanese. There is a passage in "Uji" that illustrates this point. Dōgen writes, "Reaching is impeded by reaching and not impeded by not-reaching. Not-reaching is impeded by not-reaching and not impeded by reaching."[43] When I first read this section, I thought it meant something like, "Reaching gets in the way of reaching, and does not get in the way of not-reaching. Not-reaching is hindered by not-reaching, and not hindered by reaching." Then I made this make sense to me. But this is not what this passage means.

The word here being translated as "impeded" is *ge*, and it means something like "to be defined by" or "affirmed by." In the Sōtō Zen Text Project translation of these sentences, the footnote reads in part, "Reflecting a recurrent use in Dōgen's writings of the passive *keige seraru* ('to be obstructed or impeded') in the sense 'to be identified or defined.'"[44] Dōgen uses this word many times in Shōbōgenzō.

With this new information, I realized that Dōgen's point refers to all things' particularity, which in this case he expresses as "reaching is defined by reaching." In other words, you are you, not someone else. Your you-ness defines you. You are not a dog or a rock. Furthermore, you are not just human; you are a particular human with a particular set of causal conditions, personality, and so forth. And because you are both form and emptiness, you are not some blob of oneness. It is not our goal in practice to disappear. We have a self;

there is a there, there. Dōgen is saying we are defined by, affirmed by, our is-ness. For this reason, we come to see the Dharma through ourselves as it plays out in our own life in relationship with myriad things. Because we are in a body, in our life, we come to understand the Dharma within the context of our life, not someone else's. In this way, we can enact the Dharma and thus see our interconnection with all other beings. This is a very different meaning than the one I originally concocted before I understood that the word in Japanese being translated as "impeded" actually meant "defined or identified as."[45]

Our teachers can be guides to understanding Dōgen and we can rely upon their interpretation. I also encourage you to read translations of Dōgen that have footnotes as well as commentaries by Zen teachers. If you really want to delve deeply, read commentaries by scholars. To approach studying Dōgen by interpreting his writing from the seat of our pants, making intuitive guesses as to his meaning, will lead to an inaccurate understanding.

I have found that the more I question, persevere, and investigate Dōgen's teachings, the richer my practice becomes and the deeper I experience my life. When first introduced to Dōgen, I did not understand his meaning, but I intuitively felt that he was on to something very important. I wanted to investigate further. It is not necessarily bad to read Dōgen intuitively, but if you *only* do that, you may miss a lot of what he is trying to teach us. For this reason, I encourage everyone to investigate Dōgen through intellectual study before jumping into intuitive interpretation. Once you have a pretty good handle on Dōgen's basic Dharmic worldview, then you can feel your way through the more difficult passages.

CHAPTER 1

"GENJŌKŌAN"

The Realized Koan

As in many of Dōgen's Shōbōgenzō titles, "Genjōkōan" indicates the overall Buddha Dharma of the whole fascicle. In the *Goshō*, Senne states that the title "Genjōkōan" can be applied to every fascicle of Shōbōgenzō as well as every situation or dharma (thing/person) we may encounter: "The title of each of the seventy-five chapters of this writing can be called *genjōkōan*. There can be the *genjō* of delusion, the *genjō* of realization, or the *genjō* of a whisk or a monk's staff, because the reality of each thing is manifested (*genjō*) [within each thing]."[1]

Genjōkōan is life as manifest Buddha Dharma.

Examining the meaning of the characters making up the title "Genjōkōan" can give us context for Senne's and Kyōgō's understanding. "*Gen* [現] is being neither concealed nor revealed. *Jō* [成] is not becoming through study. *Kō* [公] is equalizing inequality. *An* [按] is keeping one's lot."[2]

Gen is all things manifesting in front of us just as they are. If we cannot see them, then we may perceive them as "concealed." Then when we do see them, we believe that something has been "revealed." But their actual presencing as this life, our life, is never not present, despite our limited perceptions of how each being, thing, or situation exists as our life. For example, if you have had a traumatic experience, that experience will influence your decisions whether you are aware of it or not.

More broadly, *gen* expresses the total function of any given moment. For example, if you are standing on the shore, the water, fish, current, rocks, and you *is* total expression with all being(s). This completely expressed, concerted, and coordinated activity is realization as practice and practice as realization. The continuous effort of water, fish, current, rocks, and self verifies the Dharma's total functioning as this moment's expression. You may not see it, but it is there. Even if you see it, can you ever see *all* of it? Probably not, but this does not matter if you can respond appropriately to what is happening at that time.

Jō, according to Senne and Kyōgō, refers to "not becoming through study." I believe they are pointing out the immediacy of realized response. This is not about an intellectual deconstruction of reality; it is turning toward our and all being(s)' true nature as visceral and immediate. Our inclusive expression is like the fish leaping clear of the water and splashing down.[3] It is "just so," and nothing need be added.

Shohaku Okumura translates *jō* as "'to become,' 'to complete,' or 'to accomplish.'" He goes on to explain, "As a verb, the compound term *genjō* means 'to manifest,' 'to actualize,' or 'to appear and become.' As a noun it refers to reality as it is actually happening in the present moment."[4]

Norman Waddell and Masao Abe sum up the meaning of *genjō* as one thought referring to "the *immediate presence* (or presencing) of all things as they truly are in their suchness, untouched by our conscious strivings; their ultimate reality, realized in religious practice."[5]

As humans, we experience this immediate presencing as reality itself expressed through and as oneself, not separated from the activity and is-ness of all being(s). It is nothing more than our present life's unfolding. This is the intersection of the particular and universal. This is the kōan of genjōkōan. Thus, the koan or question becomes: How do I manifest the activity of genjō as Buddha's Way?

According to Senne and Kyōgō, "*Kō* is equalizing inequality [and] *an* is keeping one's lot." This may seem unusual because most of us have learned that *koan* means some kind of case deriving from a legal term in China or a cryptic dialogue that must be solved. Here we are given a different understanding of the word.

In this case, *kō* refers to the state in which we maintain a horizontal or equalizing relationship with all aspects of our life. Senne writes in the *Goshō* that *kō* denotes "to equalize inequality when conditions are unfair."[6] This means that even in a vertical, unequal— that is, "unfair"—relationship, the basis of respect and cooperation from our side is maintained. This is "equalizing inequality." Consequently, even in hierarchical relationships we do not forget our shared true nature.

For example, all sentient beings share the same qualities of impermanence, no-self, and suffering.[7] From this perspective, no being is higher or better than others; all manifest in equality. This can also be understood as a relative statement pointing to our shared humanity: we are all just folks trying to get through our lives as best we can. This is true of ourselves as well as our bosses or teachers with whom we may have hierarchical relationships. Keeping this teaching in mind, we are better able to respond to each and all situations with wisdom and compassion. *Kō* therefore addresses the relative or everyday aspects of our relationships, based upon universal qualities.

An (keeping one's lot) points to unique and particular qualities such as those of a person or situation.[8] For example, sometimes one is a teacher and sometimes a student (vertical relationship). At other times, the situation requires that we acknowledge and express our equality (horizontal relationship). These states coexist, and either one may come forward depending upon the need of the situation. On a deeper level, they are always functioning equally.

Taken together, *kō* and *an* express the simultaneity of "equalizing inequality" and "keeping one's lot." Both *kō* and *an* are aspects of abiding in a dharma position (*jū hōi*).[9] As a dharma position, *kōan* describes, for example, the particularity of a situation or relationship we may encounter in which our response functions skillfully with both the horizonal and vertical aspects of that encounter.

Situations in life are often both horizontal and vertical: same and unique. When we meet our teacher in practice instruction, they take on the role of master and we begin the meeting with a full prostration. If we run into our teacher in the grocery store, we don't fall to the floor in prostration; we say hello and continue shopping. That is "keeping to one's lot," responding with an action appropriate to the situation. Senne adds that inequality and equality are actually the same. He writes, "[Dōgen Zenji] is talking only about the principle of total function (*zenki*, 全機) that has no separation between subject and object; this and that." Later he adds, "Once we understand that to be equal and to be unequal are one, it is not possible to say that we equalize inequality."[10]

Senne is speaking strictly from the position of duality versus nonduality in Buddhism. Equality and inequality are in opposition to each other and therefore depend upon each other for their meaning. For this reason, we can say equality is inequality and inequality is equality. They both point to each other and are thus describing aspects of the same thing.

When Senne says, "It is not possible to say that we equalize inequality," he is pointing to emptiness or no-inherent-existence of these words or situations. He is not suggesting that inequality that causes suffering should be ignored or encouraged.[11] For this reason, Senne sums up this teaching as, "What kōan means should be inequality and keeping one's lot within the total function (*zenki*)."[12] Here, "total function" refers to knowing and acting in accord with the needs of all parties. Using this as the litmus test for realization, both keeping one's lot, equality and inequality function as a team. Viewed in the context of a dharma position or a particular time, situation, person, and so forth, inequality, equality, and keeping one's lot include all aspects of genjō, or completely manifesting the presencing moment.

Keeping one's place, or seeing and acknowledging the unique contributions of each person, as well as knowing that all beings share equality and inequality, will result in being able to wisely respond to any situation in which we find ourselves. It enables us to listen and respond to the immediate presencing of both a dharma's equality-inequality and uniqueness simultaneously. This is genjōkōan.

In *Realizing Genjōkōan*, Okumura puts it this way:

> [Using] the example of a hand . . . we can call it a hand or we can call it a collection of five fingers. As a collection of five fingers, each finger is independent and has a different shape and function. We cannot exchange the little finger with the thumb because each has its own function, shape, and unique way of being. . . . Each finger is truly independent. And yet, from another perspective as one hand, all five fingers function together, and there is no separation between them. When we see the fingers in this united way, there is really just one hand.[13]

This event called a hand can also be a slap, a fist, a wave, or a thumbs-up. It is a tool and a body part. All of a hand's functions are determined by each moment's expression and particularity: "its lot." We can see the hand as open or closed or as individual fingers. We can puzzle over questions such as, Which is equal: the fingers or the hand? But both have their function, and both are equal and unequal simultaneously.

What we experience and how we respond, in this case, have to do with the appropriate function of the parts of a hand in relationship to the person of the hand and the totality of the situation that person is in. Furthermore, this hand and its expression are also predicated by all the causal conditions throughout time that lead to the hand's response as directed by the person's mind. Is it a slap, a wave, or a thumbs-up?

This is why Okumura summarizes the meaning of genjōkōan as follows: "Dōgen however, said that to see one reality from two sides is not enough; he said we should also *express* these two sides in one action."[14] This expression, "two sides of one action," is the key to fully being and responding with all being(s) as genjōkōan.

To express two sides in one action involves responding to "what is" while seeing the universal view of the situation of self and other through the lens of no-self, interconnection, and the suffering of our human condition. Our suffering and how we negotiate that suffering are the topics Dōgen addresses at the end of the opening lines of "Genjōkōan": "Therefore flowers fall even though we love them; weeds grow even though we dislike them."

Expressing realized action will include the daily joys and difficulties of our lives. A well-known Buddhist metaphor expresses realization as having arrived at the other shore. The implication is that upon crossing the water, we will have shed our delusion, suffering, and problems. Dōgen did not see our practice as a method to get from point A (delusion) to point Z (realization). He writes in Shōbōgenzō "Bukkyō" (The Teachings of the Buddhas),

> "*Pāramitā*" means "arrived at the other shore." Although "the other shore" is not the features and traces of coming and going, the "arrival" is "realized" [genjō], the "arrival" is "the kōan." Do not think that practice will arrive at "the other shore"; since there is practice on "the other shore," when we practice, it is "the other shore." For this practice is invariably endowed with the power to appear in the realms everywhere."[15]

The arrival, or manifesting of genjōkōan, is not something attained after practice; rather, practice and "arrival" function simultaneously.

Senne makes quite clear that genjō includes everything expressing at this moment:

> There can be the *genjō* of delusion, the *genjō* of realization, or the *genjō* of a whisk or a monk's staff, because the reality of each thing is manifested (*genjō*) [within each thing]. This delusion is the delusion at the time when all dharmas are the Buddha Dharma. After all, this expression (*genjōkōan*) is used to express the meaning [that has been transmitted] in this tradition.[16]

Genjōkōan leaves nothing out. We cannot reject "flowers falling" or "weeds spreading," as they too are genjōkōan. They become part of the what of practice-realization and verification. Waking up is not predicated upon attaining some state in the future or on the other shore.[17] What characterizes this state of arrival is not about a steps-and-stages progress from delusion to realization over time. The features of coming and going are not germane in the case of realization. This shore and this practice are not different from where we are right now, even as we may be struggling with delusion or delighting in actualization.

CHAPTER 2

BUDDHIST STUDY, REALITY, AND HUMAN EXPERIENCE

When all dharmas are the Buddha Dharma, there is delusion and realization, practice, life[1] and death, buddhas and living beings.

When the ten thousand dharmas are without [fixed] self, there is no delusion and no realization, no buddhas and no living beings, no birth and no death.

Since the Buddha Way by nature goes beyond [the dichotomy of] abundance and deficiency, there is arising and perishing, delusion and realization, living beings and buddhas.

Therefore flowers fall even though we love them; weeds grow even though we dislike them.

Dōgen begins the first two sentences of this text with "When." *When* denotes a particular time that can be understood as the time(s) when we look at our life through the lens of the Buddha Dharma. If we turn our attention to enacting specific aspects of Buddhist practice, then we will understand our life's experience based upon these concepts. This is the time(s) of the first line. The second line is the time(s) we experience our life just as it is unfolding, having let go of labeling our experience. The first line denotes the activity of turning our minds to the task of labeling the "how" of our effort.

From this perspective, we are asked to parse our experience as delusion, realization, practice, birth or life, death, buddhas, and living beings.

The question of time in Dōgen's work is important because it is only within the context of a specific being-time (dharma position) that we enact our understanding. This response cannot happen in some unspecific future or past. The past may inform the present, as may our future desires, but our life can only be lived and expressed in the present moment's unfolding.

Both types of active inquiry—using categories such as "delusion and realization, practice, birth (or life) and death, and buddhas and living beings"; and dropping such categories, and living no delusion and no realization, no life and no death, and no buddhas and no living beings—are our practice of the Buddha Dharma at a specific time. Inserting the word *when* indicates a time when both, or one or the other, of these views are necessary. And there is going beyond concepts to arrive at "just this is it."

Sometimes it is helpful to relate to the labels of delusion and realization, birth and death, buddhas and living beings. Sometimes we must let go of these categories, resulting in the mind of no delusion and no realization, and so on. Letting go of a particular scenario we may be attached to is actualizing, for example, no birth and no death. This no birth and no death is no-inherently-existing-birth and death. This is the view of realizing our inter-being and connection with all of life as one continuous holistic process. Regardless of our idea of labeling or not labeling, and regardless of our focus, both views are functioning at the same time. This understanding may not completely mollify our attachment to this life, for example, but it will transform our view and response.

At some point, our own experience will require us to engage the dichotomies Dōgen presents and what that may mean to us. Furthermore, we realize that as human beings we will always experience "flowers fall[ing] even though we love them." This is our human condition. When and how we implement our understanding will naturally be like a multilane highway in which we change lanes depending upon how we want to negotiate our journey. Yet regardless of the lane we choose, the whole road is always present.

When all dharmas are the Buddha Dharma, there is delusion and realization, practice, life and death, buddhas and living beings.

As I mentioned in the introduction, Dōgen's early texts are in the service of teaching people the basics of his understanding of Buddhist philosophy and practice. He wrote "Genjōkōan" as a letter to a lay disciple named Yo Kōshū, who may have met Dōgen on his travels to or from China.[2]

Because the initial audience for this text was a layperson, it would be logical to assume that it was Dōgen's intention to write his instructions in a clear and straightforward fashion. This would be in line with his earliest texts, such as 1227's "Fukanzazengi" (Recommending Zazen to All People) and 1231's "Bendōwa" (On the Endeavor of the Way).[3] It is for this reason I have decided to comment on the opening lines in the simplest and most direct way.[4]

In "When all dharmas are the Buddha Dharma," "Buddha Dharma" (shobō no buppō)[5] literally means "to study the Buddha's teachings." Dōgen thus begins this fascicle by saying, in effect, "Look, when we study reality from a Buddhist perspective, we break it down into these elements—delusion and realization, practice, life and death, buddhas and living beings." To this day, in discussing our practice life, we often investigate these categories.

When we ask, "What is delusion?" the question is inevitably accompanied by "What is awakening?" As we begin practice, we are often driven by the desire to end our own delusion, which we experience as personal suffering. Consequently we become attracted to awakening and wish to distance ourselves from delusion. It is not uncommon to want to reject our current situation as being mired in delusion and imagine that the future goal of practice is enlightenment. It is helpful to be clear about Dōgen's belief in the efficacy of your life in all of its complexity.

In "Shōji" (Birth and Death), Dōgen writes,

Your present birth-and-death itself is the life of Buddha. If you attempt to reject it with aversion, you thereby lose the life of Buddha. If you abide in it, attaching to birth-and-death, you also lose the life of Buddha and are left with only its outward appearance. You attain the mind of Buddha only when there is no hating of birth-and-death and no desiring of nirvana.[6]

Here Dōgen clearly states that the aim of practice is not to reject our life in order to attain "the life of Buddha." In fact, this life itself is a buddha's life. Our question is not "How do I reject this life in order to attain enlightenment?" but rather "How do I realize that this life's problems and mistakes are the very source of Buddha's Way?" Clarifying the meaning of realization and its relationship to our messy life is key to correctly understanding Dōgen's presentation of practice-realization. Therefore, "practice" in this sentence is the very activity of living out Dōgen's teachings, which is not different from the effort we make to wake up in the midst of our relational, intimate life. This practice is genjōkōan.

I believe that since Dōgen wrote "Genjōkōan" as a primer for those entering practice, he opens by meeting us at our own beginning—at a place of assuming that oppositional concepts are real. Of course, Dōgen does not stop there, nor does he really understand delusion and realization, life and death, or buddhas and living beings as incompatible positions. But for now, he is meeting us where we are.

In this opening sentence, Dōgen juxtaposes buddhas and living beings (and for "living beings" we could also say "sentient beings"). What is a buddha? What is a sentient being? Is *buddha* a synonym for some rarified being that is other than this delusional sentient being? Dōgen writes in "Uji" (Being-Time) that realization and delusion are both parts of our self's response. He writes that our buddha-ness (sixteen-foot golden Buddha-body) is not different from our daily life, and at the same time the delusional self (demonic asura) is also our life.[7]

Where does our skillful, wise self go when we are acting like a jerk? And when we are being calm and wise, what happens to the part of ourselves that is caught in grasping and delusion? Both are presencing; we are simultaneously buddha and sentient being.

This opening sentence touches on all aspects of our practice. Each pair of what seem like opposites becomes the Buddha Dharma deconstructed. This deconstruction is how we talk about our life of practice. This is how we are able to pick apart our experience as we strive to understand the meaning of these concepts individually.

As we study and incorporate each aspect of Buddhism, we begin to see that they are actually one thing. It is like a quilt: We work one piece at a time, but there is a larger project—the quilt itself. We pursue a design one section at a time, but to make a quilt we must join the pieces. When all the pieces are sewn together, we see one thing: a quilt. This quilt becomes all of reality manifesting. This sets the stage for what Dōgen writes next.

When the ten thousand dharmas are without [fixed] self, there is no delusion and no realization, no buddhas and no living beings, no birth and no death.

Again, the sentence begins with "When." "When" indicates a particular time that we are experiencing the same dharmas listed in the first sentence as the "ten thousand dharmas," now from a different perspective. Here we are told that these same dharmas—delusion and realization, buddhas and living beings, and birth and death—can also be understood nondualistically. These living beings (sentient beings, human beings, us) don't really have an inherently-existing-self, and there aren't reified states such as delusion or awakening separate from all of reality's arising. This is also true for buddhas and living beings, as well as birth (arising) and death (cessation), and everything named or unnamed, concealed or revealed.

Everything—every person, every situation—has independence and particularity (first sentence) while manifesting as one process with all beings (second sentence). For this reason, each one of us and all things are simultaneously coming and going, experiencing delusion and awakening, being buddhas and sentient beings, with every other person, being, and thing in this world and in this universe. We are the whole of everything while we are experiencing just one thing—birth, death, delusion, realization, buddhas, human beings, and so on.

In the first sentence, we look at practice through the lens of each piece of the quilt. In the second sentence, we sew it together and find that each piece is actually one thing called a quilt. We can deconstruct the quilt, as Dōgen does in the first sentence, but if we want to see the quilt in its entirety, we must cease to understand it as pieces and enact its function as a whole. A quilt cannot function as a quilt without this aspect of wholeness, even as "quilt-ness" is dependent upon its pieces. Finally, the pieces have to unite as one whole cloth in order to keep us warm and cozy.

Now we see the whole. Dōgen says when we take this larger perspective—which was never not there to begin with—then we cease to focus only on the pieces. We say no (inherently existing) self, no (inherently existing) delusion, no (inherently existing) enlightenment, no (inherently existing) buddhas, no (inherently existing) living beings, no (inherently existing) arising, and no (inherently existing) cessation. This is not different from the message of the Heart Sutra, wherein Avalokiteśvara says to Śāriputra, "All dharmas are marked by emptiness; they neither arise nor cease, are neither defiled nor pure, neither increase nor decrease."

This nondualism or no-inherent-existence of the pieces—arising, ceasing, delusion, awakening, living beings, buddhas, and so on— is about life as process. Life is both the individual pieces and the totality of the pieces. When we view the whole, we see that while there are particular pieces, in actuality they function as one thing. In fact, the pieces have always been that one thing. Knowing and manifesting this knowledge through one's actions is enacting no-self as a particular self. All things (dharmas) are both particular and real while causally connected in a process called life manifesting.

There is the time of working on each piece and the time of working on the whole. Even after a practitioner has experienced the time of working on the whole, it is okay to respond to each piece as it arises, because that is often how life meets us. Keeping this in mind, we also realize that we need both working together to bring forth a skillful response. This is why it is said there are no enlightened people, just enlightened moments. Realization is a collaborative effort of the self and all being(s). But in order to respond with our awakened mind, we must function from the place of knowing that we are never separate from the whole of reality. We have to hold both particular and universal, as well as go beyond both.

A contemporary example is when we encounter a person with whom we have very different beliefs, to the point that we really have come to dislike and disrespect this person. We are upset whenever we see them, and we certainly don't feel a lot of love or equanimity toward them. Yet our practice requests of us that we cultivate goodwill toward others. Practicing goodwill enables us to respond with compassion and wisdom, which results in a skillful response. How can we develop these responses when we don't feel kindly toward that person?

If we have faith and belief in the second sentence of Dōgen's "Genjōkōan," then we understand we are not separate from this other person. This involves understanding the meaning of delusion in the first sentence as delusion about the interconnection between ourselves and this person we dislike. This reminds us that we are not fundamentally different. If we are not different from them, then how do we work with our desire to push them away? How do we work with our certainty that we are not compatible with this person?

We can ask, "At this time of discord, how do I find the time of harmony? Because the time of harmony and discord are the same time, how can I reconcile my problem?" This kind of deep inquiry is not easy. A part of us will probably resist acknowledging that looking at the other person with the compassion of interconnection may bring up a defensive response in our mind. Nevertheless, we persevere and gently work with our mind to solve this dilemma.

We do this by examining the meaning of no-inherently-existing-self, how causal conditions arise, and what it means to look at humans and buddhas together. We can't do this work without fully immersing ourselves in both the whole picture (second sentence) and the individual aspects of practice (first sentence).

Since the Buddha Way by nature goes beyond [the dichotomy of] abundance and deficiency, there is arising and perishing, delusion and realization, living beings and buddhas.

In the example above, our salvation, our practice, arises because following the Buddha Way involves being willing to challenge our own fixed views. We are asked to see that this person is more than "abundance and deficiency" while we believe they are deficient in what we want or abundant in what we don't want. They may have the same feeling about us. We see that all of the dichotomies exist: "Yes, they are a pain in the ass; yes, I am caught, angry, disappointed. And yet what about going beyond those labels—can I do that?" We must have faith that we can respond from a place beyond what holds us captive.

This doesn't mean that we don't set boundaries when we believe that something is harmful in another's behavior. When we can act from the place of not being caught by our own attachments, we can then set those boundaries skillfully. We can discern if harm is actually being caused and, if it is, set boundaries without being either punitive or too lax.

In the Buddha Way, we come back around to addressing the specificity of "arising and perishing, delusion and realization, living beings and buddhas." But this time we are able to integrate particularity (first sentence) and universality (second sentence) into a skillful response "beyond [the dichotomy of] abundance and deficiency" (third sentence).

In "Since the Buddha Way by nature goes beyond[8] (J. chōshutsu) [the dichotomy of] abundance and deficiency . . . ," "since" means that because the way of Buddha goes beyond what is this or that, it transcends any labels that create fixed views antithetical to awakening. Yet, at the same time, in this life, how and what we express is through the medium of "arising and perishing, delusion and realization, living beings and buddhas." Do not understand this sentence to mean that we should view our life solely through the lens of the doctrine of emptiness. We don't want to suffer, and sometimes we believe that if we focus entirely on some state beyond abundance and deficiency—that is, emptiness—we will transcend our life and find some peace of mind. But in Mahayana Buddhism, we are not trying to transcend anything. We are fully in the mud and muck of our life, realizing its particularity. It is through becoming acquainted with how life actually works that we are able to find peace. It is a process of transformation through, not transcendence of.

One of my favorite quotations is from Dōgen's Shōbōgenzō "Kattō" (Twining Vines). He observes, "In general, although sacred beings all aim to learn the cutting of the roots of the complicated,[9] they do not learn that cutting means cutting the complicated with the complicated, and they do not know that the complicated is entwined with the complicated."[10]

The entwining vines are practice-realization and problems-delusion. They are in a symbiotic relationship. They appear to be opposites but actually define and drive each other's activity. We must go into our problems to find liberation from them. We cannot cut off the roots of problems; we have to face and work through our relationship with difficulties. For this reason, we don't want to reject troublesome situations.

In Sōtō Zen we have many activities within our rituals. We learn to hit bells, bow in a certain way, and many other practices. We do this, in part, because these activities bring out problems. Perhaps we struggle with fear of making a mistake or, conversely, we become arrogant in our abilities. When this happens, the forms of ritual become the twining vines of practice. As we work through our obstacles, we discover intimacy with other practitioners and the objects we engage, thereby dropping our self-conscious clinging and freeing ourselves to work with all aspects of the ritual. These, in turn, become the mandala that goes beyond abundance and scarcity. We unselfconsciously hit the bell, chant the chant, and so forth without judgment of self or other.

Therefore flowers fall even though we love them; weeds grow even though we dislike them.

We are right in the middle of clinging and aversion. We just can't help it as human beings. Yet knowing this is so, we still make an effort to bring forth our bodhi mind in response.

This sentence is perhaps my favorite passage in "Genjōkōan" because, despite our intellectual understanding, we are human, and we get caught over and over again. In his teaching on this line, the influential Sōtō Zen monk and teacher Shunryu Suzuki Roshi said,

> [T]his is life. And if you do not try to understand this point fully, those profound teachings [are] nothing to us. So actually, it is necessary to practice—to continue our practice in [the] realm of duality as unenlightened people. We are all unenlightened people, and we should strive for enlightenment. We should do that. While you are striving for it, you will really understand what Dōgen meant. Unless you do that, you will have no result. You will not find out any meaning of life.[11]

Suzuki Roshi's commentary strikes me as very sensible. I take him to mean that no matter how much we want to spend our time trying to avoid our problems, we will still have to face our own difficulties. Effort in practice is to continue as we grapple with our likes and dislikes, our desires and fears. If this practice resonates with you, then it becomes a lifeline and can transform your relationship to suffering.

Going beyond the dichotomy of abundance and scarcity, accepting impermanence in the midst of clinging and accepting aversion as we strive to find equanimity is not apart from our bodhisattva practice. It is said a bodhisattva fully participates in life while not engaging in unwholesome attachments. A bodhisattva is grounded in their daily life and is not caught by their delusion or that of others. Bodhisattvas see the practice of leaping beyond and staying put. This is to be *in* our life—we are completely engaged with our life but not *of* or caught by our delusions. We don't ping-pong back and forth between too much and too little. We avoid getting caught; we go beyond both, leaping clear of the obstacles of our karmic tendencies or habits. We can hold both sides of a situation. This is the opening message of "Genjōkōan," after which Dōgen begins to examine the nuts and bolts of understanding reality and actualizing suchness.

CHAPTER 3

WHAT DOES REALIZATION LOOK LIKE?

Conveying oneself toward all things to carry out practice-
enlightenment is delusion. All things coming and carrying
out practice-enlightenment through the self is realization.
Those who greatly realize delusion are buddhas. Those
who are greatly deluded in realization are living beings.
Furthermore, there are those who attain realization beyond
realization and those who are deluded within delusion.
When buddhas are truly buddhas they don't need to
perceive they are buddhas; however, they are enlightened
buddhas and they continue actualizing buddha.

In this section, Dōgen clearly defines what realized action looks like
in the middle of our messy lives. This teaching flows nicely from the
previous line, "Therefore flowers fall even though we love them;
weeds grow even though we dislike them."

Conveying oneself toward all things to carry out practice-enlightenment
is delusion. All things coming and carrying out practice-enlightenment
through the self is realization.

To convey oneself "toward all things to carry out practice-
enlightenment" refers to pushing our own agenda to the detriment

of others. This is a delusory response. The "self" of this sentence is the self caught in its own desires, to the point that there is no room to see others as having their own needs and wants. When we bring forth the self that is caught in delusion, caught in likes and dislikes, and try to "carry out practice-enlightenment," the results will not be in accord with the Dharma. In delusion, we are responding from the position of "What's in it for me?" rather than "How can I help?"

Remember that problematic person who was such a pain in the ass in the previous chapter? If we always approach that person with the notion that they are the problem, and we are not open to the causes and conditions of our relationship with them, then we think it's okay to reject them—to shut them out. This "conveying oneself," or perpetuating the delusional mind, is antithetical to "carrying out practice-enlightenment." We may deceive ourselves by blaming the other. We say, "Oh, that person isn't practicing, therefore they are the problem." If we think this way, we are interpreting our situation from the delusional mind or the mind of likes and dislikes. "Conveying oneself toward all things," in this case, is reifying our own view. All we are doing is solidifying our own notion of the situation or our own ideas about practice in a self-serving way.

Facing the truth or allowing the idea that more may be happening than our narrow view would mean that we have to let go of an idea of who we are and our story of what is happening around us. This is scary and threatens our sense of self. This inability to accurately discern our current situation is getting caught in "flowers falling" and "weeds growing."

As humans, we are very attached to our likes and dislikes, mainly because they are a major source of perceived self-stability. Buddhist practice is difficult because our small mind, while trying to protect itself from the fear of being erased, much prefers to remain caught up in black-and-white thinking.

If we say "I'm always right" about something, then it has a kind of certainty. This "right" becomes a definition of who we are. It becomes a kind of core delusion we hang on to that often leads to harmful action because it pits those who agree with us against those who do not. And those who do not become the "bad" standing in contrast to our "good." As we cling to these definitions of self, regardless of the situation or needs of the other person, we can fall into a kind of personal authoritarianism or rigidity because we are trying to protect a self that actually does not need protection. It does not even exist the way we think it does.

As Dōgen points out in the first line of "Genjōkōan," we use the stages or categories of learning practice—"delusion and realization, practice, life and death, buddhas and living beings"—to deconstruct our delusional thinking. This is not an intellectual practice; it is very real. Practice is about all the feelings that we encounter when the metaphorical and real blossoms in our pretty flower arrangement start to wilt. It is the reality of all the weeds that spread in our garden, beyond our control, that keep popping up over and over again.

When I was a first-year student at Tassajara Zen Mountain Center, there was a woman who just drove me nuts. I couldn't stand her. One day she and I were yelling at each other across a courtyard in front of the study hall. Everyone could hear us, and this was supposed to be a silent time. The head monk had to come out and tell us to stop. At that time, I was working very hard to find some way to come to terms with my anger in general, but specifically with this person.

My primary study guide for this practice was the chapter on patience in Shantideva's *Guide to the Bodhisattva Way.* Cultivating patience is the Buddhist antidote to anger. Enacting the teachings from a book to bring about transformation is hard. Reading about how to practice is not practice—we have to walk the walk. I had to open my mind to the myriad dharmas of my life and imagine the causes and conditions of my enemy's life.

I would sit down and say to myself, "I hate her!" Another voice would say, "Remember your practice—remember that each of you is struggling with all the causes and conditions of your life that brought you together. Remember that she is suffering too." Then I would say to myself, "So what?!?" And again I would recall, think about, and apply the Buddha Dharma's teachings.[1] Back and forth

I did this until I understood in a real way how this worked. This woman was a Dharma gift to me, although at the time it didn't feel that way.

If I had continued to wallow in my conviction that I was the victim of this woman's perceived misdeeds, then I would not have escaped the suffering of my delusion. Every time I reinforced my belief in what was wrong with her and what was right about me, without the tempering aspect of practice, I was caught in delusion. I was conveying myself toward all things to carry out practice-realization, seeing through the eyes of my delusional interpretation of her and my world. This is the very definition of suffering.

Learning in practice is very much about our own experiences, not someone else's. This is why Dōgen writes, "All things coming and carrying out practice-enlightenment *through the self* is realization." We do not practice in another person's mind or body. It is this self that comes forward and enacts the Dharma. And it is this particularity that is met by and carries out practice-realization with the myriad dharmas practicing with the self—not for the self's agenda.[2]

Norman Waddell and Masao Abe, in their translation of this section, offer a quotation from Dōgen's *Gakudō Yōjinshū* (*Points to Watch in Practicing the Way*) almost identical to the one we are discussing:

> The Dharma turns the self; the self turns the Dharma. When the self readily turns the Dharma, the self is strong and the Dharma weak. When, on the other hand, the Dharma turns the self, the Dharma is strong and the self is weak. The Buddha Dharma originally includes both of these.[3]

This Dharma is all of reality, and we experience this self as our own particularity through the lens of our senses: this particular mind, worldview, experiences, and so forth. But in our practice we are asked to go beyond our limited view of the self and recall that we are never apart from all of reality's functioning. "Conveying oneself toward all things" is trying to "turn the Dharma." "All things coming and carrying out practice-enlightenment" is being "turned by the Dharma." Ideally our activity is reciprocal, resulting in "The Buddha Dharma originally includes both of these."

There are times that we make our best effort to accord ourselves with the Dharma and must persevere in the midst of what may seem like a fruitless effort. In 2024, as I write this section, we are faced with catastrophic climate change. In the United States, back in the 1970s, President Richard Nixon created the Environmental Protection Agency because he acknowledged that we were creating huge problems for the earth that needed to be addressed. Fifty years later, we are still unable to grasp the enormity of our attachments to having it our way.

The vow of a bodhisattva is to continue to practice in the midst of suffering, regardless of the delusion that may be unfolding. If we do not persevere in our attempts to address climate change, then it is inevitable that catastrophe will continue and worsen. As Dōgen writes in Shōbōgenzō "Kūge" (Flowers of Emptiness), the bodhisattva's practice can only unfold in the middle of the fire. He writes that "the time and place that blue lotus flowers open and spread are in the midst of fire and in the time of fire."[4] In other words, our bodhisattva practice is called upon and blooms in times of difficulty—that is the very definition of the bodhisattva's vow to benefit all being(s). We should continue our practice without necessarily clinging to a certain outcome.

When we are able to open ourselves to more than our limited view, then we become reunited with reality, or the Buddha Dharma. We strive to fully participate as a partner in the dance of life: call and response, step and sway, give and take.

In the *Goshō*, Kyōgō rejects a relative understanding of the paragraph under consideration. He writes,

> Commonly speaking, it seems [Dōgen Zenji is saying] that to practice-verify the myriad things using the self is delusion, and that the myriad things coming toward the self and carrying out practice-verification is realization. Such understanding is not

right. If we understand in such a way, "self" and "myriad things," and "delusion" and "realization," become separate things. This [interpretation] is not correct.[5]

Kyōgō seems to disagree with a commentary that makes a distinction between the delusional self and a realized self. He focuses on the second sentence of "Genjōkōan": no-inherently-existing: self, delusion, realization, buddhas, living beings, birth, or death.

A possible complication of Kyōgō's universal view is that we may deceive ourselves in thinking that we do not need to address our unskillful actions or that this nondualistic view gives us a free pass to act in ways that are not inclusive of another's needs. This is a nihilistic misunderstanding of the nonduality of self and other. Consequently I think it is important to take up the relative teaching.

Those who greatly realize delusion are buddhas. Those who are greatly deluded in realization are living beings. Furthermore, there are those who attain realization beyond realization and those who are deluded within delusion.

When we become aware of our delusion and practice with that delusion, we are not caught by it. This is "those who greatly realize delusion are buddhas." Being caught is "those who are greatly deluded in realization are living beings." Dōgen describes these two states as "buddha" and "living beings."

It would be easy to think he is saying there are enlightened beings—buddhas; and then there are delusional folks—living beings. *Shujō* (衆生), the Japanese word translated here as "living (or sentient) beings," refers to all beings as sentient beings bearing the qualities of buddha-nature.

In Shōbōgenzō "Busshō" (Buddha-Nature), Dōgen writes,

What is the essence of the World-Honored One's words, *All sentient beings without exception have the Buddha-nature?*[6] It is his utterance of the Dharma teaching: "What is this that thus comes?" Whether you speak of "living beings (*shujo*)," "sentient beings," "all classes of living things," or "all varieties of living beings" it makes no difference. The words entire being . . . mean both sentient beings and all living beings. In other words, entire being is the Buddha-nature. I call the whole integral entity of entire being "sentient being."[7]

We are buddhas and living beings simultaneously. Dōgen's labels of delusion and realization enable us to understand that there is a difference between delusional, unskillful response and realized response. Dōgen tells us that when we "greatly realize delusion," we are responding from the mind or position of a buddha. When we are caught in our delusional logic, then we are "greatly deluded living beings." In other words, sometimes we are caught circling around in an eddy of muddy water; other times we respond sitting atop the lotus blossom. Both states rest upon the substratum of buddha-nature.

Time is implied in this section of "Genjōkōan," which could easily begin with when we convey ourselves toward things, when we are greatly realized about delusion, and so on. Dōgen distinguishes buddhas from living beings only by their ability to avoid being caught in delusional thinking about any given situation, person, thing, or time.

We are buddhas and living beings simultaneously. Living beings are buddhas, and buddhas are living beings. Both are presencing in each of us and all being(s). Our basic nature is buddha-nature, and buddha-nature is another way to refer to the interconnected, impermanent, nondual processing called life. This is why Dōgen writes that we are "greatly deluded in realization." Realization is reality's presencing as suchness. We are suchness; we are not separate from reality's functioning. Therefore, we are caught in delusion in the midst of realization.

This is not about the someone else you may become in the future. In "Shōji" (Birth and Death), Dōgen explicitly spells this out: "Your present birth-and-death itself is the life of Buddha. If you attempt to reject it with aversion, you thereby lose the life of Buddha."[8] In the same text he writes, "To seek Buddha apart from birth-and-death is like pointing . . . northward when you want to go south."[9]

This is a reoccurring theme in Dōgen's understanding. We are not trying to jettison our life in favor of some other life we do not currently inhabit. Our practice can only happen right here and now. So, we must wake up to our delusion and accept it as the very means by which we are able to sit amid the fire of the blue lotus of our life and our society and respond skillfully. In this way, we meet and are verified by myriad dharmas: the situations and people of our life.

Furthermore, there are those who attain realization beyond realization and those who are deluded within delusion.[10]

Is Dōgen talking about one person who is both in delusion and realization or two separate people? Because Japanese pronouns can be ambiguous, this sentence can be translated both ways.[11] Kazuaki Tanahashi translates this sentence as, "Further, there are those who continue realizing beyond realization, who are in delusion throughout delusion."[12] In this translation, a person can occupy the state of "realization beyond realization," and the same person can occupy the state of being "deluded within delusion." These states or dharma positions are simultaneously present in all of us. We can be completely in the state of delusion or completely in the state of actualizing realization, depending upon our mind and circumstances.

In his commentary on this sentence, the Meiji-era Sōtō monk Nishiari Bokusan writes,

> What is it you realize? You realize delusion. Also it says, "greatly deluded about delusion." Look. When you are deluded, what are you deluded about? You are deluded about enlightenment. In this way, when you say "delusion," and when you say "enlightenment," in the end, it is a borderline between the self and myriad dharmas.[13]

His point is that "realization beyond realization" and "deluded within delusion" are dependent upon each other; they coexist. Although they might appear to butt against each other, without one there cannot be the other. Consequently we have the borderline that Nishiari talks about.

When you are "realization beyond realization," you are unaware of awakening because it is just the state you are experiencing without defining that experience as awakened. Yet there is delusion and there is realization, and it is the contrast between the two that defines them. This contrast is real, as delusion and realization result in different outcomes.

The borderline Nishiari refers to hearkens back to the lines, "Conveying oneself toward all things to carry out practice-enlightenment is delusion. All things coming and carrying out practice-enlightenment through the self is realization." Dōgen distinguishes between self and all things, but self and all things are also not different. It is this borderline or delineation between one thing (self) and myriad dharmas (all things) that creates the conditions for both realization and delusion. These are individual responses in concert or discord as (and with) all being(s) responding and making the world. This intersection is also the place in which delusion or realization about reality arises and manifests.

Practice-enlightenment is not myriad things and the self merging into each other, because realized action is enacted by particular persons or dharmas. Instead, the intimate state of individuation within the whole of reality's functioning, in relationship with myriad things, is what responds with a buddha mind.

Kyōgō complements this teaching when he writes,

It seems the person appears specifically and abruptly, but this person refers to the person of "The entire ten-direction world is the true human body." We should understand that being [on the ground of] realization is called a "person," and being within delusion is called a "person."[14]

The "entire ten-direction world is the true human body" is the universal aspect of our life. "The person appears" is our particular self manifesting in relationship to the "entire ten-direction world." This existence model can be applied to the first two sentences of "Genjōkōan"—there is particularity with distinctions: "When all dharmas are the Buddha Dharma, there is delusion and realization, practice, life and death, buddhas and living beings"; and there is unity as inter-being: "When the ten thousand dharmas are without [fixed] self, there is no delusion and no realization, no buddhas and no living beings, no birth and no death."

Within the same person there is "realization beyond realization" and being "deluded within delusion." In other words, all of us are going beyond realization, and all of us get caught in delusion to the point that we don't see it as delusion. There is a border between the states of delusion and realization, yet that border is borderless when we realize that "the ten thousand dharmas are without [fixed] self." It is this fluid state that enables us to be freed from our karmic hindrances in the instance of realization beyond realization.

When buddhas are truly buddhas they don't need to perceive they are buddhas; however, they are enlightened buddhas and they continue actualizing buddha.

Buddhas who do not need to label themselves as realized are realization beyond realization. Ideally, fully enacted practice-realization is unselfconscious. When we respond to our life with realized mind, we just respond to our life. We are not thinking, "I am a buddha," nor are we thinking, "I am a demon." Chances are good that each one of us engages in small acts of enlightened response daily. For example, if we spontaneously open the door for someone whose hands are full, we don't think to ourselves, "That was an enlightened action!" Yet realization arises from putting ourselves in the other person's shoes and responding from the mind of inclusion. This realization, presencing as one event, is the world unfolding.

You do not perceive yourself as buddha, yet you are enacting a buddha's response.

Our buddha mind (as well as our delusional mind) is always activated within the context of a particular time, place, and being with others. There are also causal antecedents. Realization is relational, not the property of a person. It is a myth to assume that an individual achieves enlightenment once and for all. Furthermore, while we may be responding with buddha mind, we are not its verifiers. This is "the myriad dharmas proceeding to practice and verify the self is awakening."[15] These myriad dharmas are everything inter-being or practicing buddha-nature. Out of that intimate dance of interaction comes verification of the self's activity as awakened activity. But as soon as the self pats itself on the back for its good works, that self slides into delusion.

Only the particularity of each person can interact with other dharmas (situations, persons, other creatures, things). These relational interactions and their effects exhibit delusional or awakened behavior. What defines (or verifies) either category is not losing sight of reality's nondual nature. We do none of this on our own. Therefore, to congratulate the self as realized is delusion. As Kyōgō writes, "When all buddhas are truly all buddhas, there is neither self nor perception. . . . This 'verification' has no separation between subject and object."[16]

The last clause of this section of "Genjōkōan"—"however, they are enlightened buddhas and they continue actualizing buddha"—points out that even if buddhas are not aware that they are buddhas, they *are* buddhas. Consequently these functioning moments of buddha-nature are verifying that there are buddhas. Kyōgō writes, "This 'verification' has no separation between subject and object. Though it is said that 'they continue verifying' [Okumura's translation is 'continue actualizing'], there is no one who verifies. Buddha's verification is like this. 'To continue verifying' is called verification."[17]

No subject-object relationship can readily be identified, according to Kyōgō. Using actualization instead of verification, Kyōgō's last sentence above becomes "To continue actualizing is called actualizing."

Shō (證), translated here as "verification" or "actualization," is the same character used in "practice-realization" (修證).[18]

Practice-realization accords us with the whole functioning together. This activity is the entire world manifesting and supporting each dharma, thus continuously verifying the Dharma, even if we can't see the verification.

There is a sense here of a kind of perpetual motion between the practice of buddhas that affects and continues the practice of buddhas. "To verify" is active—a verb signifying altruistic functioning in practice-realization. There is this buddha, or that buddha, or buddhas verifying the activity of all of buddha-nature, presencing through the practice-realization of all and one simultaneously.

Here is an example from my life, which I think sums up the complexity and unfolding of this kind of inter-being of practice-realization. I am at my local grocery store the day before Thanksgiving. The express line is not open, there are only a few clerks, and the line is very long—maybe twenty people. I'm about four people from the back, and I have two items. The clerk from the coffee bar comes over to my area of the line and points to four of us who have few items and says, "Come over to the coffee register and I'll check you out."

We all peel off and head to the coffee-bar register. I am the last in line. A man rushes up behind me and says in a whiny voice, "What about me? I was ahead of you." I reply, "Don't complain; just go ahead of me," which he does. The woman in front of him, having heard our exchange, also lets him go in front of her. Now he is in the front of the line.

I could see the delusion of the guy who complained. He thought he had been slighted when he hadn't. The clerk didn't see him. Nevertheless, his delusion annoyed my delusion, so I said, "Don't complain."

I realized my delusion because "Don't complain" was unnecessary and judgmental, but I said it nevertheless. Although I was not perfect, I was good enough. I let him go ahead of me, although somewhat begrudgingly. Clearly my actions were not completely awakened. They were in the ballpark but did not have the quality

Dōgen later characterizes as "realization beyond realization." My response was spontaneous but not necessarily skillful.

Often in practice we don't see what we are doing is off the mark. The first thing we have to do is see that. What do we see? We see that we are only perceiving our situation from our own perspective. We are carrying the self forward. Feeling irritated, I characterized the other person as perceiving himself as a victim. Responding without any thing extra would have been to say, "Please go ahead," without the judgmental comment or thought on my part.

It is my observation that the person Dōgen is calling "buddha" and the person he is calling "sentient being," as well as the times of their "realization" or "delusion," are fluid. Very likely, the guy who complained does not always complain. This complaining is empty of inherent existence. In a different scenario, surely he is the one responding with his buddha mind. Consequently we go back and forth with varying degrees of success.

Perhaps when the woman ahead of me heard our exchange and said "Please go ahead of me," her buddha was actualized. Maybe it was already actualized and she immediately said, "Go ahead." But her ability to say "Go ahead of me" was still contingent upon me saying "Go ahead." My saying "Go ahead" was dependent upon the guy's complaint, and so on back through the causal chain of events. In our stumbling manner, we were buddhas actualizing each other.

Each one of us has affected the outcome of this situation and in some hidden way carried forward the practice of no-self by acknowledging the needs of one another. By doing so, we may be buddhas who "continue actualizing buddha," although we had no intention of doing so or even defining our actions in such a way.

Sometimes a person engages realization beyond realization, while at other times we activate being deluded within delusion. Sometimes a person functions as a bodhisattva in both states; sometimes we go back and forth or do both simultaneously. These states are not oppositional; they are situational and informed by our level of awareness.

Both delusion and realization are our actual state. We swim in both. Good swimmers—that is, bodhisattvas—swim effortlessly without thought while totally immersed in the delusional samsaric world. Sometimes we greatly realize delusion, and sometimes we are greatly deluded in realization. And sometimes we facilitate the practice of others as we continue to actualize buddhas, resulting in both self and other cofunctioning in realized activity.

CHAPTER 4

PERCEPTIONS AND VERIFICATION

In seeing color and hearing sound with body and mind, although we perceive them intimately, [the perception] is not like reflections in a mirror or the moon in water. When one side is illuminated, the other is dark.

"Seeing color and hearing sound" refers to two stories of awakening: Zen Master Reiun Shigon seeing peach blossoms, and Zen Master Kyōgen Chikan hearing the sound of a piece of tile hitting bamboo. Both practitioners were students of Zen Master Dayuan of Dawei.[1] Dōgen writes about their stories in Shōbōgenzō "Keisei Sanshiki"[2] (Sound of the Stream, Form of the Mountain):

> One day, [Zen Master Reiun Shigon,][3] while on a ramble in the mountains, stops for a rest at the foot of a hill and views the villages in the distance. It is spring, and peach blossoms are in full bloom. Seeing them, he suddenly realizes the truth. He makes the following verse and presents it to Dai-I, his teacher.
> > For thirty years, a traveler in search of a sword.[4]
> > How many times have leaves fallen and buds sprouted?
> > After one look at peach blossoms,
> > I have arrived directly at the present and have no further doubts.[5]

Reiun saw the peach blossoms blooming and had an awakening experience because, having dropped the self that perceives the blossoms as other than the self, he perceived them for themselves. This is the same realization that Master Chikan had upon hearing a tile hit bamboo.

Master Chikan studied many years with his master (also Reiun's), Dai-I.[6] First he had to let go of intellectual study, which was blocking his understanding. He countered this tendency by devoting himself to service. Finally, in consultation with Dai-I, he moved to a hermitage where he tended his garden. Dōgen writes,

> One day, while he is sweeping the path, a piece of tile flies up and strikes a bamboo with a crack. Hearing the sound, he suddenly realizes the great state of realization. He bathes and purifies himself, and facing Dai-i-zan Mountain, he burns incense and does prostrations. He says, *Great Master Dai-I! If you had explained it to me before, how would this thing have been possible? The depth of your kindness surpasses that of a parent.*[7]

These integrated forms and sounds are the same as realization beyond realization. Reiun and Chikan did not label their experience nor break it down into discrete functions; they just experienced the one perception without subject (what sees or hears) and object (what is seen or heard). Having experienced the intimacy of not-self, not-other, their responses to their situations arose in accord with the totality of cooperative function.

But do not take away from this teaching that awakening is an experience of merging with what is perceived. We are simultaneously both the same and different from the perceived object. Intimacy does not remove our particularity or the particularity of the object of perception. What it does, rather, is break down the dualism that hinders our ability to respond skillfully to our situation. A buddha who does not realize they are a buddha is functioning in the mode of nonseparation while maintaining their integrity as a separate being. We are not merged with the other; we are in accord. We respond with empathy to another's pain; yet, at the same time, you are still you and they are still they, while both are we.

Dōgen expresses this later in "Genjōkōan" when he writes, "Realization does not destroy the person, as the moon does not make a hole in the water." There is realization, person, moon, and water. It is the integration based upon the shared inter-being, interconnection, and no-inherently-existing-is-ness that is expressed as realized or intimate response. Realized response is not some kind of melding that erases all particularity. We hold both as being true: oneness and particularity.

Dōgen continues his discussion of a buddha's intimate awakening with "[The perception] is not like reflections in a mirror or the moon in water. When one side is illuminated, the other is dark."

When we have an intimate experience of seeing and hearing without dualistic ideation getting in the way of immediate response, this experience is different from when we are looking in a mirror and seeing our reflection or looking at a puddle and seeing the moon reflected in the water. Looking in the mirror and looking at the moon reflected in water, we see both moon and water, and we see both reflection and mirror. In the case of intimately seeing and hearing, we do not see both sides simultaneously because we are fully engaged with a nondual perception of self and other. Yet, at the same time, both sides are still presencing or individuating, although we are perceiving one thing. Dōgen makes this point by saying "one side is illuminated; the other side is dark."

To experience something intimately (in this case, seeing color or hearing sound), we do not understand the object of our perception as disconnected from ourselves. This intimate perceptual understanding causes us to drop the self's agenda.

Such perceptual immersion does not erase our selfhood or the selfhood of the perceived other. Hee-Jin Kim writes of this section of "Genjōkōan,"

> The Way was "intimately understood" in and through what we expressed and enacted by the mustering of our body-minds. Humans and the Way were no longer in a dualistic relationship like that of the moon and the water, or the mirror and the reflection, or the knower and the known. . . . Nonduality did not primarily signify the transcendence of duality so much as it signified the realization of duality.[8]

Kim's "realization of duality" is when we acknowledge both self and other as having intrinsic agency in a situation. As he points out, we are not trying to transcend our duality or particularity in the service of awakening. Holding both particularity and nonduality is what allows realization to manifest.

Kim ties together Dōgen's intimacy of hearing and seeing, revealed and hidden, with entering the presencing moment completely. He writes,

> This statement epitomizes the principle of "the total exertion of one dharma": when one dharma is disclosed, all other dharmas are concealed. This is closely related to the "principle of simultaneous establishment of concealment and disclosure."[9]

"Total exertion of one dharma" (*ippō-gūjin*, 一法究盡) is often translated as "total exertion of a single thing." In the context of "Genjōkōan," Senne writes, "We should just say that the moon is reflected in the moon and the mirror is reflected in the mirror."[10] That is, if you fully understand the moon, then you will understand both what you can see and what you cannot see. What we experience is a total immersion in each moment's unfolding.

Kyōgō's commentary reiterates this view. If we fully engage the specificity of our current situation, everything else will fall into place as the "moment's intimate arising." He further observes,

> When we say body/mind, there is nothing outside body/mind. When we say the color or the sound, there is nothing outside

the color or the sound. This is the meaning of "when one side is verified another side is dark."[11]

When we fully engage sound, there is just sound. When we fully engage color, there is just color. "Just" refers to ippō-gūjin, or total engagement with one thing, as fully encompassing the totality of experience. That one thing verifies what is illuminated yet does not negate the aspect that is not seen.

To completely experience one thing is to realize all things as we investigate the one. How can this be possible? The conceptual development behind this view can be found in Huayan philosophy, which posits that all things are mutually penetrating and have mutual identity.

Mutual identity is meant to convey the observation that all things share the qualities of (1) having no inherently separate existence, (2) being subject to causal relationships, and (3) being impermanent. Mutual penetration posits that if everything shares the qualities of mutual identity, then they are also in a state of physically penetrating, comingling, and cofunctioning together. For example, when you eat something, it becomes part of you on a cellular level. What began as something outside becomes inside or beyond inside—it becomes you.

Consequently, if you fully understand one thing through the lens of mutual identity, mutual penetration, or comingling, then you will know something essential about reality's functioning. From this understanding will come awakening.[12] This is why Kyōgō says, "When we say body/mind, there is nothing outside body/mind." This can be said of any dharma. Therefore, Dōgen points out that this is not about the moon's relationship to water or a reflection's relationship to an object of reflection. When we fully integrate body-mind-sight-sound, we experience and manifest our understanding. We know on a cellular level the importance of this single immersion in the intimacy of one thing, which is the dharma gate to all things and our relationship to them. From this comes awakened response.

Does this happen in daily life? I argue it does and that it happens exactly as Dōgen describes in this section of "Genjōkōan." This experience of paying attention to one thing is not like deeply examining or pondering the essence of something in the abstract—a type of attention often portrayed by Auguste Rodin's famous statue, *The Thinker*. It is an interactive experience in which we fully pay attention and remain open to intimate inclusive functioning with the totality of an experience.

Let's take the example of driving your car in traffic. If you drive your car as if you were the only person on the road, this will create serious problems for yourself and others. This is being greatly deluded in realization. If you drive your car cognizant of the rules of the road, then you will be skillful and harmonized with others. This is realizing the shared experience of inter-being mutual driving.

If you are aware of the problems that arise for you when you are driving, such as impatience or critical mind, and you know that this can manifest in your driving, then you can counter your instincts to act out. This is the same as being greatly realized about delusion.

Awakening to and remediating your difficulties will result in skillful, integrated driving. If you don't drive this way, then you are blindly caught in delusion and might cause problems or even an accident. On the other hand, if you drive in such a way that you are integrated and without the hindrances of your attachments, then you may be totally unconscious of any effort you are making. Consequently you are inter-being with traffic and other drivers. No problem. This mind is realizing beyond realization because there are no labels or steps; it just is.

Because of this, your actions also create a kind of karmic ripple (as does your delusional driving) that, unbeknownst to you, creates efficacious driving by others. Hence, you go on actualizing buddhas, as do others who are doing the same thing. Very nice.

You might even have a *kenshō* experience while driving, which would correlate with "seeing color and hearing sound with body-mind" in the way the Zen masters Reiun and Chikan experienced.

This visceral awakening would be created through deeply experiencing the intimacy of the totality of one's experience as a driver. Now that would be very interesting because, to me, a true kenshō does not disrupt one's activity. One is aware of a deep compassion and connection with others. This awareness is a nonintellectual body-mind experience that allows us to dance with others. You don't need to make it special, but you are deeply moved by the intimacy and interconnection of your situation. The activities of inter-being and appropriate response are realized and enacted in everyday life.

Whether you have a special experience or an ordinary drive to the office, if you are integrated with others through dropping self-delusional clinging, then you will be a realized driver manifesting buddha-nature. Furthermore, your actions will affect others, whether you or they are conscious of it.

In order to achieve a state of realized driving, we must be totally engaged with this one thing—driving. Dōgen might say that driving drives driving when we drop our own agenda and fully immerse ourselves in driving; this is "one side is illuminated and the other is dark," or the total exertion of a single thing. When driving drives driving, we are unconsciously aware of what we are not seeing, such as the causes and conditions of other drivers. Driving is an activity with many moving parts. Yet as soon as our attention is required, we pay attention to what we are directly perceiving. For example, we stop at a red light, or our attention shifts from listening to the radio to hitting the brakes when a car in front of us slows abruptly. Responding to the car in front of us is our complete attention to one thing. And at the same time, it is a response that mirrors the totality of our and others' driving experience.

Giving Dōgen the last word, he writes in "Gabyō" (A Painted Rice Cake):

"The total experience of a single thing" does not deprive a thing of its own unique particularity. It places a thing neither against others nor against none. To place a thing against none is another form of dualistic obstruction. When total experience is realized unobstructedly . . ., the total experience of a single thing is the same as the total experience of all things. A single total experience is a single thing in its totality. The total experience of a single thing is one with that of all things.[13]

CHAPTER 5

DROPPING BODY AND MIND

To study the Buddha Way is to study the self. To study the self is to forget the self. To forget the self is to be verified by all things. To be verified by all things is to let the body and mind of the self and the body and mind of others drop off. There is a trace of realization that cannot be grasped. We endlessly express this ungraspable trace of realization.

In this next passage, Dōgen explains how we intimately experience "seeing color and hearing sound with body and mind" by looking at the true nature of the self in relationship to others. This is "to forget the self is to be verified by all things."

Dōgen clearly states that the study of this dharma called the self, if investigated through the lens of the Buddha Way, will lead to awakening. This self, when illuminated, reveals the true relationship between self and other. Dōgen calls this dropping off body-mind of self and other. Realized action is validated by all parties when we are freed of dualistic notions of self versus other. Both sides can function in accord. You can't label this experience when you are in the middle of it, but we might call it mutual interconnected process continuing without end.

In Shōbōgenzō "Jisho-zanmai" (Samadhi as Experience of the Self), Dōgen again points to the importance of studying the self as a Dharma gate to awakening:

> To take up the hundred weeds is to take up the self. To take up the ten thousand trees is to take up the self. We learn in practice that the self is inevitably efforts like these. In this learning in practice, we get rid of the self,[1] and we experience the self as exact accordance.[2]

And later in the same text,

> If we exhaustively explore the self, we will already have exhaustively explored the external world. And if we exhaustively explore the external world, we will already have exhaustively explored the self. Unless received from a master, this Buddhist standard cannot be realized in bodily experience.[3]

To study the Buddha Way is to study the self.

What is the relationship between "when one side is illuminated, the other is dark," or a deep investigation of one thing, and "to study the Buddha Way is to study the self?" Perhaps the most important point of this line is that we study the *self* rather than studying someone else. This is to focus on the nature of ourselves, which will open up the true nature of all being(s).

Quoting Shōbōgenzō "Gabyō" (A Painted Rice Cake), Dōgen clearly makes the connection between the deep study of one thing and the understanding of all things:

> Thus, it has been said [by Yün-chu], "If you understand one thing even a little, you understand all things." . . . When understanding one thing does not obstruct understanding all things, this is understanding both one thing and all things.[4]

While studying the self from a Western psychological perspective may be quite helpful, Dōgen is specifically talking about using Buddhist tenets and methods for awakening. His teaching is in some sense an application of the Huayan teachings on mutual penetration and identity to the self. We study the self and thus know this one thing, but we don't stop there, because if we really do penetrate the "one thing," we realize "all things."

Still, we will have to hold both what is seen (illuminated) and what we cannot immediately see (dark). This nonperceptual perception is intimately knowing and responding to what is presencing at this time. At the same time, when we realize and act upon our sameness, we recognize that each dharma (person, situation, and so forth) has its own particularity. That too is part of the equation of awakening.

How do we actually study the self in the Buddha Way? Much of the rest of "Genjōkōan" explores this question. The first step in studying the Buddha Way is to look at ourselves but in a very specific context as elucidated in the opening lines of "Genjōkōan": "When all dharmas are the Buddha Dharma, there is delusion and realization, practice, life and death, buddhas and living beings. When the ten thousand dharmas are without [fixed] self, there is no delusion and no realization, no buddhas and no living beings, no birth and no death."

Studying the Buddha Way is both the practice of the Buddha Way as well as the learning of the Buddha Way. Both arise hand in hand. Nevertheless, learning can be parsed as having different aspects: intellectual, observational, practice, and intuition. If you are reading this book, you are making the effort to understand the Buddha Dharma as Dōgen understood it and to apply that learning to your practice.

My initial introduction, as an American Zen student, to understanding the nature of dharmas and self was through studying the Heart Sutra, which we recited almost daily. In this sutra we read, "Form is emptiness, emptiness is form, form itself is emptiness and emptiness itself is form." Because the Heart Sutra is difficult to understand, we begin by intellectually decoding these teachings. As we integrate intellectual with intuitive understanding into our practice, we begin to observe the veracity of the teaching and to respond to our life through that lens. Intuitive understanding reflects the experiences we have had outside the intellect, yet understanding may also be dependent upon intellectual study to clarify what we intuit.[5] We can think of intellect, observation, practice, and intuition as all functioning simultaneously within the context of what is needed. So, we should not think that intellectual study is bad and intuitive response is always good, or vice versa. All four aspects function together: intellectual, observational, practice, and intuition. This inquiry is done through the self's perception, understanding, and practice.

As we study the teachings of Buddhism, we find out about the self's true nature and place in the world of dharmas. We come to see that we are impermanent and inter-being with all of reality. We are one with reality as part of a great process of becoming, and we are at the same time a particular being or dharma. Through this investigation we realize the meaning of studying the self. We may not believe it at first, but we go forward with faith in these teachings.

We may ask, "Who am I? How do I function in this vast mandala called reality?" We ask the questions that Dōgen presents: "What is delusion? What is realization? How do I approach practicing the Dharma? What is my birth and death in the Buddhist context? Am I a buddha and/or a living being? How does my understanding bring about transformation?" All of these questions may arise, and all of them will be offered in relationship to our own practice and our own view of self.

These questions become folded into our practice in a seamless way. Shohaku Okumura writes of study,

> Even when we say, "I study the Buddha Way," there is still a subject and an object that are separate. . . . When we truly practice

the Buddha Way or study the self, there is no separation between "I," "the self," "the Buddha Way," "study," and "practice." . . . Yet when we think or speak, we use concepts and we must therefore say, "I study the self," or "I study the Buddha Way." So the important point is that we should just study and just practice.[6]

As we study, observe, and practice the Buddhist doctrine concerning the absence of a separate, disconnected self operating outside the realm of causality, we begin to respond to our situation with greater intuition and intimacy. This is when study becomes practice. We begin to know that what is not revealed is contiguous with what is seen. Through that inquiry we begin to understand the second sentence of the opening: "When the ten thousand dharmas are without [fixed] self, there is no delusion and no realization, no buddhas and no living beings, no birth and no death."

But we cannot reach this understanding without entering the Dharma gate of the duality of our own experience.

To study the self is to forget the self.

Engaging in this study, we begin to see the truth of our not-separateness. Yet this can be a tricky idea because the self is still a particular self. You are you, not the other, yet you are also not different from the other. Dōgen refers to this relationship in "Uji" (Being-Time): "I encounter a man. A man encounters a man. I encounter myself. Going forth encounters going forth."[7] Each person or each thing connects with another particular person or thing. We can see each other in each other because we are the same and, at the same time, we do not lose the independent aspect of a person or dharma. In that exchange or inter-being, I see myself. Life's presencing cofunctions with life's presencing.

When we are able to manifest this practice, which is not different from studying the Buddha Way, we have forgotten the self. A forgotten self is the self that no longer perceives itself as the center of the universe but rather as one of the many elements of the universe. In the "Uji" quotation above, Dōgen is describing the intimacy of such an encounter as "going forth encounters going forth."

Seeing yourself as the universe does not mean you are some kind of demigod who makes the world. Rather, you make the world in concert with the whole of the world, and you are not separate from that world's making. In that relationship arises responsibility for your actions in accord (or discord) with others.

Senne says something interesting and seemingly opaque here when he writes, "To forget means to know without touching things."[8] He does not elaborate on the meaning of his comment, but "to know without touching things" may refer to a state in which one knows and responds to others or a situation without needing to verbally assess what is needed. This would be a state of forgetting the self.

To forget the self is to be verified by all things. To be verified by all things is to let the body and mind of the self and the body and mind of others drop off.

Forgetting the self results in "buddhas [who] are truly buddhas [but don't] perceive they are buddhas." Having forgotten, dropped, or let go of the mistaken idea that we are separate entities disconnected from the world's inter-being, we can then be verified by the world itself. This does not require that we self-consciously acknowledge our realization. In fact, realization is predicated upon forgetting realization as a separate thing.

Dōgen defines *verified* as "to let the body and mind of the self and the body and mind of others drop off." *Shō* (證),[9] translated here as "verified," can also be translated as "confirmed" or "enlightened."[10]

From this point of view, we understand that to be verified does not mean that things or persons come up to you and say, "Well done. You're great. I verify your realization." It means that as we are integrated with the totality of our life, our situation, our dharma position, we cease to only view those we encounter as others to be manipulated or used. We see ourselves and others as integrated, whole beings in concert making something happen. This is dropping body and mind.

Dōgen describes how this looks in "Yuibutsu Yobutsu" (Only a Buddha and a Buddha):

> How, then, are we to understand that this state of buddha is the same as us? To begin with, we should understand the action of buddha. The action of buddha takes place in unison with the whole Earth and takes place together with all living beings. If it does not include all, it is never the action of buddha. Therefore, from the establishment of the mind until the attainment of realization, both realization and practice are inevitably done together with the whole Earth and together with all living beings.[11]

And in the same section he writes, "The human being under investigation is not I and is not [another] person."[12]

If we push forward our small self's agenda, thinking that we are practicing Buddha's Way, we are mistaken. When we meet everything with an open and spacious mind, with the knowledge that we are one process functioning, then we are practice-realizing together as all beings. This is the same activity as dropping body and mind. Let's now look more closely at this key term in Dōgen's writing:

Dropping body-mind or body and mind (*shinjin-datsuraku*, 身心脱落) is most often associated with sitting zazen or shikantaza, just sitting. Dōgen makes this connection often. He writes in *Eihei Kōroku* (Dōgen's Extensive Record), Dharma Hall Discourse 432,

> The family style of all buddhas and ancestors is to engage the way in zazen. My late teacher Tiantong [Rujing] said, "Cross-legged sitting is the Dharma of ancient buddhas. Practicing meditation (sanzen) is dropping off body and mind."[13]

What exactly does this instruction mean? It does not mean to lose one's awareness of one's surroundings while sitting. In the same Dharma Hall Discourse, Dōgen specifically says, "Zazen is dropping off body and mind. It is not the four formless absorptions,[14] nor the four dhyāna."[15] Elsewhere in *Eihei Kōroku*, Dōgen is recorded as saying, "Without turning your back on a thousand people or ten thousand people, drop off body and mind, go to the hall and sit zazen."[16]

Later in the same discourse, Dōgen is reported to have said,

> Dropping off body and mind is good practice. Make a vigorous effort to pierce your nostrils. Karmic consciousness is endless, with nothing fundamental to rely on, including not others, not self, not sentient beings, and not causes or conditions. Although this is so, eating breakfast comes first.[17]

In an accompanying footnote to this translation,[18] Leighton and Okumura indicate that we can understand practice (*sanzen*) as either formal meditation practice or Dharma practice in general. This is born out when Dōgen admonishes his students not to forget to eat breakfast and not to forget "a thousand people or ten thousand people."[19]

Returning to "Genjōkōan," Dōgen writes, "To be verified [or enlightened] by all things is to let the body and mind of the self and the body and mind of others drop off." The activity of being enlightened by all things involves dropping or shedding body-mind of both self and other.

Dōgen is not suggesting that the goal of practice is to cease to have a personality. Rather, this admonition is about incorporating and integrating oneself with all other dharmas (persons, things) that are presencing at the same time-being of our particular situation. It is not "turning your back on a thousand people or ten thousand people."

As Dōgen clarifies in Dharma Hall Discourse 432, we are not talking about a dissociative state in which one has lost their sense of self, surroundings, community, or interactions. This is a state of inclusiveness. Formal zazen practice, when done properly, opens us to unselfconsciously enter the world or community of dharmas around us. Thus we drop body and mind.

There is a trace of realization that cannot be grasped. We endlessly express this ungraspable trace of realization.

When a bird or insect flies through the sky, there is no trace of their passage, yet this does not negate that the passage has happened. What is there to grasp? What we call a bodhisattva's or buddha's practice cannot be said to begin and end there. As we cannot grasp such things, we should not grasp after them.

Kyōgō writes,

> When we consider this from the perspective of duality between "delusion" and "realization," there is a boundary. There is nothing that can be called the trace of realization. Since the "trace of realization that cannot be grasped" has no boundary, it is stated, "endlessly keep expressing." "The trace of realization that cannot be grasped" should be understood as the trace of original realization without beginning.[20]

To label our experiences as delusion or realization is to create a boundary by which we define what is "good" (realization) and "bad" (delusion). Because of this dividing line there is just the one or the other. Labeling or grasping is a step beyond the actuality and actualization of reality's functioning. Reality's functioning is a process deeper than the labels we put on top of that functioning and therefore it "cannot be grasped." What cannot be grasped is without boundaries. It is the world's presencing, without beginning or end.

Dōgen writes in "Yuibutsu Yobutsu" (Only a Buddha and a Buddha) about the difficulty of having a preconceived idea of realization and, by implication, the difficulty of delusion. "Even though we had imagined it, it is not a realization. . . . Realization itself is nothing like we imagined. That being so, to imagine it beforehand is not useful."[21] We all make the mistake of imagining what our realization might look like, and we measure our activity by how we meet this standard. This is grasping after the traces of realization.

This grasping is not all bad, as Dōgen indicates later in "Yuibutsu Yobutsu" when he says that our misconceptions are not completely without function: "It was different from how we had supposed it to be, . . . [which] does not mean that our thinking . . . had no power in it."[22] The power in it is our motivation to become realized, so we keep trying to grasp realization. Later we discover what cannot be grasped, but we cannot avoid grasping initially.

For example, we may have a nondual experience in which we feel our self has disappeared and we are directly experiencing the boundaryless state of self and other. This kind of experience can be helpful in practice, but no matter how strong a visceral inclination we have to remain with or repeat it, we should not try to replicate it. To make this kind of effort is to grasp after traces.

In Senne's commentary on this section, he makes a confusing reference to Shōbōgenzō "Shoaku-makusa" (Not Doing Evil Deeds): "Evil deeds are not doing, not doing is evil deeds; good deeds are doing, doing is good deeds. The entirety of the 'ungraspable trace of realization' is called 'expressing endlessly.'"[23]

"Shoaku-makusa" is a discussion of the meaning of a verse that is quite close to what in contemporary Zen we call the three pure precepts. Dōgen writes, "Not to commit wrongs / To practice the many kinds of right / Naturally purifies the mind; / This is the teaching of the buddhas."[24] In this difficult fascicle, Dōgen wants to make the important point that good and evil are not basic states of response or being. This is expressed near the beginning of "Shoaku-makusa":

> Good and evil are temporal, but time is neither good nor evil. Good and evil are dharmas, but dharmas are neither good nor evil. It is the dharmas are equal, the evils are equal; it is the dharmas are equal, the goods are equal.[25]

What we understand to be good or bad behavior is not an expression of the world's (or our) essential nature because suchness is fundamentally the world's essential being. Therefore, we cannot grasp or define suchness as good or bad.

Senne's pointing to good and evil are examples of delusion and realization being ungraspable. We cannot hold on to some idea of realization or delusion that is outside the context of the time or being of our current situation. That is the meaning of Dōgen's "Good and evil are temporal, but time is neither good nor evil. Good and evil are dharmas, but dharmas are neither good nor evil."[26] Time and being (dharmas) in and of themselves are not good or evil. It is the circumstances and our ability to respond skillfully that will become helpful or harmful.

CHAPTER 6

LOOKING FOR THE PATH OF THE AUTHENTIC SELF

When one first seeks the Dharma, one strays far from the boundary of the Dharma. When the Dharma is correctly transmitted to the self, one is immediately an original person.

These sentences in "Genjōkōan" mark a shift from Dōgen explaining the nature of realization, or how to recognize actualized response, to directly addressing our problems in practice.

For the first time in the fascicle, Dōgen specifically refers to "people" as *nin* (人). *Nin* is a Buddhist term used to refer to our status as a person caught in the wheel of birth and death. A paraphrase of the first sentence might be "When a person (*nin*) [who is caught in delusion] makes the effort to practice, they will probably not be able to find where the practice of the Dharma begins."[1]

In the second sentence, the person who has correctly received the Dharma is identified as "an original person," or in the Sōtō Zen Text Project translation, "The person of the original lot."[2] The Japanese for "an original person" or "the person of the original lot" is *honbun nin* (本分人), which refers to one's buddha-nature.[3] Kyōgō comments, "'Original person (*honbun nin*, 本分人)' means something like the principle of original enlightenment (本覚). The expression, 'to become far from' means that when the dharma has been correctly transmitted, [the dharma] never separates from the person's body and mind."[4] Kyōgō's understanding seems to accord with something Dōgen says in "Uji" (Being-Time):

> Although the views the ordinary, unenlightened person now holds and the conditions that cause them are what the unenlightened person sees, it is not the unenlightened person's Dharma; it is only the Dharma temporarily causing him [to see that way.][5]

The logic of Dōgen's teaching is that we are never apart from the Dharma since we are already buddha-nature. Therefore, even when we can't find the Dharma because of our ignorance or attachment to erroneous views, the Dharma is still presencing. For this reason, a person can immediately become awakened to their true nature as soon as they actualize what is already presencing.

Our goal may be to enact the Buddha Way, as Dōgen has described in the previous lines of "Genjōkōan," but we must understand that having a description of that goal is not enough—particularly because our ideas about the path or our attachment to erroneous views of self may take us astray from it. You think you know what enlightenment is, but you have no real context for your opinion. Hence we may stray away from the Buddha Dharma, even as we seek to awaken to its true nature.

Before realization, we think there is a border or boundary that we must pass through. The boundaryless boundary is not known to us. But as soon as we correctly receive or understand the Buddha Dharma, we realize we are not separated from it. Senne writes, "To seek after the Dharma is 'to become far from it.'" He follows this statement with, "We may think that we should not vainly seek after the Dharma. However, without seeking, there is no Dharma that has been correctly transmitted."[6] Senne essentially wants to encourage us to continue our journey, even if we might start off going in the wrong direction. Because if we keep seeking, we will succeed in finding what we seek.

The issue here is not that we seek the Dharma. The problem is looking for realization by going down the wrong path, misguided by our preconceived ideas about the Dharma. Here's an example from my experience. Twice I have run into people at the grocery store who have come to our Zen center a few times and then stopped. They feel it necessary to tell me that they have not come back because when they meditate, they cannot stop their thoughts. Therefore, in their mind, they do not have the capacity to sit.

This is a perfect example of a preconceived idea about the Dharma that takes us away from practice. This person believes that zazen requires one to have no thoughts while sitting. What they imagine is far from Dōgen's meditation instruction. Since it is common to have thoughts during zazen, it is not a requirement of zazen that one does not have thoughts. It is the way we *relate* to that thinking that is the focus of zazen.

When the Dharma is correctly transmitted to the self . . .

Although in this passage Dōgen does not explicitly state his belief that one must study in person with a teacher, elsewhere he clearly communicates the importance of the student-teacher relationship. In Shōbōgenzō "Menju" (Face-to-Face Conferral), for instance, Dōgen writes,

> If we do not meet a master during our lifetime, we are not a disciple; if we do not meet a disciple, we are not a master. Definitely to see each other and be seen by each other, to have conferred face to face and to have inherited the dharma—this is the realization of the way[7] on which the ancestors confer face to face.[8]

Zen is, at its heart, a lineage of buddhas and ancestors transmitting the teachings from one person to another through a vertical lineage, which is also a multitemporal, nondual lineage transmission.

Direct person-to-person, student-teacher learning is about our daily or regular interactions within the context of sangha and teacher. The forms and practices of Zen reveal the difficulties and misunderstandings that we may have about and with practice. Conferring with a teacher is critical for our development.

Dōgen illustrates this transmission of the Dharma from teacher to student at the end of "Genjōkōan" through the dialogue between Master Baoche and his student. The student-teacher relationship is not often easy, and there may be problems. Nevertheless, find a teacher and situation that seems wholesome and stick with it. Since you don't know what enlightenment is, you should probably not worry about that. Just find a teacher who seems compatible and whom you respect.

. . . one is immediately an original person.

As discussed at the beginning of this chapter, an "original person" is a person who enacts the Dharma. "Original" refers to our essential nature as that of a buddha or reality's functioning. We tend to anthropomorphize buddha and thus think it refers only to persons. But buddha-nature refers to the interconnection and inter-being of all of reality working together to make the world. Manifesting the depth and compassion of this model is what we call the buddha mind.

Manifesting our original person happens in real time, not in the past or some future time. In "Busshō" (Buddha-Nature), Dōgen discusses the simultaneity of buddha-nature's appearance and practice, writing, "The buddha-nature and realization of buddha inevitably experience the same state together."[9] Although we are buddha-nature, Dōgen writes that buddha-nature is not expressed except through action ("realization of buddha-nature"). This manifestation is actualization of buddha-nature as expressed through the self. The synchronization of buddha-nature manifesting as buddhahood can only happen in the present now of our interactions.

Also in "Busshō" Dōgen writes,

"If the time arrives" means "The time has already arrived; how can one doubt it?" . . . The "if arrives" is the same as the "already

arrived"; if the time has already arrived, the Buddha-nature need
not come. Accordingly, as the time is already here, it is itself the
presence of the Buddha-nature.[10]

Reality, buddha-nature, true self, and so forth are not far away since
they are integral to our actual being, thus their manifestation in the
right circumstances can be immediate. For this reason, we cannot
be other than our original self, even as we may not bring forth our
true nature.

We seek the Dharma, and sometimes we wander in our delusion.
But if we persevere, we will certainly bring forth our authenticity.
This process unfolds within the context of sangha and a teacher's
guidance. Dōgen writes in *Shōbōgenzō Zuimonki*:

> Although the sound of bamboo is marvelous, it does not sound
> of itself; it cries out with the help of a piece of tile. Although
> the color of peach blossoms is beautiful, they do not bloom of
> themselves; the open with the help of the spring breeze.
>
> Practicing the Way is also like this. This Way is inherent in
> each of us; still our gaining the Way depends upon the help of
> co-practitioners. . . . Therefore, while unifying our mind and con-
> centrating your aspiration, practice and seek the way together.[11]

Our sangha and teachers keep us moving toward and through the
gateless gate of attaining the Buddha Dharma. Through their help
we awaken to the beauty and suchness of our and all beings' true
nature.

CHAPTER 7

RIDING IN A BOAT

If one riding in a boat watches the coast, one mistakenly perceives the coast as moving. If one watches the boat [in relation to the surface of the water], then one notices that the boat is moving. Similarly, when we perceive the body and mind in a confused way and grasp all things with a discriminating mind, we mistakenly think that the self-nature of the mind is permanent. When we intimately practice and return right here, it is clear that all things have no [fixed] self.

In the passage examined in the previous chapter, Dōgen observes that as we seek for realization, we can be very far away from what we are seeking. One reason this happens is because we are confused about the self's impermanence and inter-being with reality. Since impermanence and the nature of the self are intimately entwined with bringing forth our original person, Dōgen now takes up this teaching.

If we are to be freed from the delusion of a fixed self, then we have to ask, "What is it we perceive as a self?" Dōgen does not deny that we have a particular self when he admonishes us to forget the self or drop body-mind. He is indicating that the self's attachment to itself as having a fixed nature separated from all being(s) is incorrect and problematic.

Furthermore, Buddhism has always taught that the constellation of characteristics that our mind perceives as the fixed and immutable self is a collection of impermanent, constantly changing causal factors. When we deeply consider this teaching, we discover there is no permanent self.

Dōgen now offers an example of why we might be deceived into thinking an impermanent, causally created self is an unchanging and separate entity. This misunderstanding is similar to what we perceive when standing on a boat watching it pull away from the shore. The analogy of the boat refers to how our physical perceptions give us the impression that, for example, the shore is moving, when actually it is the boat that is moving. If you have had this experience, you know how strong this particular misperception can be.

As Kyōgō and Senne both point out in their commentaries, we should not take this analogy to mean that the boat is a metaphor for an unmoving permanent self-nature (an eternal soul or essence) and that the shore refers to our body's physical impermanence.[1] Senne sums up the problem by writing, "This analogy does not mean that the boat is self-nature and the coast is body and mind."[2]

Rather, Dōgen uses this powerful example to illustrate how strong and overriding our mental and physical perceptions of having a separate, unchanging self can be. When you stand on the deck of a boat leaving the wharf and watch the dock, even though you might absolutely know that the boat is moving, it is disorienting when your perceptions tell you that the shore is moving. Only when you look down at the water do you have direct perceptual confirmation that in fact it is the boat that's moving, thus correcting the mistaken perception that the shore is moving. Watching the shore move is the same as thinking the self is permanent. To "intimately practice and return right here" is to look down at the water and realize that the boat is moving—the self is changing.

Senne comments, "Right here in '[return] right here' is not a particular place. 'Right here' refers to the Buddha Dharma. The principle of 'all things have no [fixed] self' refers to, for example, 'when the triple-world is only one mind,[3] all dharmas are true form.'"[4] This realignment of the self's true nature will turn us toward the boundary of the Dharma in the previous chapter.

If we can deeply observe the present moment's arising, we will perceive that everything is interacting and thus permeable, and nothing has a fixed or disconnected self. Perceiving the totality of the presencing moment (water, boat, shore), we realize our own codependence and cofunctioning with all things throughout time and causal conditions. This is what Senne references with the phrase "the triple world is only one mind." "One mind" refers to the trajectory of all dharmas co-causality. Dōgen writes in Shōbōgenzō "Sangai-yuishin" (Three Worlds Are Inseparable from Mind), "All things that arise or fall is the [universal] mind."[5]

We don't have a permanent self, separate from or unaffected by all other things/beings. If we function with the model of a fixed disconnected self, we will convey the self forward, thinking we are enlightened and separate from what is happening around and with us. But if we realize our cofunctioning and codependence with others and thus respond to our situation in concert with others, then we practice-enlightenment through the self, which by definition includes everything.

Another way to talk about this is to look at the way we deal with our own difficulties and ideas. If we relate to our mental sequential causality as if it were a permanent stream of consciousness, we think of our self as having permanency. This perceived permanency of our causality or karmic imprints (thoughts) feels immutable, and we might conclude that we can't break the chain of these perceptions. This is relating to "the body and mind in a confused way and grasp[ing] all things with a discriminating mind."

In Western psychological terms, we believe that our pattern of thought-habits defines who we are to such an extent that we cannot change our behavior. Buddhism is optimistic about our ability to get unstuck from our mental habits and patterns.

In our day-to-day interactions and thoughts, we reify the self as it pertains to situations, other people, and almost everything we encounter. We also hope, even expect, that the things we like will stay the same and the things we don't like will change. Freeing ourselves from the mental trap of concretizing the self is difficult but not impossible.

Dōgen states that if we pay attention (intimately practice) and ground ourselves in what is happening (return right here), we will realize that impermanence (nothing at all has unchanging self) is a primary characteristic of all of reality's manifesting. We will see that the boat (self) is moving and not the shore. This works well as a metaphor for the self's understanding of itself, and it is perhaps a good time to point out that everything else is without a permanent, separate self as well. So, in this sense, the shore *is* moving, as is everything else.

Believing in the permanence of self is about not only clinging to a certain view of causality or being afraid to die but also having the idea that our thoughts define us in some kind of fundamental way. If we think it, then we are it. We cling stubbornly to these self-images, not wanting to change. We also resent anyone who implicitly or explicitly contradicts our desire to hold on to this self-image, often pushing them away.

As I write this book in the era of Donald Trump and QAnon, there are a lot of people holding on to various far-fetched conspiracy theories. Why do we hold on to theories and ideas that are not factually based? What compels us to hold on to ideas that cause suffering and division? Perhaps because holding on to views that we believe define us as moral, special, or part of a community allows us to maintain a sense of self that is solid and safe. In seeking certainty and affirmation, we silo ourselves with others who share our views.

Another example of perceiving the self as fixed is when we decide that our view is the correct view, outside of any circumstances we might encounter. This "correct view" is the self isolating itself, believing itself to be unmoving. Such a view solidifies our idea of who we are, regardless of the needs of a situation. We might think, for example, that a person should never steal and that a person who steals is always a bad person. But there are situations in which a person might legitimately take what is not offered, such as an impoverished person who takes food to feed their family. If you believe that you are better than a person who finds themselves in a situation in which they engage in behavior that you do not approve of, then you are probably functioning within the context of a fixed view.

As Senne writes, "When we conceive our body and mind in confusion and discriminate all myriad things, we mistakenly think that the self-nature of our mind is permanent. It is clear that myriad things have no fixed self."[6] If we believe that we have a fixed permanent self, then we cannot forget the self, be enlightened by all things, or drop off body and mind. When we are aware that we are not separate and immutable, then we are engaged in intimate practice, returning right here, and we attain a kind of skillful fluidity that enables us to respond in accord with our current situation.

Our practice is, in part, about waking up to how our perceptions and thoughts may trick us. Just realizing that we are moving (no fixed self) is a huge step in practice. Once we are convinced of and have faith in the truth of this, then we can begin to deconstruct and reconstruct our sense of who we are as individuals and in the context of community. As we directly experience our current moment of time as the self's being in concert with all being(s), we realize that the boat is moving. The how of that experience is what Dōgen discusses in the next section of "Genjōkōan," on the relationship between firewood and ash.

CHAPTER 8

WHAT DO I EXPERIENCE AS A PARTICULAR SELF?

Firewood becomes ash. Ash cannot become firewood again. However, we should not view ash as after and firewood as before. We should know that firewood dwells in the dharma position of firewood and has its own before and after. Although before and after exist, past and future are cut off. Ash stays in the position of ash, with its own before and after. As firewood never becomes firewood again after it has burned to ash, there is no return to living after a person dies.

Dōgen ended the previous section by reiterating the basic Buddhist teaching that we and all beings have no separate, unconditioned self. But if this is true, what exactly do we experience as self? How is it that we perceive ourselves as existing in a solid way? The answer to these questions is found in the concept of *jū hōi* (住法位): abiding in a dharma position which is an important aspect of Dōgen's understanding of how we see and understand particularity.[1]

In this section of "Genjōkōan," Dōgen doesn't directly address the topic of how we experience the self as permanent. Instead, he discusses the nature and, by implication, the importance of the independent aspect of a dharma position. It is this independent aspect of a dharma position that we mistake as a separate and/or permanent self.

84 |

A dharma position is a person, a thing, a dharma, a situation, or any conceptualized discrete being-time. What is significant about the independent aspect of a dharma position, here firewood or ash, is that it is only from this position that we can awaken or enact realized response: the theme of "Genjōkōan." Firewood is complete in itself as the dharma position of firewood. Ash is complete in itself as ash. You are totally you in this moment of you. At the same time, each person (dharma) has a before and after. Each of us has our own life experiences that affect our present. Yet, there is just this moment of self, ash, or any dharma fully expressed.

In "Uji" (Being-Time), Dōgen writes, "The horses and sheep now arrayed throughout the world are each dharma stages [positions] dwelling in their suchness."[2] Horses, firewood, sheep, persons, the self—all are dharma positions. Each dharma position is manifesting "things as they are," or suchness. It is only within the context of fully expressing and experiencing a dharma position, our current now, that we can become awakened or enact practice-realization. This awakened response is actualizing "dwelling in suchness."

A paragraph later in "Uji," Dōgen points out that no matter what we may think about our present experience, it can be nothing other than a fully expressed moment:

> One does nothing but penetrate exhaustively entire time as entire being. There is nothing remaining left over. Because any dharma left over is as such a left-over dharma, even the being-time of a partial exhaustive penetration is an exhaustive penetration of a partial being-time.[3]

Firewood experiences and is fully itself in each moment of being firewood. This is to "penetrate exhaustively entire time as entire being." This is also true for us and how we respond to things. Our response—or life in each moment—is fully expressing itself, and as such, dwelling in suchness.

Each moment, each dharma position, is freed from all other moments of our life. It is independent, 100 percent itself, while simultaneously inter-being with all being(s). This is important to realize, otherwise we are caught in ideas or causal conditions that limit our response to life, and we cannot engage with a fresh and unhindered reaction.

Your life is uniquely your life. This particularity called you has its own experiences, memories, desires, futures, and so on that have created an original personality with specific ideas and ways of seeing the world. In this way, we have a unique before and after. Our past experiences and our future life are particular to us while being part of the whole of creation. But, if we mistake this independent aspect as permanent or a fixed self, we will limit our ability to engage our awakened mind.

Because we are talking about how something exists in the present moment, not how it might have been in a previous dharma position, Dōgen writes, "past and future are cut off." Kyōgō comments, "Although there are before and after, the boundary between before and after is cut off. This refers to the principle of 'Life is manifestation of total function; death is manifestation of the total function.'"[4] Each dharma position is completely expressed within this moment's arising. This is manifesting total function. From this perspective, our perceptions of past experiences and our desire for future events are dropped in service of a more flexible attitude toward our present experience; in this way, we "cut off" our attachment to experiences and past and future desires.

It is only from this perspective that we can meet others with an open mind and a freed heart. We can become curious about that person and not walled off from them because we have placed them in some ideological box. Nor do we place ourselves in a prison of karmic shackles. We are not trapped in a karmic cycle of self-identity. Refusing to internalize self-labeling such as "I am stupid" or "I'm the smartest person in the room" frees us to redefine our experience. If a dharma position did not have an independent aspect, this would not be possible. Because of a being-time's particularity, we can cut ourselves loose from habitual reification of the self and create a path of transformation and freedom from suffering.

Furthermore, it is only in the present that we can become liberated through expressing realized action. We must be aware of our delusion and confident in our ability to do something different. A being's present manifestation, or a person's experience of self, does not negate the past or future of that self or dharma; nor does it deny causally created karmic response and effect. Rather, it contextualizes them as factors or influences that do not necessarily dictate our response at this time. In each moment we are free to respond to what is arising. This happens, according to Buddhist teaching, by fully realizing the impermanence of one's self and thereby freeing oneself from karmically conditioned, unworkable, and unskillful actions.

Dōgen ends this section with "There is no returning to living after a person dies." A moment of our experience of self is like firewood. It is real, functional, and not permanent. This moment, this person, will become something else. We are something different in each moment as we maintain continuity of past and future. For example, we are aging. We are morphing slowly (or quickly) into an older person or a sick person or a well person. Or we are changing jobs, ending and making new relationships, and so on. Our ideas about things are changing. Everything is in flux. All our states of being are impermanence manifesting, although our felt experience of this self can be very solid.

Just as ash cannot become firewood again, we cannot become ten years old again. We can't relive the past except in memory. It is of note that Dōgen chose to use something very solid (firewood) as his example. From the position of firewood, things feel very solid, yet this firewood becomes something very ephemeral, ash.

As I end this chapter, it might be interesting to ask the question, "Why shouldn't I view ash as after and firewood as before? We all know that when you burn a piece of wood it becomes ashes." The reason that we break the causal chain between before and after is twofold.

First, if we understand before and after or cause and effect from a universal, nondualistic view, we understand that the whole world

throughout time(s), being(s), and space is constantly interconnected, and that interconnection is sequential and nonsequential
simultaneously. It is multidimensional rather than a straight line.
From this perspective, all time and being—everything—coexists
simultaneously.

Second, and perhaps more important for our practice, is that if we
open up to this understanding and let go of the idea of everything's
sequential causality, then we begin to question our perception of
self and other. Both self and other become one while remaining two.

For example, right now in America, unmovable politics and rigid
beliefs are causing people to become very polarized in their views.
We have divided ourselves into camps with labels such as Repub-
lican, Democrat, independent, Evangelical Christian, Muslim, Jew-
ish, Buddhist, black, white, of color, cis gender, LBGTQI+, pro- or
anti-abortion, and many others. As I name them, you might have
specific ideas about who falls into each category and what that
person's beliefs are likely to be—specifically in relationship to your
understanding of what is right and wrong. If your ideas about a
person's beliefs are fixed, you might believe that they are fixed in
their ideas. This is a kind of sequential processing of ideology. We
think if a person falls in this category, it follows that they must
uniformly believe such and such (firewood becomes ash). For this
reason, I (unmoving boat) might assume they are wrong (shore
is moving), thus I think I cannot communicate with this person.
I might hate this person's beliefs, which results in rejecting that
person, even though I have never met them.

Viewing this situation as a dharma position, we understand we
can hold independent positions yet meet each other without fixed
views. We are aware that Buddhist doctrine teaches that all being(s)
are more same than different. We acknowledge that we are joined
on a cellular level and through innumerable other forms of connection. We are brothers and sisters, with not only each other but
all of reality. We are human beings together, and therefore we are
all community. We may disagree, but we do not need to demonize
one another. We are the earth's process as and with all being(s),

and from this perspective we are one process—the Triple World of one mind. This is the view of the universal inter-being of all peoples and things. When this becomes our view, the labels drop away and we can find ways to communicate and function with and for one another's welfare. This is compassion arising from wisdom, resulting in skillful means. From this perspective, we can see that becoming attached to the idea that burned firewood always results in ash is a problem.

CHAPTER 9

WHO DIES, WHO LIVES?

As firewood never becomes firewood again after it has
burned to ash, there is no return to living after a person dies.
However, in Buddha Dharma it is an unchanged tradition
not to say that life becomes death. Therefore we call it
no-arising. It is the established way of buddhas' turning the
Dharma wheel not to say that death becomes life. Therefore,
we call it no-perishing. Life is a position in time; death is
also a position in time. This is like winter and spring. We
don't think that winter becomes spring, and we don't say
that spring becomes summer.[1]

Dōgen clearly connects his example of firewood and ash with the
impermanent nature of the self. When we die, we don't continue as
before. The self does not come back as itself after we die. He writes,
"As firewood never becomes firewood again after it has burned to ash,
there is no return to living after a person dies." This is a commonsense
point about birth and death. We don't come back to life after we die.
If birth or death is only fully realized as each moment, there cannot
be "birth" or "death" as a finite state. There is just this moment's
expression through our own body-mind, which is in constant flux.

From the view of impermanence, how could what we call the self
be reborn as itself after death? This is not possible. Dōgen is saying
that "it is an established way in Buddha Dharma" not to reify death
or birth as fixed or permanent positions. Dōgen chooses at this

90 |

point to clarify that he is not suggesting that we have some kind of unchanging essence that is reborn as itself after death, which may be an idea that we have about the Buddhist doctrine of rebirth. Dōgen seems to be warning us not to view the doctrine of rebirth as a perpetuation of the self.

In his commentary, Kyōgō also addresses the question of death, rebirth, and the absence of some permanent abiding essence within each person when he writes, "To think that we will not be reborn after death is a non-Buddhist [view of] *danken* 断見."[2] His point is that there is a kind of continuation, but it is not a perpetuation of a permanent self.[3] Since everything is impermanent and interconnected, there cannot be a final end, only transformation. An example of this would be a green burial in which a person's body is transformed into fertilizer.

From the Buddhist perspective of rebirth, Kyōgō may also be contrasting the Mahayana idea of rebirth with the Theravada view that a practitioner's goal is to cease rebirth by exiting the karmic wheel of birth and death.[4] Kyōgō doesn't want a person reading this sentence in "Genjōkōan" to come away with either the view of a self's complete cessation without transformation or the idea of a permanent soul that outlives the body.

In the next set of sentences, Dōgen attempts to complete his presentation of how a thing or person exists as impermanence by speaking of no-arising (birth) and no-perishing (death). How should we understand a dharma's or person's life, death, and presencing in relationship to codependent function? In response, Dōgen discusses no-arising and no-perishing.

However, in Buddha Dharma it is an unchanged tradition not to say that life becomes death. Therefore we call it no-arising. It is the established way of buddhas' turning the Dharma wheel not to say that death becomes life. Therefore, we call it no-perishing.

Having established that things do not return to life after death, Dōgen now states that in Buddhist teachings it is not said that life terminates in death, nor that death becomes life. This may seem a contradiction, but it isn't.

No-arising and no-perishing together mean that, from the perspective of no-inherently-existing-self, everything is interconnected. Inter-being is a process of becoming and no-becoming, constantly morphing, yet still taking shape as form. From the perspective of inter-being and transmogrification, things do not arise and cease; they are the processes of the world's worlding, which is sometimes apparent to us and sometimes not.

From this nondual view of existence, we cannot say there is birth and death, nor can we say that death becomes life again. All being(s) arising and dissolution are within the context of always having been coexistent and inter-being with each and every thing. From this perspective, what we see as beginning, end, birth, and death are all stages of a continuous, beginningless, and endless process. Although, any point in that process could be labeled birth or death (or some other being-time) as they are also independent aspects of a dharma position. And at the same time, any part of that process can be called no-inherently-existing-death (no-death) or no-inherently-existing-birth (no-birth).

Senne comments, "We just say total-firewood and total-ash in the same way as life is manifestation of the total function and death is manifestation of the total function."[5] The term "manifestation of total function" here is borrowed from Dōgen's Shōbōgenzō "Zenki" (The Whole Works), which in turn quotes Chan Master Yuanwu, who said, "Alive, the manifestation of the full function; dead, the manifestation of the full function."[6] Alive and dead are dharma positions cut off from past and future, completely no-inherently-existing-alive and no-inherently-existing-dead.

In case 289 in Dōgen's collection of three hundred koans, we find a koan associated with this teaching: "Daowu's 'Alive or Dead.'" Daowu and his student Jianyuan[7] visited the home of a deceased person. Jianyuan rapped on the coffin three times and said to his teacher, "Alive or dead?"

Daowu said, "I won't say alive. I won't say dead."

Jianyuan said, "Why won't you say?"

Daowu, said, "I won't say, I won't say."[8]

Is the body dead or alive? From the relative dharma position, this body is dead. From the absolute position, one cannot say dead or alive. The teacher won't say because, as students, we have to realize for ourselves how to negotiate the seemingly contradictory states, for example, of birth and death.

Knowing and seeing a dharma position's nonduality does not negate a conventional worldview. We can view this process as birth, death, firewood, self, or whatever the case may be. We can talk about the progress from birth to death or even the doctrine of rebirth.[9] Birth and death are dharma positions; both independent and nondual.

In the koan cited above, the student views the corpse's dharma position only from the independent and relative positions of alive or dead. Yet, at the same time, a dharma position is fully presencing in this moment, which includes all being(s)-time(s). Consequently, there is no-perishing and no-arising, just inter-being codependent functioning process. There are no fixed positions; there are just myriad things presencing, fully apparent and functioning. That is why Daowu says, "I won't say."

Life is a position in time; death is also a position in time. This is like winter and spring. We don't think that winter becomes spring, and we don't say that spring becomes summer.

Even though it is an error to reify birth or death, we can say that something—a person, a cup, a process, or whatever the case may be—fully exists and functions in their dharma position. Thus, Dōgen writes, "Life is a position in time; death is also a position in time." It is as if Dōgen has circled back to his original statement about the independent aspects of firewood and ash. But now we are aware of the nuances of a dharma position's particularity and coexistence with and as all being(s). Perhaps he returns to his initial position because he wants the reader to return to the presencing moment as the place and time of realization.

When we are in the middle of winter, we don't view it as the beginning of spring; we experience it as the "dead of winter." When we are experiencing the "dog days of summer," we don't say it's the end of spring. Winter is 100 percent winter. Spring is 100 percent spring.[10] It is only in the present moment of a dharma position's arising and our experience of it that we can awaken. Therefore, we really want to experience spring without comparing it to summer or winter. We really want to fully immerse ourselves in the experience we are having and live out that experience as our realized effort to enact the Dharma.

Dōgen tells a story in Shōbōgenzō "Shohō Jissō" (The Reality of All Things):

> Xuansha, Great Master Zongyi,[11] was on his way to the
>   dharma hall when he heard the swallow's voice.
> He said [in his dharma talk], "The swallow's voice deeply
>   speaks of reality and well expounds the heart of the
>   dharma."
> Then, he descended from the teaching seat.
> Later, a monk asked him for teaching by saying, "I don't
>   understand it."
> Xuansha said, "Go away. No one believes you."[12]

Dōgen comments on this story:

> You may think that Xuansha's statement, "The swallow's voice
> deeply speaks of reality" means that swallows alone deeply speak
> of reality. But it is not so. He did hear the chirping of swallows
> on his way. It is not that swallows were speaking of reality. It is
> not that Xuansha was speaking of reality. They were not divided
> into two, but at that very moment there was speaking of reality."[13]

The moment that Xuansha hears the swallows is a dharma position that includes the whole of Xuansha's experience as the totality of what is arising at that moment—in this case, the swallows, the talk he was giving, the student's question, and so on. The whole story can be understood as a dharma position, as can each of the individual moments described. Each position is independent yet simultaneously inter-being as one event.

Dōgen ends his commentary on this dialogue: "Indeed, even if you are an ordinary person . . . you experience the reality of all things. When reality is actualized in this way at this time and place, you are directly connected to the life vein of buddha ancestors."[14]

Our experience and expression of realization is predicated upon our ability to fully presence ourselves for this time and place, which enables us to be "directly connected to the life vein of buddha ancestors." Why did Xuansha say that "no one believes you"? Because we are never apart from reality's suchness, and each dharma position abides in and as suchness, even if we cannot understand this from our current perspective. If we pay attention to our immediate experience and make our best effort to respond with bodhi mind, having an intellectual explanation of our experience is unnecessary in our effort to actualizing Buddha's Way.

CHAPTER 10

ENLIGHTENMENT

The Long and Short of It

When a person attains realization, it is like the moon's reflection in water. The moon never becomes wet; the water is never disturbed. Although the moon is a vast and great light, it is reflected in a drop of water. The whole moon and even the whole sky are reflected in a drop of dew on a blade of grass. Realization does not destroy the person, as the moon does not make a hole in the water. The person does not obstruct realization, as a drop of dew does not obstruct the moon in the sky. The depth is the same as the height. [To investigate the significance of] the length and brevity of time, we should consider whether the water is great or small and understand the size of the moon in the sky.

As we saw in the previous chapter, Dōgen explains how we experience the self as a particular individual while realizing our inter-being, cofunctioning, cooperative self as part of the universe's functioning. When we realize and can act from both, it is said that we are actualizing realization in the presencing moment. In this next section of "Genjōkōan," Dōgen addresses the question of how the particular self and realization cofunction. One does not cancel the other.

When a person attains realization, it is like the moon's reflection in water. The moon never becomes wet; the water is never disturbed.[1]

In Zen, the moon is often used as a symbol for enlightenment. In this case, water can be understood as a particular manifestation of the realized self. The moon can be reflected in any body of water, and each of those waters—a lake, a drop of dew, and so on—has its own characteristics, and each of those instances is a locus of enlightened response. This is true for people as well, such that water can easily be used as a metaphor for self. When we as a person, a self, respond with realized action, this is the moon reflected in the water.

This moon (realized action enacted by a self in concert with all beings) can be reflected in all and each of reality's dharma positions and thus is part of reality's fabric. Yet—and this is Dōgen's point—this responding awakened self is not deindividualized by the moon's presence. We do not disappear as a particular person with specific characteristics when we manifest and actualize our buddhahood. Shunryu Suzuki, in his commentary, says that if you like sake in your unenlightened states, you will still like sake in your enlightened states.[2] Indeed, when we read stories about Zen masters, they all have distinct personalities and do not lose these unique qualities in realization.

As we become more familiar with how to enact realized responses, we are not going to suddenly become a different person. This is important for us to understand and accept. We often have a fantasy that everything we don't like about ourselves is going to disappear without a trace, suddenly, as we are engulfed by and disappear into enlightenment. It doesn't work that way.

Realization is attentive response to a particular arising situation. As has been said before, we are not enlightened as individuals; we manifest realization in response to a situation or encounter. It is unlikely that we will always respond with 100 percent buddha mind; on the other hand, we will be less and less likely to respond with 100 percent delusional mind as we sincerely apply ourselves to practice.

If we look at Suzuki Roshi's example, what happens if the person who likes sake gets drunk and engages in delusional behavior? Does that mean this person is no longer capable of a realized response in the future? Since it is our particular personalities and karmic traces that are the genesis of our delusion (and realization), Dōgen comments in Shōbōgenzō "Daigo" (Great Awakening),

> Furthermore, is "great enlightenment" one hand and "still suffer-ing from delusion"[3] another [on the same body]? However that may be, we must realize that hearing the statement "A person of great enlightenment still suffers from delusion" is the ultimate penetration of our inquiry. Note that "great enlightenment" is ever joined with "still suffering from delusion."[4]

Delusion and realization do not necessarily cancel each other; as Dōgen writes earlier in "Genjōkōan," "Those who greatly realize delusion are buddhas. Those who are greatly deluded in realization are living beings. Furthermore, there are those who attain realiza-tion beyond realization and those who are deluded within delusion." In his commentary on "Daigo," Dōgen makes clear that a person can get caught in delusion and then respond later with an awakened mind. How well we know ourselves is going to determine the bal-ance between being skillful or causing problems for self and others.

Another element is time. Also in "Daigo," Dōgen instructs us about time by pointing out that realization is meeting a situation "at this moment" with an awakened mind, and therefore "great awakening" is not a permanent state. Dōgen writes in "Daigo," "The *nowadays* [of awakening] is the right now of each of you. Even if you think of the past, present, and future millions of times, all time is this very moment, right now. Where you are is nothing but this very moment."[5]

Sometimes when we study the Buddhist doctrine of emptiness and understand this to be a description of the awakened mind, we imagine that it means we merge into something called emptiness and our personality disappears. Emptiness refers to something being empty of inherent existence. This means that a thing, a situation, a dharma position, a person, does not function or exist outside of the whole of reality. A dharma position has particularity while having unity, and it functions within the context of the whole. Emptiness has very little to do with merging into something else and becoming oneness without particularity.

When we skillfully respond within the context of reality's functioning, at this very moment's arising, then we have answered with buddha mind. By the way, we are never without bodhi mind; we are just not able to enact that mind when it is clouded by delusional thinking. To imagine that one's personality disappears upon enlightenment is delusional thinking.

It is true that as we practice more and more, we will begin to transform. For example, we might become more patient, inclusive, and forgiving. Our suffering does not disappear; it is our relationship to it that becomes equanimity.

Although the moon is a vast and great light, it is reflected in a drop of water. The whole moon and even the whole sky are reflected in a drop of dew on a blade of grass.

The beauty of buddha-nature and buddha-nature expressed is that it is always a "vast and great light." Realization is manifest in everything, in its entirety. Enlightenment does not require some special field to shine in. It can manifest fully in the smallest and most impermanent fleeting dharma position.

Because nothing is missing from the very beginning, buddha-nature will shine forth when the circumstances align. In this case, it is the moon, a dewdrop, light, sky, grass. All those dharma positions are metaphors for the immense variety of possibilities. Each instance of actualized response reveals reality's suchness.

When things line up in accord with the Buddha Dharma, you are expressing enlightened response. This is going to happen in your daily life—driving the car, attending a meeting, or standing in line at the grocery store—because this is the where and how of our life's

activity. Every bit of reality is the whole of buddha-nature expressing, and every bit of our lives reflects this, even if we don't know it
and are not in tune with it. There is no moment, person, situation,
or dharma position that is too small to reflect reality's totality.

Realization does not destroy the person, as the moon does not make
a hole in the water. The person does not obstruct realization, as a
drop of dew does not obstruct the moon in the sky.

These lines reiterate Dōgen's first teaching in this section of the
fascicle: "When a person attains realization, it is like the moon's
reflection in water. The moon never becomes wet; the water is never
disturbed." We do not disappear upon engaging our life skillfully,
nor does the moon's reflection break the water. Conversely, a person's unskillfulness does not obstruct realization's arising, just as a
droplet of dew, as it reflects the whole of the moon, does not swallow
up or block the moon's presencing. Realization is the activity of all
reality presencing in the now of our experience.

Let's again look to "Daigo," where Dōgen writes,

> There is no delusion that obstructs great awakening; taking up
> three pieces of great awakening, we make a half piece of slight
> delusion. . . . The great awakening of the buddhas has a great
> awakening because of living beings; the great awakening of liv-
> ing beings has a great awakening to the great awakening of the
> buddhas. This has nothing to do with before or after. The present
> great awakening is not self, is not other. It has not come. . . . It
> has not gone.[6]

Our lives—our likes and dislikes, our personalities, our joys and
traumas—will not necessarily disappear, and our skandhas do not
dissolve into emptiness. We are still here sometimes "greatly realizing delusion," sometimes "greatly deluded in realization," and
sometimes "attain[ing] realization beyond realization." In fact, if we
were not still here, we could not enact a realized response. Nothing

would be present to respond or react to; everything would be a big blob of energy.

When we act unskillfully, when we cause harm, we don't break buddha-nature. Buddha-nature is the altruistic state of the world. You may doubt this because in this *sahā* world[7] we engage in so much hate, greed, and delusional thinking.

But if you turn this around and think about all the processes throughout endless eons, still functioning now, that enable us to breathe, eat, move, do anything—you can begin to see that the whole world is engaged in altruistic actions creating itself, which includes ourselves and all dharmas. Delusion is not apart from this activity.

Dōgen called this activity *gyōji* (行持), variously translated as: "activity-unremitting,"[8] "Continuous Practice," "Pure Conduct and Observation of Precepts,"[9] or "sustained practice." Dōgen writes in Shōbōgenzō "Gyōji" (Continuous Practice),

> The working of this activity-unremitting [gyōji] upholds the self and the other. Its import is such that through one's activity-unremitting the entire earth as well as the whole heaven of the ten directions share in its working. . . . Because of this activity-unremitting, there exist the sun, moon, and stars, because of activity-unremitting there exist the great earth and empty sky.[10]

This continuous practice or activity-unremitting is manifest in the buddhas and ancestors, as well as all being(s), as they accord with the total functioning of all aspects of our world. Later in "Gyōji" Dōgen writes,

> One may try to put aside activity-unremitting in order to conceal the delusive thought of escaping from activity-unremitting, but this putting aside of activity-unremitting is itself [a form of] activity-unremitting.[11]

Even our delusional actions or thoughts cannot "make a hole in the water," nor obstruct realization or the moon in the sky.

Everything is included, and this state of altruistic realization and practice cannot be defiled by delusion.

Realized action is in response to the needs of a particular situation, and comparisons may not be helpful. Dōgen now turns to this topic.

The depth is the same as the height. [To investigate the significance of] the length and brevity of time, we should consider whether the water is great or small and understand the size of the moon in the sky.

In his commentary on this section, Kyōgō writes, "We should examine the principle that we do not argue about greatness and smallness of water to understand the vastness and narrowness of the moon in the sky." He adds, "When we discuss time on the basis of the Buddha Dharma, we should not be caught up in its length and shortness."[12]

Recalling the opening sentence of this section of "Genjōkōan," we remember that Dōgen is talking about "when a person attains realization." He is discussing practice and realization's manifestation as this moment's response—our thoughts and actions in response to the situation to which we are responding. Therefore, it is not a matter of comparing. We don't need to compare anything, especially our current situation, with our ideas about realization. If our response is based on what is happening right now, comparisons are not helpful.

Time is like this as well. The time of realization is the time right now, not some other time or place. Nor is its manifestation predicated upon a predetermined length of practice.

Kyōgō writes,

[Dōgen Zenji] uses this analogy to teach us the principle that dharma and our body and mind do not obstruct each other. The "height" and the "depth" are simply the same length. "Length and shortness of this time" and "greatness and smallness of water" should be examined in order to grasp the vastness or narrowness of the moon in the sky. This means that we should examine the principle that we do not argue about greatness and smallness of water to understand the vastness and narrowness of the moon in the sky.[13]

We don't need to compare because the Dharma and our body and mind (or self) are essentially not different and do not obstruct each other. Senne observes, "For example, when all things are the Buddha Dharma, delusion and realization, life and death, are all equally the Buddha Dharma and there are neither superiority nor inferiority between them."[14]

Kyōgō follows this same logic when he writes that height and depth are the same. The moon fits into the depth of the water, and the water is the height of the moon. Since the moon in its entirety is reflected in any reflective surface, no matter how large or small, the size or time of that reflection is unimportant. If we get caught in making these comparisons, we will lose our way. This is the "view the ordinary, unenlightened person sees," nevertheless the Dharma, moon, water, and so forth are always presencing in each dharma position, responding to what is needed.

Kyōgō points out that a kalpa is not long and one moment is not short because the kalpa and the moment are both manifest in a Zen master raising a fist or hitting their staff on the ground.[15] This is so because time, like being, is a dharma position holding all of eternity. This moment of the teacher raising a fist or hitting a staff on the ground contains all moments presencing as one dharma position. This is not just true for teachers; it is true for firewood, ash, ourselves, and all being(s) and time(s).

All these instances of expressing realization (or delusion) hold both the long and small of time. They are a dharma position's momentary arising that is, at the same time, all time presencing. In "Uji" (Being-Time), Dōgen observes, "As the time right now is all there ever is, each being-time is without exception entire time."[16] Attaining realization, or responding to each moment's request, happens "as the time right now," and this present time also holds all of time as well. From this perspective, it is all happening here and now, and we do not need to parse it as then, now, or in the future. It is not long or short.

Senne adds to this conversation by pointing out that human beings tend to want to make these comparisons. He says, "Therefore it seems that there are length and shortness, greatness and smallness in the water, but heavenly moon and the entire sky reflect themselves on the water whether or not they are long or short, great or small."[17]

We don't need to explore the characteristics of realization through comparison with delusion, relative, absolute, form, or emptiness. Practice-realization is directly responding to what is now, not in comparison to what was then or what will be. It is not in comparison to an idea we have about realization. It is not a question of is this realized action bigger, better, or more important. Nor is it about the person who is realized. All these attitudes are traps.

If we make comparisons, we become caught in labeling things as good or bad, or making up rules about what should happen or what something or someone should look like. Maybe we think the flashy teacher is enlightened, while the humbler, less charismatic teacher is not. Consequently we don't look to see if this person is responding to the whole of their situation, following the precepts, or if their actions are in accord with the needs of the sangha or students. We are blinded by the light of their rhetoric or posture. It is better to drop our ideas, stop making comparisons, and look at the effect of our or another person's actions in relationship to the whole of a situation.

Another way to view this section is as an exhortation to avoid dismissing our practice as too small. We are prone to feel that if we are not appearing in the media, our effort is not enough. For example, we may watch the news and see someone who runs a worldwide NGO that goes to every disaster and war zone in the world dispensing aid. We may think that is real practice. But real practice includes helping our neighbor, donating to organizations that help others, being considerate of one another in both private and public; it includes all the small ways we better the lives of others through our actions. This too counts and ripples throughout society.

As Dōgen points out at the beginning of this paragraph, "The whole moon and even the whole sky are reflected in a drop of dew on a blade of grass." No matter how small the situation (a drop of dew) or how vast (the whole ocean), the moon is still fully reflected. Realization is not predicated upon any comparative criteria.

CHAPTER 11

THERE'S ALWAYS SOMETHING

When the Dharma has not yet fully penetrated body and mind, one thinks one is already filled with it. When the Dharma fills body and mind, one thinks something is [still] lacking. For example, when we sail a boat into the ocean beyond sight of land and our eyes scan [the horizon in] the four directions, it simply looks like a circle. No other shape appears. This great ocean, however, is neither round nor square. It has inexhaustible characteristics. [To a fish] it looks like a palace; [to a heavenly being] a jeweled necklace. [To us] as far as our eyes can see, it looks like a circle. All the myriad things are like this. Within the dusty world and beyond, there are innumerable aspects and characteristics; we only see or grasp as far as the power of our eye of study and practice can see. When we listen to the reality of myriad things, we must know that there are inexhaustible characteristics in both ocean and mountains, and there are many other worlds in the four directions. This is true not only in the external world, but also right under our feet or within a single drop of water.

"When the Dharma has not yet fully penetrated body and mind, one thinks one is already filled with it." One example of our misapprehension may be when we attempt to see the world only from the side of emptiness or no-inherently-existing-form, and we believe that this view is the goal of practice and the definition of enlightenment. Having had one, several, or many nondual experiences, we might think this is enough and there is nothing more. This view is problematic because the mind of a buddha or bodhisattva is not about attaining special experiences; it is about benefiting all being(s). In the *Eihei Kōroku* teaching "Awakening Shines through All Things," Dōgen says to the assembly, "Loving emptiness and hating existence is not the way."[1]

Kyōgō's observation on this section is more general. "This 'body and mind' refers to living beings in delusion. Even when we think that someone has already attained realization though that person has not yet gotten it, we think that the Dharma fills [that person's body and mind]."[2] In general, any time we believe that we have achieved something definitive and we think or say, "I am enlightened," we will be off the mark. Our practice is grounded in our response to the variety and forms of life's co-arising.

Dōgen's understanding of realization is *shushō ittō*, or the oneness of practice-realization. Only focusing on emptiness, a person loses connection with their life as form—as practice. *Shō* refers to realization or verification,[3] and *shu* is practice. *Ittō* indicates the pairing of practice with realization and realization with practice. Our practice or actions in our daily lives are the manifestation and actualization of *shō*. Practice and realization are synonymous.[4]

When the Dharma fills body and mind, one thinks[5] (J. *oboyu*) something is [still] lacking.

A sincere practice is one in which we don't take things for granted. Instead, we always remain curious and diligently work to practice and understand Buddha's Way. The activities that make up our days and nights are infinite in variety, and they are the dharmas that fill our body and mind. Considering this practice as our daily activity, we realize that it goes on endlessly. When we see that this is the case, we realize that in each moment we are challenged to go further. In this way we understand that practice-realization will always be the koan of genjōkōan. Realizing practice never stops; there is always the next moment and the next moment. In short, the more we know, the more we realize we don't know.

Dōgen next gives the example of a boat out in the ocean to illustrate how our limited perceptions give us an erroneous view of the innumerable, constantly arising moments of response.

For example, when we sail a boat into the ocean beyond sight of land and our eyes scan [the horizon in] the four directions, it simply looks like a circle. No other shape appears.

If we go far enough out to sea or on a large lake in a boat, we lose sight of the particular characteristics of the shore. We see the horizon as a flat, circular oneness in which we are the center.[6] It is rather like having an experience of nonduality in which the self and other drop away and we no longer see the particularities of our experience. Everything appears as one great circle. When we have this experience, we may think "This is enough. I am completely 'filled with the Dharma' and there is nothing more to do."

This great ocean, however, is neither round nor square. It has inexhaustible characteristics.

Dōgen's use of "neither round nor square" may be a reference to partial teachings (square) and complete (round) (hōen, 方圓) teachings. Square teachings would be those that are applicable to a particular situation (relative teachings) but that do not express the complete understanding of the Dharma, as do absolute or round teachings.[7]

In this context, the great ocean goes beyond definitions such as relative or absolute. Life cannot be categorized by one or the other, and realization goes beyond these dichotomies by directly expressing a situation's needs. The ocean is home to many creatures and is subject to many views. The shore has many characteristics. There is no end to the variety of beings and circumstances. This great ocean is life in its totality. Senne writes, "To see a circle in the ocean without mountains is about our eyes. As for the virtues of the ocean, to be seen as a circle is one of the virtues of the ocean. And yet the virtues of the ocean are inexhaustible."[8]

The ocean is not just one big circle, nor is it square: these are inferences humans might derive from limited sensory perceptions. We can't fit our experiences into neat boxes, nor do they cleanly abide in universal generalizations. We want to recall that each being, thing, situation—each dharma position—is simultaneously unique and universal. This ocean of reality is made up of many, many varied and diverse beings. Dōgen writes that when we understand the vastness of each being-time as a unique presencing, we know that "something is [still] lacking."

[To a fish] it looks like a palace; [to a heavenly being] a jeweled necklace.[9]

Every creature sees and interprets their world differently. These perceptual shifts remind us that we cannot globalize our personal experience as being true for all. It is this widening of our own view that awakens us to our kinship with other beings who perceive the world differently than ourselves.

This is not only true for fish and heavenly beings but also for people. In the United States, we currently clash over disparate views of abortion rights, environmental concerns, and other issues that we hold dear to our perception of this oceanic world. Which view is correct? If you believe abortion is murder, then we could say you are like the fish who sees the ocean as a palace. If you believe that it is women's right to choose, then perhaps you are seeing a jeweled necklace.

From the view of practice-realization, we can only begin to find consensus or peace with our varied opinions when we acknowledge that each of us has a different perspective based upon our experience, karma, culture, and expectations. Without some kind of willingness to honor each unique characteristic, we will never come to meet each other. Meeting each other may lead to a solution that honors all those involved.

[To us] as far as our eyes can see, it looks like a circle. All the myriad things are like this. Within the dusty world and beyond, there are innumerable aspects and characteristics; we only see or grasp as far as the power of our eye of study and practice can see.

Sailing out into the ocean, on his way to China, Dōgen probably had the experience of looking out over the water and seeing a circle of horizon. He knew that the shore resides somewhere beyond the sky and water's meeting, but what he could see was just one vast circle. Clearly this experience triggered in him a deep understanding about the relationship between what we see and what might be true.

There is much more going on than we can know through our senses: the "dusty world" of our perceptions. What we do know is either limited or expanded by our previous life experience and even our particular sensory functions. In the case of learning the Buddha Dharma, our realization will be greater or smaller based upon our current understanding.

A buddha knows that they cannot see beyond their eye of study and practice and factors this limited view into their response. This teaching is incredibly important for us because we are often caught in our own perceptions of a situation based upon limited experience. We are sure we are correct; consequently we neglect to hold the larger picture in our mind. In fact, we can't see the larger picture because we have never been exposed to a greater view than the narrow one we currently hold.

Dōgen has already pointed out the necessity and fallibility of our perceptions several times in this text. Earlier he refers to our perception of color and sound as the bases of awakening. Then he uses mistaking the movement of a boat to be the movement of the shore as an example of how our perceptions deceive us. He cautions us not to conflate firewood and ash, nor to think of spring becoming summer.

Both our delusional and realized perceptions are dependent upon the strength of our study and practice of the Buddha Dharma. In just this paragraph, he talks about or implies the six senses: seeing the ocean, grasping the Dharma, listening to reality, smelling the ocean, and perhaps even tasting the sea foam. Our sixth sense is consciousness, which cognizes perceptions, interprets them, and imputes understanding to our experiences. All of this is the tactile basis of the instructions in "Genjōkōan" for the self to perceive, awaken to, and drop the self, thereby meeting and hearing the "innumerable aspects and characteristics" and "the reality of myriad things."

When we listen to the reality of myriad things, we must know that there are inexhaustible characteristics in both ocean and mountains, and there are many other worlds in the four directions. This is true not only in the external world, but also right under our feet or within a single drop of water.

"When we listen to the reality of myriad things," we can intuit the unfathomable complexity and completeness of our world. From Dōgen's point of view, there is no beginning or end. There is just this endless process of the Dharma unfolding.[10] A realized response begins with listening. If our minds are occupied with ideas about what each thing, person, or situation is, regardless of the actual experience, we will never find the point of pure response that goes beyond this or that. We must listen to enact true practice.

In "Mujō Seppō" (Insentient Beings Speak Dharma), Dōgen teaches that hearing the voices of this myriad world is paramount to our understanding:

Hearing dharma is not limited to ear sense and ear consciousness. You hear dharma with complete power, complete mind, complete body, and complete way from before your parents were born . . . through the entire future, the unlimited future. You can hear dharma with body first and mind last. Such ways of hearing the dharma are all effective. Don't think that you are not benefited by hearing the dharma if it does not reach your mind consciousness. Effacing mind, dropping body, you hear the dharma and see the result. With no mind and no body, you should hear dharma and benefit from it. Experiencing such moments is how all buddhas and ancestors become buddhas and attain ancestorhood.[11]

This is stopping and actively listening to our life. This is living zazen. Dōgen reiterates the importance of listening in *Shōbōgenzō Zuimonki* (*Treasury of the True Dharma Eye: Record of Things Heard*), but in this quotation he emphasizes the importance of the teacher's role in our awakening:

When we listen completely purified in body and mind, we can hear intimately. When we listen in this way, we will be able to clarify the truth and resolve our questions. True attainment of the Way is casting aside body and mind and following our teacher straightforwardly. If we maintain this attitude, we will be true people of the Way. This is the primary truth.[12]

In this passage of "Genjōkōan," "There are inexhaustible characteristics in both oceans and mountains," Norman Waddell and Masao Abe translate "characteristics" as "virtue,"[13] which shifts the meaning of the passage in interesting ways. Ocean virtue (*kaitoku*, 海徳) can be understood as a reference to the many characteristics of a thing—in this case, the ocean. But if we explore the meaning of virtue, our view is expanded to see the vast, efficacious nature of all being(s). Virtue imparts the qualities of benevolence, morality, goodness, strength, and agency to all things. All of these are qualities that Dōgen attributes to the buddha-ness of dharmas.

Dōgen opens the fascicle "Sansui Kyō" (The Sutra of Mountains and Water) by extolling the virtues of mountains and water:

The mountains and water of the present are the realization of the words of eternal buddhas. Both [mountains and water] abide in place in the Dharma, having realized ultimate virtue [*kudoku*]. . . . They are vigorous activity in the present.[14]

The oceans, mountains, and "single drop of water" referenced in this section of "Genjōkōan" are not different from the mountains and waters of "Sansui Kyō." Each is a dharma position fully endowed with the "words of the eternal buddhas." Can we hear their teaching being vigorously taught in the presencing moment? Can we perceive the virtue of their presencing?

A drop of water is so ephemeral that it appears and disappears in a matter of seconds or minutes. Yet each completely holds the totality of the moon's reflection or the Dharma's continuous practice.

We know from modern microbiology that there really are worlds in a drop of water. If we deeply listen with our body, heart, and mind, not just with our ears, we begin to "hear" the myriad teachings of our life's companions—we hear the voices of the ocean and a small drop of water. Zen teacher Nishiari Bokusan brings us back to our immediate practice when he writes, "Vastness without limitation is immediately underfoot. You may think a great ocean is vast and distant but it is no other than the cup of tea you are drinking right now."[15]

One of Dōgen's primary teachings is that we live in a world of vast interconnected networks all functioning together to manifest what we experience as solid form. Furthermore, this network or working of reality is essentially an altruistic endeavor. Virtue is the essential goodness of total function. Seeing this, we relate to such vastness in the immediacy of each moment's arising in our present circumstances, time, or dharma position. Vital to this mandala of activity is our own particular participation as practitioners of the bodhisattva ideal.

The logic of how a bodhisattva manifests buddha-nature is Dōgen's teaching throughout all of his writing. Nishiari reminds us that following the Dharma as far as our eye of study and practice can see is dependent upon knowing that "vastness without limitation is immediately underfoot." Recalling this teaching opens our eyes to looking (listening) more closely than we have before, with more curiosity and generosity. This looking-listening-seeing is "the cup of tea you are drinking right now," and it is the drop of dew on the grass outside your front door. It is bubbles in your sink and the troubles that greet you. Each instant is a sutra written as mountains and oceans, teacups, and problems. These are the sutras of our immediate experience, of the "many other worlds in the four directions." It is also the song of our life as it is "right under our feet" or within the smallest drop of water.

In Shōbōgenzō "Bukkyō" (The Teachings of the Buddhas), Dōgen points out that

> the sutras are the entire world of the ten directions. There is no moment or place that is not sutras. The sutras are written in letters of the supreme principle and of the secular principles. . . . The entire world of the ten directions are no other than letters of the sutras and the surface of the sutras. Regard them as the instruments of the great way and as the sutras of the buddha house.[16]

A single drop of water, mountains, oceans, a teacup, washing your clothes, eating dinner, arguing over abortion—everything, every situation and activity of daily life, should be approached as Buddha Dharma. When we can hear the inexhaustible great virtue of our life, then our practice will come forth as realized practice. Sutras are the wisdom of those who came before us, and sutras are being written every day. Dōgen teaches that each moment of our life is a sutra. It is sacred, mundane, absolute-relative, practice-realization, nothing special, the whole ball of wax: it's all happening right now, right here, under our noses.

We will not find an end to the newness and challenge of each moment's unfolding. As we meet the myriad things, having dropped our agenda and stopped clinging so tightly to our ideas, and if we sincerely heed these teachings, we will never come to the end of study, curiosity, and effort in the Way. Our world will keep opening in front of us, and our life will renew itself moment by moment. Dōgen illustrates this in his example, in the next section of "Genjōkōan," of fish swimming and birds flying in their elements.

CHAPTER 12

FISH, BIRDS, AND HUMANS PRACTICE

When a fish swims, no matter how far it swims, it doesn't reach the end of the water. When a bird flies, no matter how high it flies, it cannot reach the end of the sky. Therefore, since ancient times, no fish has ever left water and no bird has ever left the sky. When the bird's need or the fish's need is great, the range is large. When the need is small, the range is small. In this way, each fish and each bird uses the whole of space and vigorously acts in every place. However, if a bird departs from the sky, or a fish leaves the water, it immediately dies. We should know that [for a fish] water is life, [for a bird] sky is life. A bird is life; a fish is life. Life is a bird; life is a fish. And we should go beyond this. There is practice-enlightenment—this is the way of living beings.

When I first encountered the opening two lines of this section of "Genjōkōan," I was confused. It seemed to me that fish can reach the end of their environment, and birds can and do live on land. But, of course, this is not Dōgen's point. He is further exploring the idea that "when the Dharma fills body and mind, one thinks something is [still] lacking."

We swim in the Buddha Dharma. All of reality is a buddha—buddha-nature. This has been true since the beginning. As you may recall, there is a famous statement that Dōgen makes in Shōbōgenzō "Busshō" (Buddha-Nature) in which he says we *are* buddha-nature; all beings are buddha-nature. Furthermore, this buddha-nature is not something we need to acquire. All beings are buddha-nature, and nothing is left out. The Dharma is air, water, fish, birds, humans, and all of this is practice-realization. The Buddha Dharma is all of reality. Since this is the case, how could we ever run out or reach the end?

When the bird's need or the fish's need is great, the range is large. When the need is small, the range is small. In this way, each fish and each bird uses the whole of space and vigorously acts in every place.

Practice-realization accommodates the totality of our life. The fish cannot swim to the end of their capacity, nor can the bird run out of sky. Likewise, as we practice, we cannot run out of practice. Life itself is practice; every situation is practice. So we should not think that some parts of our life merit our effort and others do not.

Each fish and bird "uses the whole of space and vigorously acts in every place" refers to our daily life. This vigorous action is our practice and our realized response to each moment's unfolding. We never stop being who we are; we do not become another person, somewhere else; we are just this one unique life that cannot reach the end of Buddha Dharma. Recognizing this allows us to use the whole of our life as an arena for practice. Leave nothing out and nothing is left out. Because this is true for us, we don't have to go somewhere else or be someone else to practice. "We only see or grasp as far as the power of our eye of study and practice can see"—a line from earlier in "Genjōkōan"—doesn't mean what we can see or reach never expands or contracts. It is all practice actualizing as our life. We are making our best effort to enact the Buddha Dharma by responding to our life with skillful actions. This is our bodhisattva effort in practice.

Furthermore, in the context of each situation, person, and choice we encounter, we respond. This response is our practice activity.

Another translation of the line about a bird's or fish's need and range is "when the need is large the use is large, and when the requirement is small the use is small."[1] "Need" and "use" denote two aspects of our response. One is that there is a call for action in order to complete what is needed. In a Buddhist context, this would be to restore a cofunctional working equilibrium through a skillful response. The other is to put something to use, to have a purpose. In bodhisattva practice, we answer with what is needed, and we have the tools to enact practice-realization.

Let's now tie in some previous lines from "Genjōkōan." As we study the Buddha Way, we study our own actions, our own responses to what is needed, through Buddhist practice. Are we carrying the self forward "to be verified by all things?" Or do we "forget the self" to meet a situation's need? When we appropriately integrate self with other, the awakened mind's function or business will remain the same regardless of the size of the field we encounter. In this way, we use "the whole of space and vigorously [act] in every place."

Dōgen is not making a judgment about the worthiness of a situation's need. The practice is realized activity meeting the myriad things, resulting in each action answering to the needs of any given situation. In Shōbōgenzō "Tsuki" (The Moon), Dōgen quotes Shākyamuni Buddha: "The true dharma-body of the Buddha is just like the empty sky; in response to things, it manifests itself in various forms, like the moon in the water."[2]

When the water is great, the moon's reflection will be larger. When the water is small, the moon will appear smaller. The size of the moon has not changed, but the moon's response is calibrated to the need of the water. This is the reciprocal Dharma between water and moon.

Your embodied sensitivity to a situation as it arises will dictate your response. If your agenda dictates your response, the response (or use) will not necessarily meet the need. If you allow the situation to meet you, your response will meet the need. There are no large or small encounters. There is just each moment's need. Comparisons are not helpful. When we make comparisons in determining our actions, we are categorizing a situation as worthy or unworthy of our best effort. This is incorrect. Each situation requires our total commitment to practice-realization. This is the total engagement of a single thing or dharma position.

In Shōbōgenzō "Zenki" (The Whole Works), Dōgen includes a similar passage:

> Realization [現成, genjō][3] is life, and life is realization. At the moment of this realization there is nothing which is not the total realization of life, and there is nothing which is not the total realization of death. This momentary pivot-state can cause life to be and cause death to be. The very moment of the present in which this pivot-state is realized is not necessarily great and not necessarily small, it is neither the whole world nor a limited area and is neither long lasting nor short and pressed. Life in the present exists in this pivot-state, and this pivot-state exists in life in the present.[4]

As we fully exert our effort in practice at this moment, we completely inhabit each moment of our experience. Functioning in Buddha's Way, this pivot point expresses genjōkōan, or fully expressed practice-realization. This is true as we experience life and as we experience death. It is true as we wash dishes, sit zazen, or attend meetings; no situation is too small or too large. Just right now, just this.

However, if a bird departs from the sky, or a fish leaves the water, it immediately dies. We should know that [for a fish] water is life, [for a bird] sky is life. A bird is life; a fish is life. Life is a bird; life is a fish.

Water and air are the Buddha Dharma. As practitioners, we swim in the water and breathe the air of practice-realized or practice-verified. We can go further and say that water, air, practice-realization or -verification, practitioner, fish, bird, all things-being(s), reality—all are one great function. If we reach the end of the air or water, that means we have ceased to practice. If our practice ceases, some part of our awareness of our place and function in the world dies.

We might just quit practicing for various reasons, or we might think we have reached the pinnacle of realization. Either way, our practice is on life support. When we cease to care about making our best effort in every encounter, using our knowledge and experience of life as practice, then we have departed from the medium of our practice life.

This very medium is life. We are life and life is us. That is why Dōgen says, "A bird is life; a fish is life. Life is a bird; life is a fish." Each unique person, bird, fish, and all dharmas are life itself, and all of life is the particularity of a person, bird, fish, and all dharmas inter-being. In this way we cannot check out of practice. It is our air and water; it is the field in which we disport ourselves.

And we should go beyond this. There is practice-enlightenment—this is the way of living beings.

There are several interesting translations of these two sentences:

> Waddell and Abe: "We could continue in this way even further, because practice and realization, and for all that is possessed of life, it is the same."[5]
> Sōtō Zen Text Project: "Other than these, there should be further steps forward. That there are practice and verification, and that they have 'those with lifespans, those with lives,' are like this."[6]
> Kazuaki Tanahashi: "You can go further. There is practice-enlightenment, which encompasses limited and unlimited life."[7]
> Hee-Jin Kim: "Besides these [modes of life], there are still others. They all have exertion-and-verification and life-span like this."[8]

The first clause of this sentence seems to be fairly clear: we can go beyond these analogies of fish, water, birds, and air. Because the text says little about practice on its surface, it could be taken out of context to be understood as a description of the lives of fish and birds.

Now, Dōgen says, let's go on; let's make the connection between this example and practicing the Buddha Dharma. He could also be saying, go beyond the idea of making continuous effort and attain realization beyond realization: attain bodhisattva-buddha-practice-realization beyond all ideations and striving. Kim's translation, in toto, seems to simply say all living beings engage in the activity of practice-realization or practice-verification.

Unlike Kim's summation, a literal translation of this sentence is a little harder to understand. In the Sōtō Zen Text Project example, it refers to "those with lifespans, those with lives"; and Tanahashi's translation is "limited and unlimited life." The Japanese is *jusha myōsha* (壽者命者),[9] meaning "old-age person" (*jusha*, 壽者) and a "live person" (*myōsha*, 命者). "Old-age person" has the connotation of a person who has experienced many rebirths; and "live person" might refer to this lifetime. *Myōsha* (live person) has to do with agency and destiny. Hee-Jin Kim writes, "Dōgen . . . seems to be using the term [*jusha myōsha*] in a more general way rendered in this translation as 'life-span.' But life-span here is akin to what we call eternal life. That is to say, every mode of life has its own 'life-span,' which exists always as the indivisible oneness of exertion and verification."[10]

Perhaps Kim is saying that our lives are eternal in that we are part of a process of the world's functioning throughout time and space (unlimited life), and that we are each a particular life, a particular form being, experiencing our current reality (limited life). This life (exertion as practice) and buddha-nature (verification) come together as one activity: practice-realization or practice-verification.

Tanahashi renders this "limited and unlimited life," which is the same as Nishiari's understanding of this term.[11] Limited and unlimited life, according to Nishiari, refers to the idea that as we are cycling through rebirth (unlimited life), we will, "if we inherit the Buddha Way," function both as the limited and unlimited life in this lifetime. We will be able to function in the world of samsara and yet also be able to go beyond these dissatisfactions.

Senne makes an interesting comment about this sentence in "Genjōkōan": "A bird should use the sky as its own legs or wings without being limited in its life."[12] Any being—a bird or a person, for example—is endowed with particular physical attributes and perceptions. Therefore, this body-mind is what they (or we) have to negotiate the world. Perhaps this is the reason Dōgen refers to past lives and present lives. Our past rebirth will determine our present manifestation, which will become the ground of our practice-realization or practice-verification.

Okumura translates this sentence as "There is practice-enlightenment—this is the way of living beings." This is our life of practice. This is what it means to be a living being—one who is reborn into the sahā world and answers the call of realization or bodhi mind. Since we are endowed with the mind of a buddha, the question is, do we practice with this mind, thereby bringing forth practice-enlightenment? According to Dōgen, this should be our function and vow as bodhisattvas. It is the way (the Buddha Dharma) of living beings.

In Shōbōgenzō "Keisei Sanshoku" (Sound of the Stream, Form of the Mountain), Dōgen writes,

> Though we may have spent our previous years and months in vain, while this life is not yet exhausted, we should forthwith make a vow. I pray that, together with all living beings, from this life through life after life to come, I shall hear the true dharma; that whenever I hear it, I shall not doubt it and fail to believe in it; that when I encounter the true dharma, casting aside the worldly dharma, I shall receive and keep the buddha dharma, and finally attain the way together with the whole earth and sentient beings. When we make a vow in this way, it will naturally be the cause and condition of correctly bringing forth the [bodhi] mind. This mental attitude is not to be neglected.[13]

CHAPTER 13

WALKING THE WALK

Therefore, if there are fish that would swim or birds that
would fly only after investigating the entire ocean or sky,
they would find neither path nor place. When we make this
very place our own, our practice becomes the actualization
of reality [*genjōkōan*]. When we make this path our own, our
activity naturally becomes actualized reality [*genjōkōan*].
This path, this place, is neither big nor small, neither self nor
others. It has not existed before this moment nor has it come
into existence now. Therefore [the reality of all things] is thus.

If we try to practice Buddhism without experiential immersion
in our life, we will only find a dead end. Practice is enacted not
through intellectually investigating the whole of a situation, like
a drone hovering over terrain; it is found by being on the ground.
Another analogy is that trying to practice only after investigating
all of Buddhism would be like stipulating that you will not enter a
new relationship without seeing how it will unfold in the future.

When we make this very place our own, our practice becomes the
actualization of reality [*genjōkōan*]. When we make this path our
own, our activity naturally becomes actualized reality [*genjōkōan*].

Practicing the Buddha Dharma must reflect our own life. We need
to make this very place our own and make this path our own. This

hearkens back to Senne's commentary on the previous section, in which he writes that a bird "should use the sky as its own legs or wings." As practitioners, we must see our own life as the path and place of actualizing or harmonizing as and with our presencing life. The past of your activity has left, the future of your activity has not arrived. Our activity can only be manifest as this moment's actualization of practice-realization. As soon as we presence ourselves for our immediate experience, the whole of reality, just as it is, meets us right now. This is not a special or unattainable state. You probably do it all the time without thinking. These are the times when we fully, skillfully, spontaneously respond, "Oh, let me help you!"

Since this paragraph contains Dōgen's first use of the word gen-jōkōan within the fascicle, it is helpful to revisit its meaning. Gen-jōkōan is to actualize practice-realization (or practice-verification) at and as this place on this path. This is responding to things as they are, or gen. Therefore, many possibilities arise.

Senne writes,

> The word genjōkōan can be used together with any term. When we expound the dharma of being (u, 有), we can say, genjōkōan of being (u). When we talk about the dharma of nonbeing (mu, 無), we can say genjōkōan of nonbeing (mu). When we explain the dharma of neither-being nor-nonbeing (hi-u-hi-mu, 非有非無), we can speak in the same way.[1]

And perhaps more concretely, he states,

> There can be the genjō of delusion, the genjō of realization, or the genjō of a whisk or a monk's staff, because the reality of each thing is manifested (genjō) [within each thing].[2]

Jō refers to gen being fully allowed to express itself. Another way to say this is to be "actualized by myriad things," which results in total immersion in or intimacy with just this, or the state of "your body and mind as well as the bodies and minds of others drop[ping] away." This actualization is completely dropping into your life as it is unfolding now.

Kōan is more difficult to define, but in the context of fully engaging our current circumstances, it can be understood as: (1) a kind of question that leads to a deeper understanding of our life as the Buddha Dharma. (2) To find equanimity in inequality. Okumura summarizes this as "to equalize the unfair or unequal situations among beings that arise in the world of disorder and discrimination."[3] And (3), again quoting Okumura, "it refers both to the equality of all things (*kō*) and to the uniqueness or particularity of each and every being (*an*)," resulting in "an intersection of equality (universality, unity, oneness of all being) and inequality (difference, uniqueness, particularity, individuality)."[4]

Genjōkōan is simply encountering various situations in which there are differences that become equalized by realized action. For example, when a person drops something and, without making judgments, you immediately pick it up and hand it to that person, you are genjōkōan-ing. That person is particular and not the same as you in their particularity. Equalizing those differences happens because you are unconsciously focused on your sameness with them, resulting in your immediate desire to help them by picking up what they dropped and handing it to them. Understanding fully, you intimately respond to the needs of that situation. This is not different from when people help others, without judgment or qualification, when there is a disaster.

Like birds in the sky and fish in water, we practice-actualize by making the place, time, or situation our own. We take responsibility for our life and responses. To use the illustration of a map, it's good to study the map, but if we want to use the map to find our way, we must walk the terrain. We can certainly use the map as a guide, but we have to actually enact the teachings or walk the land. If you try to skip this step you will "find neither path nor place" in the Buddha Way.

As we have seen, Okumura's translation of the second and third lines of this section read, "When we make this very place our own, our practice becomes the actualization of reality [*genjōkōan*]. When we make this path our own, our activity naturally becomes actual-ized reality [*genjōkōan*]," giving us an immediate sense of the how and where of practice. It conveys the simultaneity of place, activity, and actualization. These three elements happen concurrently, not sequentially. There is the path (place), there is the time of walking the path (practice), there is practice-realization manifesting as and in one dharma position: this is the total exertion of the fundamental point (genjōkōan).

Dōgen writes in *Eihei Kōroku* (*Dōgen's Extensive Record*), "We could say that the situation of Buddha's house is the oneness in which essence, practice, and expounding are one and the same."[5] And in "Uji" (Being-Time), he writes that when we have found our place in practice, "there is an arising of the religious mind at the same time, and it is the arising of time of the same mind. So it is with practice and attainment of the Way. We set our self out in array, and we see that."[6]

Kim's translation of the sentences of "Genjōkōan" under con-sideration puts emphasis on our daily life as practice. He writes, "When you attain your place here, everyday activity naturally becomes the realized-kōan; when you attain your way now, every-day activity naturally is the realization-kōan."[7] This is path, place, practice-realization or practice-verification as one, manifesting as daily life. We should not reject any of the aspects of our life in favor of a perceived idealized practice.

Incorporating genjōkōan into everyday life underscores the importance of sangha and having a teacher. Both are necessary for our growth as Zen students and people. It is in the sangha environ-ment that we run up against difficulties that can be addressed using Dharma teachings and the language of those teachings. Everyone in the sangha is onboard, practicing with any difficult relationships that may arise. Our teachers facilitate our understanding of how to enact this practice-realization in the context of our own experiences and problems, not as an abstract teaching about practice. This is the enactment of the mandala of the Three Treasures: Buddha, Dharma, and Sangha.

Really, where else would you find your place but within the context of your own life? If the Dharma did not apply to our immediate experience, it would have no relevance to us. Finding your place is facing toward the Dharma and enacting your particular birth and death through the Dharma. If we try to escape our life, then we will not find realization. In fact, according to Dōgen, this life is nirvana.[8]

As much as we would like to avoid suffering and pain, there is no substitute for learning by falling down and getting up over and over again. Even as we make mistakes, they are not outside the Buddha Dharma. They are a Dharma gate that can become the place and time of genjōkōan. If this were not so, we would be unable to access practice-realization. This is how we genjōkōan, or actualize the fundamental point of practice. We can stand on the side of the pool and practice our strokes, but unless we enter the water, we cannot say we know how to swim.

This path, this place, is neither big nor small, neither self nor others. It has not existed before this moment nor has it come into existence now. Therefore [the reality of all things] is thus.

"This path, this place" is where you are now. It is the Dharma position of each moment's enactment at this time. We don't need to make comparisons that engender judgments. If we don't make comparisons, then we can't say, "This is big and that is small." When we fully engage with another dharma or with our current situation, we must meet it as it presents itself. This is not to say that we can or should try to eschew comparison altogether. Comparisons can be good, for instance, when we ask ourselves if we are acting in accord with Buddhist precepts.[9]

Since many beings have practiced the Buddha Dharma before us and will do so after us, Dōgen mentions that our practice is not ours entirely, yet it is not another person's either.

It has not existed before this moment nor has it come into existence now. Therefore [the reality of all things] is thus.[10]

"It has not existed before this moment nor has it come into existence now" specifically refers the path of our spiritual journey. Our practice, while unique to us, is also being practiced with all buddhas throughout time and space at this presencing moment. Dōgen does not mean this metaphorically; he means it literally.[11] Our practice, though unique, is born and practiced with all previous and future buddhas, bodhisattvas, and ancestors.

I find this a fascinating and mind-boggling premise. Whatever we experience has never been before, yet it is not new, and at the same time reflects and affects the totality of life. Dōgen states this clearly in Shōbōgenzō "Yuibutsu Yobutsu" (Only a Buddha and a Buddha) when he writes, "An ancient buddha said, 'Mountains, rivers, and the earth are born at the same moment with each person. All buddhas of the past, present, and future are practicing together with each person.'"[12]

Dōgen explains how it is that our practice is born the same moment as that of all buddhas and ancestors:

> All buddhas of the past, present, and future have already practiced, attained the way, and completed realization. How should we understand that those buddhas are practicing together with us? First of all, examine a buddha's practice. A buddha's practice is to practice in the same manner as the entire earth and all beings. If it is not practice with all beings, it is not a buddha's practice. This being so, from the moment of arousing the aspiration for enlightenment to the moment of attaining enlightenment, all buddhas realize and practice the way together with the entire earth and all beings.
>
> You may have doubts about this. But the ancient buddha's word was expounded in order to clarify your confused thinking. Do not think that buddhas are other than you. According to this teaching, when all buddhas of the past, present, and future arouse the aspiration for enlightenment and practice, they never exclude our body-and-mind. Understand this.[13]

In each moment, a particularity arises—in this case, our own life of practice. Because our lives are unique, this moment has not existed before. Yet because of codependent arising and the nonduality of time and space, the singularity of our life is born with all the buddhas and ancestors whose lives preceded us in sequential time. We are born with and are part of a larger inter-being of nondual presencing reality. This larger codependent inter-being is the state of "nor has it come into existence now."

The aspiration to practice is born anew with each person, even as the buddhas and ancestors were there before us. Furthermore, according to Dōgen, our aspiration to practice arose at the same time as that of previous buddhas and ancestors. But in the moment of a dharma position's arising as it encounters and interconnects with others, something unique comes forth. When that particular presencing of the independent aspect of the self (or any dharma) is gone, then that moment dies with it. At the same time, each self, each being, each unique dharma position is never apart from the holistic arising (and disappearance) of reality's continued passageless passage. Thus, Dōgen quotes the ancient buddha: "Mountains, rivers, and the earth are born at the same moment with each person."

Human beings have particular mental traits that Buddhist doctrine considers efficacious and desirable for awakening. For this reason, a human rebirth is key to realizing the Buddha Dharma. In Shōbōgenzō "Fukanzazengi" (Recommending Zazen to All People), Dōgen admonishes, "You have gained the pivotal opportunity of human form. Do not pass your days and nights in vain."[14] And he extols the virtue of human rebirth in Shōbōgenzō "Shukke Kudoku" (The Merit of Leaving Home):

> This is the virtue of being human [that makes it] superior to other destinies. . . . Not only have we already received the human body, hard to receive; we have been granted an encounter with the buddha dharma. We should quickly cast aside all involvements and immediately leave home and study the way.[15]

Implied in these encouragements to value and take advantage of our human rebirth is the specificity of our life as a unique being who is able to engage the Buddha Dharma. Our independent path will not come again in this particular configuration.

Our human life has not existed before, yet it is not unique, nor has our life just come into existence. If we are willing to go beyond the intellectualization of nonduality of self and other, buddhas and sentient beings, we may have a strong sense that we are being supported in our practice by a whole lineage of former, present, and future practitioners. We may have faith that our life of practice is strengthened by the vows of others as well as our own. As Dōgen further taught in Shōbōgenzō "Yuibutsu Yobutsu," "When all buddhas of the past, present, and future arouse the aspiration for enlightenment and practice, they never exclude our body-and-mind. To doubt this is to slander buddhas of the past, present, and future."[16]

This is the power of countless practitioners who support our practice as we are supporting the practice of others. It is their vow and aspiration that has awakened our own path of practice. This activity-unremitting is manifesting from the past as it is also happening in both the present and future. Our effort is supporting the effort of all buddhas and ancestors who have come before us and will follow in the future. It is the bodhi mind as this very body and mind that has supported and will support all living beings throughout time and space. This is the simultaneity of the Buddhist multiverse.

CHAPTER 14

ENCOUNTERING, PRACTICING, PERMEATING, AND REALIZING EACH MOMENT

In the same way, when a person engages in practice-enlightenment in the Buddha Way, as the person realizes one dharma, the person permeates that dharma; as the person encounters one practice, the person [fully] practices that practice. [For this] there is a place and a path.

Dropping metaphors, Dōgen directly addresses practice-enlightenment as the Buddha Way. He defines the nature of practice-realization or verification (shushō ittō, 修證一等) as making the effort to fully understand the nature of a dharma. When we are able realize the true nature of one thing (one dharma) we will also know practice. This practice is complete engagement with a single thing (ippō-gūjin).

In "Bendōwa" (On the Endeavor of the Way), Dōgen defines practice-realization as:

It is practice inseparable from the outset from realization, and since fortunately we [practitioners] all transmit a portion of wondrous practice ourselves, even our negotiation of the Way as beginners obtains a portion of original realization at a ground that is utterly free of human agency. You should know that in order to keep from defiling this realization that is inseparable from practice; Buddhas and ancestors[1] teach unceasingly that we must not allow our practice to diminish.[2]

Here Dōgen states categorically that practice of the Buddha Dharma is the manifestation of the bodhisattva path, or realization actualized. All things are buddha-nature, therefore "your initial negotiation of the way is itself the whole of original realization." "Whole of original realization" refers to a fundamental is-ness before causal conditioning that may be obstructing practice. Being endowed with buddha-nature is being endowed with original realization. But the caveat here is that practice must accompany original realization in order for it to manifest as awakened action. For this reason, we must diligently apply ourselves to practicing the Buddha Dharma. It is not enough to be buddha-nature; we must manifest our essential nature through practice.[3]

The contemporary Zen teacher Daijaku Kinst offers a definition of practice-realization that speaks directly to practitioners: "Fundamentally, we can understand practice as the activity a person takes up that allows her to deepen her understanding, realization, and expression of Buddha's teaching, thereby reducing suffering for herself and others." Kinst continues, "'Enlightenment' or *bodhi* means 'to see things as they are' . . . to be awake . . . [which] carries with it the notion that by awakening, delusion and its consequent suffering cease."[4]

These two "goals" of our effort—practice and realization—resulting in the transformation of suffering, are not separated. When joined, practice-realization is no longer understood as a means to an end. We practice not to attain enlightenment but as expressed realization. Practice becomes the place and path of actualized activity.

When we are called to practice Buddha Way, it is a call spoken by the self to the self. Our essential is-ness, buddha-nature, suchness speaks and encourages us to follow the bodhisattva path. When we engage that path, we are expressing what is already present as us. We and all being(s) are at heart altruistic and not separate from the whole world's functioning.

. . . the person realizes one dharma, the person permeates that dharma; as the person encounters one practice, the person [fully] practices that practice.

Dōgen writes in Shōbōgenzō "Shoaku-makusa" (Not Doing Evil Deeds),

> One who knows a single dust mote knows all the worlds; one who penetrates a single dust mote penetrates all the worlds. One who has not penetrated the myriad dharmas has not penetrated a single dharma. Because when those who study penetration fully penetrate it, they see the myriad dharmas and see the single dharma, those who study a single dust mote study all the worlds without remainder.[5]

This knowing is the occasion when a "person permeates that [one] dharma." This is a full-on encounter as inter-being, interpenetration, and mutual identity with and as practice-realization or practice-verification. This knowing arises from engaging each moment as practice. Each moment is not different from a single dust mote, and completely engaging one practice is knowing the one thing. Consequently, as we put our attention to that one moment's presencing as our reality, " . . . we experience that 'when one side is illuminated, the other is dark.'" At the same time, the other side is still presencing, and by seeing what is apparent, we also, by implication, realize what is not seen.

Our effort is to immerse ourselves in any activity that we encounter. If you are washing dishes, then wash dishes in a way that fully engages you to the point that your "I" is no longer separate from the what of your activity. Dōgen would call this washing washes washing.

Dōgen describes practicing one dharma in "Tenzo Kyōkun" (Instructions for the Cook). He emphasizes that the job of head cook in a monastery (tenzo) is primarily one of practice as well as practicality. Dōgen writes, "Since ancient times, masters with Way-seeking mind, lofty people who had awakened their hearts, were appointed to this job. After all, isn't this the single color of diligently engaging the Way?"[6]

"Tenzo Kyōkun" is a hands-on guide on how to approach practice-realization through daily activity. One example is Dōgen's description of cleaning sand from grains of rice.

> You should not attend to some things and neglect or be slack with others for even one moment. . . . While examining the rice, watch for sand; while examining the sand, watch for rice. If you minutely observe from different viewpoints without absent-mindedness, then naturally the food will integrate the three virtues and include the six tastes.[7]

When the tenzo pays attention to every detail of the activity of winnowing rice from sand, the meal will naturally be delicious. Or we might say, if our activity is skillful and demonstrates the bodhisattva practice of benefiting all beings, then the outcome will be genjōkōan. This is the activity of encountering one practice and fully practicing that practice. It is dropping body-mind.

A tenzo's practice can also be applied to our relationships. As Dōgen writes in *Eihei Shingi* (*Pure Standards for the Zen Community*), "When you take care of things, do not see with your common eyes, do not think with your common sentiments. Pick a single blade of grass and erect a sanctuary . . . do not arouse the attitude of distaste or dismissal."[8]

In the American political and social commentator David Brooks's book *How to Know a Person*, the three main sections are titled "I See You," "I See Your Struggles," and "I See You with Your Strengths."[9] Essentially, this is a book about how we can fully engage with others by dropping the self and realizing one dharma by being truly interested in their lives. This is not different from the story told in case four of the *Book of Serenity*, "The World Honored One Points to the Ground," in which the Buddha locates a suitable place to build a temple, and the god Indra picks a single blade of grass, sticks it in the ground, and declares the sanctuary built.[10]

To practice one practice or "see" another person is to wholeheartedly meet each situation and treat it with the same open mind that you would treat a person you perceived as a buddha, a mentor, or a friend. Each dharma position is a sacred space and an opportunity to realize the Dharma.

Senne connects this practice with zazen, writing,

> "Attaining one dharma is penetrating one dharma" is the same as "attaining zazen is penetrating becoming-buddha." When one is sitting, one does not know the merits [of zazen]. And yet, this is zazen. Zazen is becoming-buddha. Therefore, it is said that "We should not think that what we have attained is perceived by ourselves and known by our discriminating mind."[11]

We do not know the merits of this practice because we are so engaged with the practice that there is no separation between self and zazen. This is not different from paying complete attention to winnowing rice from sand or truly seeing a person. This intimate presenting results in the self dropping away as we become one with the activity.

According to Dōgen, a practitioner's daily life is grounded in zazen mind. In Shōbōgenzō "Zazengi" (Principles of Seated Meditation) he writes, "Zazen is zazen, and it is not limited to sitting or lying down. This teaching has been transmitted person to person; thus boundless sitting and lying down are the self [beyond self]. When you reflect on your life activities, are they intimate with zazen or remote from it?"[12]

A few lines later, Dōgen proclaims, "Those who have not practiced sitting do not reach the heart of the matter. The heart of the matter is sitting time, sitting person, sitting buddha, and the practice of sitting buddha."[13] This is not different from "realizing one dharma" as fully encountering, engaging, realizing, and becoming intimate with each moment, each person.

Sitting in zazen we experience in a visceral and intimate way what it means to enter the mind of a Buddha. This mind is characterized by the famous zazen instructions, "Think of not thinking. How do you think of not thinking? Beyond-thinking."[14]

It is important to look at the Japanese for these three states of mind. Dōgen writes in "Fukanzazengi" (Recommending Zazen to All People), "Think (*shiryō*) of not thinking (*fushiryō*). How do you think of not thinking? Nonthinking. (*hishiryō*)."[15] *Shiryō* refers to our normal mental activity of thinking about things, planning, and so on. *Fushiryō* is the suspension of thinking altogether. *Hishiryō* is the mind that goes beyond thinking to the state of full Dharmic response to what is arising at any given moment.

Contrary to some meditation instructions that teach practitioners to extinguish thinking, in zazen, thoughts are to be expected. As Kōshō Uchiyama points out, they are "just a secretion in your head."[16] We are to think of letting go (fushiryō) of our thoughts by fully experiencing our current situation as it unfolds or presences. This includes the state of letting go, the state of having thoughts, and going beyond both to a state of purely living in a moment, fully actualizing a dharma position.

This instruction for our mental state in formal zazen also describes the mind-state of engaging one's reality as it arises and unfolds in daily life. This is the mind of encountering, realizing, practicing, and permeating the one dharma of our lived experience at this time.

Another way of approaching this is to say that when we engage in an activity, we are not trying to be mindful of that activity. When we "are mindful of," we create a dualistic relationship of mindfulness as awareness of something objectified outside the self's activity. Presencing or "think nonthinking" is going beyond thinking about something outside the self. When "think nonthinking" happens, we fully engage that one activity as it unfolds with and as us in that moment. If we can do this, our engagement will open to and include all practices as this one practice.

This is the meaning of Dōgen's teaching in Shōbōgenzō "Hotsu Bodai Shin" (Bringing Forth the Mind of Bodhi):

> The bringing forth the mind [of Bodhi] of a thousand million instances of bringing forth is definitely bringing forth one instance of bringing forth the mind. A thousand million people's bringing forth the mind is bringing forth one bringing forth the mind; one bringing forth the mind is a thousand million instances of bringing forth the mind. Practice and verification and turning the dharma are also like this.[17]

The "thousand million instances" are dharma positions manifesting. At the same time, "one instance" is not different from the thousand million instances. Hence, one practice, one dharma, is just the "thousand million instances" arising as this one person, situation, object, thought, and so on.

This one instance of engagement with our current situation, this one instance of practice-realization, is not done exclusively by the self; it is the community effort of all beings working in concert. We may see this, or we may not. In "Uji" (Being-Time), Dōgen tells us that all beings, even gods and celestial beings, are practicing with us in each moment:

> The deva kings and hosts of heaven—now manifested on the right now on the left—are the "existence-time" [Uji, being-time] which, even now, they continue to exert through their utmost efforts. The "existence-time" of the hosts of other waters and lands is that which they themselves now realize through their utmost efforts. Various beings and various events existing as "existence-time" in the invisible and visible worlds all realize themselves through their utmost efforts; they pass through themselves by way of their utmost efforts. Unless it is a passage of its own utmost efforts at this moment, not a dharma, not a thing, can ever realize itself or pass through itself. This we should study.[18]

And in Shōbōgenzō "Gyōji" (Continuous Practice), Dōgen encourages us to realize how important our effort, in concert with others, is to sustaining the Buddha Way:

> On the great road of buddha ancestors there is always unsurpassable practice, continuous and sustained. It forms the circle of the way and is never cut off. Between aspiration, practice, enlightenment, and nirvana, there is not a moment's gap; continuous practice is the circle of the way. This being so, continuous practice is undivided, not forced by you or others. The power of this continuous practice confirms you as well as others. It means your practice affects the entire earth and the entire sky in ten directions. Although not noticed by others or by yourself, it is so.[19]

We make effort, we engage practice-realization, through specific activity, yet that activity also includes the efforts of all beings at the same time. We may be aware of others' efforts, or we may not. If we think of our world as one great endeavor of sustaining continuous creation, then we know that all beings throughout all time have made efforts to support our current life, just as our life will continue to support others. Continuous practice is sustained in each particular activity at a specific time and place. This is why we focus on one practice, one activity, at a time.

Dōgen also said in "Gyōji," "You may not notice the causal conditions that led you to be engaged in the practice that actualizes you at this very moment of unknowing. The reason you don't see it is that becoming conscious of it is not anything remarkable."[20] We are not conscious of the results of our efforts or think what we do is remarkable, but each moment of attentive practice on our part is efficacious.

This effort does not need to be forced; it is a matter of attending to our activity with the practice mind of curiosity and generosity, not criticism or rigidity. Yes, effort is required, and that effort may at times be difficult, but it does not need to be dour.

[For this] there is a place and a path.

Dōgen ends this section of "Genjōkōan" by clearly encouraging us to investigate our own life as a Dharma gate. This life is unfolding and presencing itself to us as our life right now—not at some other time or place.

For liberation, this place and path is your current life. All you need is right before your eyes, even if it is not apparent. The whole universe is to your right and left and all around you, making effort to support your practice. This is why Dōgen writes in Shōbōgenzō "Bodaisatta Shi Shōbō" (Bodhisattva's Four Methods of Guidance), "When one leaves the Way to the Way, one attains the Way. When attaining the Way, the Way is necessarily being left to the Way."[21] We keep making our effort in practice and everything else will take care of itself.

This does not mean that everything will necessarily be fair, good, or what we want. It means that we can contribute to enriching our life and the lives of others as we negotiate our lives' ups and downs with equanimity and compassion for self and other. While we make our effort by the grace and contribution of the world's activity, it is our responsibility to practice-realize our own dharma position—moment to moment, paying attention to what is needed. If we can do this, then the Buddha Way will take care of itself.

CHAPTER 15

KNOWING IS NOT KNOWING

The boundary of the known is not clear; this is because the known [which appears limited] is born and practiced simultaneously with the complete penetration of the Buddha Dharma.

Like birds flying as and through the air or fish swimming as and through the water, we cannot see the boundaries of our life. Our day-to-day life unfolds only partially known to us. Life is unexpected, and the boundaries of what we know and what we do not know are porous. This is the Buddha Dharma unfolding as each moment-to-moment encounter with the one hundred grasses, the limitless dharmas. As we negotiate the path fully, what seems limited is still unfolding as the Buddha Dharma.

As we interact and actualize the permeability of self and other, we cannot know what will arise. Even after it has come, we cannot know the full effect or import of this communication and response. From this perspective, the beauty of a boundary is the space of fuzzy delineation between what is and what is not. This is the luminous unknowing of liminal space.

"Here is the place; here the way unfolds" is Kazuaki Tanahashi's translation of "[For this] there is a place and a path," discussed at the end of the previous chapter.[1] The specificity of "here" and "way," and the implication of "time," are quite clear. One realizes, permeates, encounters, and practices this "one dharma" in a specific place and time. Yet there is always the constant shifting from one moment to the next, the transitions of being and time.

In "Uji" (Being-Time), Dōgen observes, "Even when the time of their reaching is not yet over, the time of their not-reaching has arrived. The mind is a donkey, the word a horse, making the horse a word and the donkey the mind."[2] Putting aside the meaning of "reaching" and "not-reaching," Dōgen's reference to the donkey and horse coming and going probably refers to part of a dialogue between Changqing Huileng (J. Chokei Eryo, 854–932) and Lingyun Zhiqin (J. Reiun Shigon, dates unknown):

> Huileng of Changqing studied with Lingyun and asked him, "What is the essential meaning of Buddhadharma?"
> Lingyun said, "When the donkey matter has not yet left, the horse matter arrives."[3]

This is the unknowable transitional boundary between this and that or self and other. It is, according to Dōgen, the place, the being-time of "complete penetration of the Buddha Dharma," because it is also a space of not knowing, not having a fixed view. At exactly what point or moment has the donkey left and the horse arrived? At what point does the donkey matter and horse matter intersect? Is it the moment we can't physically see one or the other? Or the moment when their appearing ceases to have an impact on the current circumstances? Looked at from this perspective, it is difficult to say when one arrives or departs.

From the perspective of universal codependent arising, the continuous practice of all beings, all of reality, is the processes of inter-being, coming and going, abiding, and responding. This is the intimacy of fully functioning parts as whole being. When does one begin and another end? Furthermore, there is the holistic nature of time, being, response, and effect: this functioning is not just a horizontal line.

Reality's functioning—or continuous practice-realization—is never just one thing or another. The self is both particular and universal. This is the intersection of "not one, not two." Continuous practice-realization is always found at the fulcrum of a dharma position's point of contact with the totality of being-time and the specificity of our current experience. Despite our perception to the contrary, our life is always a flowing state of the indistinct boundaries of reality's coming and going.

Another translation of the sentence to consider:

> Since, in this, the place exists, and the way penetrates [every-where] the fact that the known limits are not conspicuous is so because the knowing is born together with and studies together with the exhaustive investigation of the buddha dharma.[4]

Since the Buddha Way is manifest as completely engaging one dharma at this place and time, it is the occurrence of knowing, studying, and investigating together. These three aspects of practice depend upon one another to manifest the Buddha Dharma; thus they are born together and study together. They are dependent upon one another for actualization. We cannot say one follows the other, as they arise simultaneously in dependence upon one another. This liminal transition from one space-being-time to another incubates our realization.

If you are studying for a test, when does your study become knowing? You may feel that there is a particular time you have grasped the material, but that boundary is dependent upon all the instances of this knowledge born together with the activity of study and knowing. This would include all the hours of reading, receiving instruction, and so forth that came together at the moment of your mind grasping the material. In a larger context, it includes all investigation and study being born throughout all time-being as your moment of knowing.

In his commentary on this section, Senne writes, "'To be known' and 'not clear' show that unless we are apart from the boundary of the Dharma, there is no intimacy with the Dharma. This is the meaning of 'When Dharma fills [body and mind] one side is dark.'"⁵

To be "apart from the boundary of the Dharma" refers to not being attached to knowing. We try to avoid a fixed view or boundary and instead hang out in the in-between spaces of not knowing and knowing. Between knowing and not knowing, we are poised to respond to what is happening without fixed ideas. We are prepared to study and practice together with both.

Knowing and not knowing always happen in a particular being-time of our experience. This is what Senne calls "one side is dark." This "one side is dark" refers, of course, to the much earlier sentence in "Genjōkōan": "In seeing color and hearing sound with body and mind, although we perceive them intimately, [the perception] is not like reflections in a mirror or the moon in water. When one side is illuminated, the other is dark."

This earlier section is about how, in the moment of practice realized, one perceives and actualizes intimately "seeing color and hearing sound with body and mind." When this activity is realizing one dharma, permeating one dharma, encountering one practice, and when "the person fully practices that practice," they are fully engaging one thing in order to know all things. This recognition and intimacy with one thing is the illumination of one side. Although we do not apprehend what is not apparent to us, it is not absent from our present reality. The boundaries of what is seen and not seen, or understood and not understood, are not clear because as we focus on our immediate activity, we are not concerned with differences or boundaries.

Consequently we do not have a fixed idea or agenda for the moment's arising. Nor are we aware of the devas and form beings practicing with us. What we do know, at that particular time, is the one dharma or one situation that we are trying to become intimate with. Upon achieving that state of dropping the self (resulting in "the Dharma fills [body-mind]"), there is, simultaneously, what is not apparent or is "dark," or not known to us. This is not a problem.

In everyday interactions, we experience this as deeply investigating or intimately listening to our relational life. When we vacuum the floor, intimately experiencing the activity of cleaning, we are not experiencing, for example, reading the book lying on a nearby table. Because we are focused upon vacuuming and not reading, Dōgen would go further and say vacuuming vacuums vacuuming. If we are reading: reading reads reading. Both examples remove the subject-object relationship of the "I" who "vacuums" and the "I" who "reads."

As soon as this occurs, the "known limits are not conspicuous . . . because the knowing is born together with and studies together with the exhaustive investigation of the buddha dharma." Furthermore, we, the book, and even the vacuuming are studying together, even as we probably are not making a conscious connection between the book, which seems tangential, and the activity of vacuuming the floor. All things have sentiency, meaning all dharmas preach the Dharma as they inter-are, expressing continuous practice-realization. Taking this example further, the book and the activity of vacuuming are both part of the totality of the room being cleaned, the life of the occupant who is cleaning, and all dharmas seen and unseen throughout time and space.

Hee-Jin Kim writes that Dōgen's understanding of intimacy arises from a kind of tension between delusion and realization.[6] From this tension we become intimate with and liberated from delusion into realization. This is the tension of "one side is illuminated, the other is dark." From this seemingly dichotomous relationship, the luminous aspect not only informs what is seen but also allows the hidden to intimately (silently) communicate itself.

But this can't happen unless there is engagement with the boundary of the known and the unknown as it studies together and is born with our effort to "complete[ly] penetrate the Dharma." If I struggle with sitting zazen, there is tension between zazen and not zazen. Just like delusion and realization, if communication continues, through studying together—in the case of zazen, by continually coming back to sitting—there will be a transformative dialogue, an intimate relationship, going on below the surface of my discriminating mind.

. . . this is because the known [which appears limited] is born and practiced simultaneously with the complete penetration of the Buddha Dharma.

In the best case, our wisdom, like the wind bell's clapper, hangs loosely within the sounding bell. This is the place of knowing, but it cannot be expressed without the wind and all other attendant conditions. These conditions coming together are "born and practiced simultaneously," and the bell sounds.[7] This "complete penetration of the Buddha Dharma" must arise from the totality of causal conditions throughout all of time-being. Yet if we are going to talk about our practice as human beings, then we say it is expressed through us as a particular self expressing practice-enlightenment. At the same time, we cannot lose sight that our practice is only part of an orchestra of dharmas creating a symphony. Since we cannot know all dharmas, each moment becomes a mystery intimately revealed.

We are attentively poised between our life experience, knowledge, and the unknown, as the mystery of the present is unfolding in real time. The known appears limited because our mind can conceptualize and verbalize some idea about something, but not everything. Therefore, what has been cognized consciously or captured is limited by conceptualization's linear form.

These words try to capture something about Dōgen's teachings. Yet they are not alive until you or I or someone bring them to life. How that happens is completely dependent upon the unlimited nature of each moment's function and effort. We and all beings must be in concert to bring forth the kōan of genjō. This is practice-realization or the complete expression of this place and path, which must include the liminal, transitional being-time between what is known and not known.

CHAPTER 16

INTIMACY

We should not think that what we have attained is
conceived by ourselves and known by our discriminating
mind. Although complete enlightenment is immediately
actualized, its intimacy is such that it does not necessarily
form as a view. [In fact] viewing is not something fixed.

Dōgen writes in "Muchū Setsumu" (Preaching a Dream in a Dream),

> The wheel of Dharma at such a moment sometimes turns the vast
> world of the great wheel of Dharma, unfathomably and bound-
> lessly, and sometimes turns in the smallest particle, operating
> ceaselessly even inside atoms. The principle here is that in what-
> ever *matter which is it* the Dharma [-wheel] is turned. . . . And
> whatever the place, because the Dharma [-wheel] is turned as a
> *matter which is it*, it sets in motion *the elegant ways*. Thus, the
> whole Earth is the instantaneously limitless (*mutan*)[1] wheel of
> Dharma, and all the Universe is unambiguous cause-and-effect.
> . . . Restrictions are limitless and at the same time release is
> limitless.[2]

The great Dharma wheel is always turning in each moment—in
each person, particle, and atom. All of the activity of each particular nameable thing (dharma) contributes and turns the Dharma

wheel. How could we think that knowing this intellectually is the end of the matter? The activity Dōgen describes above is genjōkōan, actualized immediately as "the elegant ways."

We do not consciously enact reality's function; it is functioning itself. We cannot say we have "attained" something that can be conclusively defined because what we can see in practice is only the tip of the mountain. We do not see the tectonic plates, the devas and beings, the causal effects that work through and with us to activate and actualize wisdom and compassion.

This is the Dharma wheel turning and moving as the universe in both the "vast world" (universal) and the "smallest particle" (particular). Yet what is vast and what is small? These are only discriminations to provide us with conceptual markers to delineate parts of one whole reality—suchness, expressed above as "matter which is it." Thus it is "unfathomable and boundless," "operating ceaselessly." This is reality, the world functioning; it is our intimate experience of is-ness right now that "sets in motion the elegant ways."

Since this is so, the Dharma immediately—in each moment, each atom—comes forth to meet us. It comes as us and to us, as we to it. We may not be able to see this happening. In fact, we probably are not aware for the most part.

In the "Muchū Setsumu" quotation above, *mutan* exactly expresses the meaning of this section of "Genjōkōan." *Mu* (無) refers to the absence of something. In Zen, *mu* is used to indicate that we cannot define something conceptually. The word signifies going beyond the boundaries of this and that. It expresses leaping into our life with the mind of not knowing, without a fixed view. *Tan* (端) refers to origin, border, end, or point.

Mutan thus suggests a borderless border or a sense that we cannot say where something begins or ends. When we do say something definitive about beginning or endings, edges or borders, those are relative, comparative terms that need to be held lightly and used skillfully. When we grasp at them and polarize our thinking, we often cause suffering for self and other.

In the quotation above, Dōgen writes, "And whatever the place, because the Dharma [-wheel] is turned as a matter that is it, it sets in motion the elegant ways. Thus, the whole earth is the instantaneously limitless (*mutan*) wheel of Dharma, and all the universe is unambiguous cause-and-effect."

The place of wherever we are is the place of the Dharma wheel's turning; it is the place of the confluence of what we know and what we do not know. This dharma position of turning, confluence, knowing, and not knowing is entering into the dance of our life as it manifests to us, through us, and as us. Practice-realization becomes the fruit of our effort and our struggles in "unambiguous cause-and-effect," allowing us to go beyond limitations and experience liberation.

Imagine hiking in a beautiful landscape. We do not often think about how it is that we can have this experience of grandeur. We are awed because we are of this earth, and we are physically and mentally endowed in such a way that we will see this vista as magnificent. The experience of feeling both filled and insignificant is the working of the causal conditions of our life as well as the totality of the earth's effort. These perfectly fitted particulars, these "elegant ways," become the total functioning of the Dharma wheel turning. The world's amazing interpenetrating, inter-beingness of creation fills us with a sense of awe.

Although complete enlightenment is immediately actualized [*genjō*], its intimacy [*mitsu*] is such that it does not necessarily form as a view. [In fact] viewing is not something fixed.[3]

Complete enlightenment, which is actualized in the immediate being-time, can be as mundane as walking down a crowded sidewalk. In the United States, we tend to walk on the right or left side of the pavement depending on which direction we are going. We are usually attentive to the flow of foot traffic around us. We pay attention to other people's movements, as they pay attention to ours. We are not aggravated by others, nor are we causing problems for others. We all flow harmoniously through and with each other, and we aren't thinking about it too much.

We may include the folks who are walking along looking at their cell phones; if we are looking at our cell phones, we are also tracking others in our peripheral vision. Or perhaps we are unaware, completely absorbed in our own activity, and so we run into someone. This is the delusional state of carrying the self forward—in quite a bodily fashion!

When we are aware on some level of our connection with others and we organically respond to that cohabitation of space, we will not be caught by our fixed ideas of how things should be and will instead respond to what is. If a person walking toward us is going to run into us, we move over. We don't judge who has the right-of-way. We just move over and keep going.

Our ability to immediately respond, without needing to talk about or intellectualize it, is the result of our intimate or innate ability to skillfully and appropriately respond to what is arising at this time. This is a practical example of *mitsu* (密), or intimacy. *Mitsu* can also be translated as "secret."

Hee-Jin Kim quotes Dōgen's Shōbōgenzō "Mitsugo" (Secret Words) in a passage that helps to clarify the meaning of intimacy:

> The *mitsu* in question means intimacy (*shimmitsu*) and the absence of distance. [When you speak of the Buddhas and ancestors], the Buddhas and ancestors embrace everything; [likewise] you embrace everything and I embrace everything. Practice includes all, a generation includes all, and intimacy includes all.[4]

Kim comments on this passage:

> Mystery, in Dōgen's view, did not consist of that which was hidden or unknown in darkness or that which would be revealed or made known in the future. Rather, it consisted of the present intimacy, transparency, and vividness of thusness.[5]

Intimacy is being completely present for and as the activity with which we are engaged, such as walking down a crowded sidewalk. Our constant adjustments to meet the current circumstances requires what Kim calls "present intimacy, transparency and vividness of thusness" or being nimble and responsive to what is. This intimate action is inclusive, curious, and open to self and other.

The concept of mitsu, or intimacy, is another key to understanding and manifesting genjōkōan as characterized by the various ideas discussed in the last chapter and in this one: (1) When we practice in the liminal space between knowing and not knowing, where "the boundary of the known is not clear," we find (2) that at this place, way, time-being, the "complete penetration of the Buddha Dharma" is "born and practiced" intimately together with all beings. Furthermore, (3) we must avoid trying to concretize or conceptualize this place of not knowing. If we can avoid this pitfall, (4) we can express, through practice-realization, intimacy with self and other. Thus, (5) we are free to abide in this place fully intimate with the totality of self and other. Intimacy is genjōkōan, and genjōkōan is intimacy.

This section of "Genjōkōan" ends with "intimacy is such that it does not necessarily form as a view. [In fact] viewing is not something fixed." Senne's commentary is as follows:

> "Not something fixed (kahitsu, 何必)," "forming as a view (kenjō, 見成)," means whether we say being (u, 有) or nonbeing (mu, 無), either is "not something fixed." We should not think that there is something fixed as "not-fixed."[6]

Kahitsu is an expression questioning a statement.[7] Senne is saying we should question our assumptions about being or nonbeing and hold them lightly or as "not something fixed." He urges us to not take this to mean that fixed is not fixed. Perhaps he's saying we shouldn't use the Zen technique of "it's not this and it's not that" to form a fixed view called "it's not this and it's not that." In other

words, there really is no place you can land based upon a preconceived ideal. How we respond is in part based upon guidelines,
such as the bodhisattva precepts, but a lived situation is going to
determine how those admonitions might be applied. Therefore,
they become koans for life, not fixed rules that dictate our actions.

CHAPTER 17

THE STUDENT-TEACHER RELATIONSHIP

[The] Zen Master [Baoche] of Mt. Magu[1] was waving a fan. A monk approached him and asked, "The nature of wind is ever present and permeates everywhere. Why are you waving a fan?"

The master said, "You know only that the wind's nature is ever present—you don't know that it permeates everywhere." The monk said, "How does wind permeate everywhere?" The master just continued waving the fan. The monk bowed deeply.[2]

Master Baoche embodies practice-realization; he is genjōkōan. But Baoche is not a generic "Zen master"; Baoche has an attitude, a personality, and he is teaching at a particular place and time.

Master Baoche reminds me of a professor I had in college who was intimately aware of each student's understanding. He would finish talking and wait for us to respond. Sometimes he would just call on one of us. It was as if he were able to sense what we were thinking. Often he answered the deeper question we had not asked or elicited from us a more nuanced understanding than we initially offered. Master Baoche has this sense about him as he sits, completely relaxed, fanning himself while highly attuned to the mind-state and needs of the students in front of him. He is not waiting, per se; he is just ready for whatever may come next.

In all likelihood, he has been fanning before we enter the story. The twentieth-century Zen master Hakuun Yasutani Roshi describes Baoche during this dialogue as "a clear-eyed teacher" who "exposes his buddha-nature" and "unsparingly reveals his original face."[3]

His fanning is the embodiment of genjōkōan as practice. It is nonintellectual. It is inter-being, like the wind-bell in Rujing's poem:

Whole body like the mouth, hanging in space;
Not asking if the wind is east, west, south, or north,
For all others equally, it chatters prajñā:
Chin Ten Ton Ryan Chin Ten Ton.[4]

This "whole body," Master Baoche, is ready to effortlessly "chatter prajñā" without discrimination toward the wind's direction or the wind itself. Yet this bell is a particular bell responding with its own sound—its own flavor of teaching. Master Baoche's "Chin Ten Ton Ryan Chin Ten Ton" has a unique sound that reflects the culmination of his wisdom as he meets the student's question.

So too is the student unique. This wind that moves the bell—it too is particular. It can be warm or cold, aggressive or calm. Whatever its character, Master Baoche will meet it and respond.

Please imagine that you are present for this dialogue, not in the medieval past but in the present. You and your monastic sangha are standing, listening, and watching your teacher. The master sits on a platform, likely having just finished delivering a teaching. Now they are just silently fanning themselves, waiting for someone to come forward with their understanding. Can you imagine what this teacher looks like? Are they old or middle-aged? Do they have a sense of humor?[5]

An unnamed student, whom you have been standing next to, asks, "Master, the nature of wind is permanent and there is no place it does not reach. Why then do you fan yourself?" Perhaps the student offers the question as a declarative statement: buddha-nature is permanent; it's everywhere. Then the student says, "Why then do *you* fan yourself?" Are they directly challenging the teacher's understanding, or is their question coming from real confusion?

Remember, you are there, so what do you do? What are you thinking and how are you responding? Do you answer the question silently to yourself? Do you make some judgment about the question itself based upon your relationship with the questioner? Are you taken aback at this student's temerity? Maybe you wait, curious to hear what the master will say in response. Maybe you are grateful that this person stepped up and asked the question you were afraid to ask.

Of course, we know the student's question is incomplete. On one level it must be, or we would not have this story. Yet if we are there, we don't know it's a story; this is our life unfolding. Therefore, we may not think it is incomplete because we may wonder about this as well.

The master responds, "You know only that the wind's nature is ever present—you don't know that it permeates everywhere."

The master's response is very kind—they give the "answer" in their response. In many Zen stories such as this, the master would have hit the student with their fan, given them thirty blows, or walked away shaking their sleeves. But this master wants to meet this student where they are in their practice. So, they respond from that position—like the wind-bell as the wind blows the clapper. "Questions" and "answers" are mutual activity; the master answers what is seen (said) and what is not seen (not said). They intimately engage the student and answer from the position of meeting and pushing this student simultaneously.

Based upon the master's answer, we know that something is missing. The question exposes a deficiency in the student's understanding. Yet it is an honest question. It is as far as their eye of practice can see. Really, that is all we can do. That is why we have masters and students. We rely upon our teachers to meet us where we are and help us deepen our understanding.

This student's question—"If realization is always active (wind), why would you need to enact that realization in each moment through practice?"—is almost identical to Dōgen's initial question: "If all sentient beings possess the buddha-nature and Tathagata exists without change . . . then why must people develop the aspiration for awakening and vigorously engage in austerities in order to realize this truth?"[6]

Since "Genjōkōan" is an early writing in Dōgen's corpus, and one aimed at a lay practitioner, perhaps this is Dōgen's answer to his own question. Steven Heine points out that Dōgen also asks this question in "Fukanzazengi" (Recommending Zazen to All People): "Fundamentally, the basis of the Way is thoroughly pervasive, so how could it be contingent on practice and realization?"[7]

Indeed, "Genjōkōan" can be read as an extended answer to this question. Clearly Dōgen has settled upon and resolved this issue for himself, therefore genjōkōan is the path one must follow to fully enact Dōgen's realization about the why and what of our effort.

Looking back at the instructions in the fascicle, we can see some of the ways the student might be incorrect in their understanding. This student

• is limited by their overly intellectual understanding.
• may be attached to their view.
• wonders if practice is unnecessary since realization attained is a permanent state.
• doesn't understand that practice is without end.

The caveat to all this criticism is that the student is asking questions. This student is living with their teacher in a monastic setting, and they are drawn to practice, even if they don't understand it. That's the point of warm-hand-to-warm-hand transmission. Student-teacher practice is about this kind of intimate investigation.

Master Baoche, confronted by this student, engages them. Complications are revealed and investigated. An intimate encounter ensues, and hopefully some truth is revealed. But even if the student did not understand, Master Baoche surely continued his engagement and teaching, hoping that the student would understand in the future.

In response to the student, Master Baoche says, "Although you understand that the nature of the wind is permanent, you do not understand the meaning of its reaching everywhere." This answer acknowledges that the Buddha Dharma and buddha-nature are always presencing as reality itself. What the student does not understand is that suchness, codependent arising, and reality as the whole works (*zenki*) is the community of all being(s) inter-being and actively presencing with and as each other's function. Practice arises and is motivated, in each moment, as we realize this truth.

Master Baoche's observation is attuned to the student's actual problem, not the question asked by the student. It is the response to the question not asked. The question behind the question may be evident to Master Baoche because he recognizes a type of practitioner or because he practices with this particular student regularly. Regardless, it is the master's ability to "hang in space" and be open to what comes: the question, the student. This is the activity of fanning, the practice-realization of genjōkōan.

"What is the meaning of its reaching everywhere?" asked the monk again. Baoche just kept fanning himself.

Now the student is curious. He wanted an intellectual answer, but instead there is the gentle sound of "Chin Ten Ton Ryan Chin Ten Ton" and the swish-swish of fanning. The fish leaps clear of the water and splashes down. We see Master Baoche's original face.

Master Baoche just shot an arrow—did it hit the mark? Because you must imagine the dialogue as happening now, in your presence. What do you see? What happened here? From Baoche's point of view he is screaming the answer. His fanning is actualizing the question and answer before any of the dialogue took place. The whole interaction between Master Baoche and the student is the activity of the whole works manifesting at this place and on this path.

The monk bowed deeply.

Did he understand or not? What can *we* see here? The monk has gone from perhaps being insolent or confrontational to respectful and deferential. Or is the monk just being a good Zen student and giving a pro forma bow in respect. Does it make a difference? Can we say that walking the walk will walk the walk? What did we learn by witnessing this interaction?

CHAPTER 18

WHAT DOES IT ALL MEAN?

The genuine experience of Buddha Dharma and the vital path that has been correctly transmitted are like this. To say we should not wave a fan because the nature of wind is ever present, and that we should feel the wind even when we don't wave a fan, is to know neither ever-presence nor the wind's nature. Since the wind's nature is ever present, the wind of the Buddha's family enables us to realize the gold of the great Earth and to transform the [water of] the long river into cream.

We ask questions: they are spoken, intellectual, intuitive, intimate. Our encounters are stones rubbing against one another, knocking off the dust of delusion. We have faith in Buddha, Dharma, and Sangha, and we are compelled to practice and understand. This is "the vital path." In order to be "correctly transmitted," it must happen as it does in the story of Master Baoche and his student—in person. Sometimes we cannot meet a teacher in person, but there must be something deeper than intellectual understanding. This is most often achieved through interpersonal relationships.

What we read and study is very important, but it is only entering the gate. Dōgen writes in "Fukanzazengi" (Recommending Zazen to All People), "Cease from practice based on intellectual understanding, pursuing words and following after speech, and learn the backward step that turns your light inward to illuminate yourself."[1]

Dōgen often taught that our salvation would not be found in words alone. But he clearly felt that writing about practice was important because, well, he wrote a lot about practice. These writings are the map. It is our teachers and interactions with our sangha that decode the map and walk the path with us.

To say we should not wave a fan because the nature of wind is ever present, and that we should feel the wind even when we don't wave a fan, is to know neither ever-presence nor the wind's nature.

A possible paraphrase of this sentence would be "If we say that since buddha-nature is reality manifesting, we don't need to make an effort in practice and that we already know buddha-nature exists without practicing, then we are ignorant about both buddha-nature's presencing and the nature of practice-realization."

The key to this sentence has to do with the metaphor of the wind. Not practicing because you believe it is unnecessary is missing the mark. To say that we will be able to manifest bodhi mind and enact the Buddha Dharma's sustained presence without practice is incorrect. While buddha-nature constantly abides, it is practice that embodies buddhahood within the context of our particular life. Practice is the activity of the realized mind.

Kyōgō and Senne each write that both the wind (buddha-nature) and fanning (practice) manifest whether a fan is fanning or not. They consider this as the more nuanced understanding: the use of a fan is optional. Senne says, "[The master] only showed [the reality] with a thing that was at hand at that moment."[2] In this case, the fan was an expedient device to demonstrate the meaning. Or we could understand this to mean that since everything is buddha-nature, anything could have been used to illustrate practice.

Kyōgō asks, "Why did the master use a fan?"

Senne says, "When you use it, just use it. When you put it down, just put it down. This means that when it is needed, we use it; when it is not needed, we put it down. If it [wind/buddha-nature] really penetrates everywhere, whether we use a fan or not should be at our will. This attitude is in accord with the principle of ever-present. When needed just use it; when not needed just leave it alone."[3]

If we understand the wind to be buddha-nature and using the fan as practice only, then we are missing a deeper teaching. Fanning is an obvious demonstration of active effort in practice. But practice-realization-response doesn't need to be evident, or it isn't necessarily demonstrable.

As Dōgen writes earlier in "Genjōkōan," "The boundary of the known is not clear; this is because the known [which appears limited] is born and practiced simultaneously with the complete penetration of the Buddha Dharma. We should not think that what we have attained is conceived by ourselves and known by our discriminating mind."

In the case of Master Baoche's fanning, he is using a teaching device, like drawing a circle in the air with a whisk. The fan and whisk have their use, and they can also be discarded when the use is no longer applicable. A master knows when and what is helpful. Once embodied, this simultaneity of practice and presencing is not necessarily apparent. Therefore, you can't say practice-realization and effort are only actualized when seen. Just because something is hidden to us does not mean it is not present.

Master Baoche is doing more than fanning; therefore, he can put down the fan and the wind of the house of the Buddha continues. This is not true for a person who has not yet understood the relationship between buddha-nature and practice.

In "Gyōji" (Continuous Practice), Dōgen writes,

> The working of this activity-unremitting [gyōji] is not always hidden; thus one arouses the mind by engaging in training. This working is not always manifest, either; thus one neither experiences it nor knows it. We must learn that though not manifest, neither is it hidden, for [activity-unremitting] is undefiled by hiddenness or manifestation, by appearance or disappearance. When activity-unremitting, although realizing itself, is hidden momentarily, you may be unaware of which dharmas of

conditioned arising have caused this activity-unremitting, but this is because to be aware of activity-unremitting is nothing especially new at all. Conditioned arising is activity-unremitting, because activity-unremitting is not caused by conditioned arising. This we must consider and study carefully.[4]

Dōgen begins above by saying that our and all being(s)' practice is not always hidden, and for this reason we are motivated to practice the Dharma. On the other hand, there are times when we do not see the workings of this practice. Then he makes the point that even if we don't realize or experience it, the activity of continuous practice, as a foundational manifestation of reality (which Dōgen calls elsewhere zenki, or total dynamic working),[5] is always active and unaffected by our ability to realize or not realize it's working.

There is a tricky sentence in this quotation: "Conditioned arising is activity-unremitting [continuous practice], because activity-unremitting [continuous practice] is not caused by conditioned arising."

"This is one of the most important passages in the Shōbōgenzō," explains Hee-Jin Kim. "Activity-unremitting is not something caused or produced by the conditions of conditioned arising . . . rather, it is inherent in each and every condition. Thus, it is activity-unremitting which makes conditioned arising what it is, not the other way around."[6]

This sustained practice of all being(s) is not produced by the causes and conditions that are arising or have arisen; rather, it is inherent in all being(s). Causal conditions are the result of zenki (total dynamic function), not the cause of zenki. This is not different than saying that all beings are buddha-nature. It is one of Dōgen's core teachings that our world functions through the practice of all being(s)' altruistic activities (buddha mind and buddha-nature), resulting in the world's manifestations. We may be aware or unaware of this activity. Other beings may be aware of or unaware of this activity. But it is this dynamic total function of buddha-nature that motivates continuous practice or activity-unremitting. It is the inherent nature of each and all beings to engage in this practice.

In 2023, as I am writing this book, PBS aired "Soul of the Ocean."[7] It features a discussion of the cooperative ecosystem of oceanic beings. For example, surgeonfish clean the shells of green turtles at cleaning stations located in specific places, usually near coral reefs. If the turtle moves fifty feet away, the surgeonfish will not clean their shell. Clarion angelfish clean algae and parasites from the skin of oceanic manta rays off the coast of Mexico. In the documentary, these specific sites and relationships are referred to as medical help.

This is a good example of Dōgen's meaning when he writes, "Conditioned arising is sustained practice, because sustained practice is not caused by conditioned arising." Dōgen's point is that the conditions arising that manifest as, for example, the green turtles being cleaned by surgeonfish are not caused by those conditions. The deeper activity is the foundational ecosystem of cooperative cofunctioning of the whole. This underlying nature is what we would call the mind of buddha or buddha-nature manifest. Fundamentally we do not practice because of the causes and conditions of our life. We practice because it is the function of all of reality presencing, and therefore we respond to our basic nature as not different from the suchness of the whole.

The turtles make a conscious effort to arrive at these cleaning stations, and the surgeonfish respond. What motivates this behavior is a deeper codependency that is not the immediate result of causal conditions. This codependent response is the continuous practice of all being(s) making the world. Because each activity makes up and is the result of the whole of continuous practice, this becomes an altruistic field of merit or virtue that is the world's suchness.

In the case of bodhisattva practice, it is incumbent upon a bodhisattva to make a conscious effort to engage and manifest this altruistic response through practice. This too is primary to Dōgen's teachings as it is to Mahayana Buddhism more broadly. Since we are endowed with this mind and this human rebirth, it is our responsibility to engage life in this way. Master Baoche's first priority was to impress upon his student that we are responsible for our effort and cannot assume that the effort of others will be enough.

Even so, there is this underlying teaching of zenki, which Senne and Kyōgō, in their commentary, want to include. This is why Master Baoche's device of fanning is in a sense arbitrary. Master Baoche, the student, the fan, and all circumstances and elements of this dialogue are gyōji. The wind is already present, whether Master Baoche is fanning or not. Yet Master Baoche is never not practicing because he embodies continuous practice, which the student has not yet understood. This is the essential meaning of the story.

Since the wind's nature is ever present, the wind of the Buddha's family enables us to realize the gold of the great Earth and to transform the [water of] the long river into cream.

Another translation of "Buddha's family" is "house of the Buddha." Dōgen, in several instances in Shōbōgenzō, mentions the furnishings or implements used by the buddhas to further the Buddha Dharma. "Know that birth-and-death is the activity of the buddha way; birth-and-death is the furnishings [essentials] of the buddha house," he writes. "It is utilized when it needs to be utilized; it is fully clarified when it is clarified."[8] Likewise, he states that "providing the teachings . . . [is] the family occupation of the house of the Buddha."[9] This includes "spiritual power and wisdom transmitted from heir to heir."[10] And in the house of the Buddha, the main method by which the Buddha Dharma is transmitted is through zazen. Dōgen writes in "Bendōwa" (On the Endeavor of the Way):

> Question: . . . on what basis does the house of the Buddha solely pursue sitting?
>
> Answer: It is impossible to know fully the ways by which the buddhas one after another from ancient times practiced and entered verification. If we ask for the reason, we should know

that the reason is just that it is what is used by the house of the Buddha.[11]

We get the sense that, for Dōgen, this family or house of the Buddha is like a guild of buddhas, bodhisattvas, and ancestors that continues its work, seen and unseen, throughout all time(s), being(s), and space(s). This work is both universal and as specific as the activity of each person, ancestor, buddha, and being. Elsewhere in "Bendōwa," Dōgen sums up the reason and hope for his transmission of the Way as a member of this Buddhist guild:

> There may be true students who are not concerned with fame and gain who allow their aspiration for enlightenment to guide them and earnestly desire to practice the buddha way. . . . Because of my concern for them, I would like to record the standards of Zen monasteries that I personally saw and heard in Great Song, as well as the profound principle that has been transmitted by my master. I wish to leave for students of the way the authentic teaching of the buddha house.[12]

As noted in the introduction to this book, "Bendōwa" was one of Dōgen's earliest works written shortly after his return from China. Dōgen saw it as his mission to carry forward the work of the house of the buddha, of which he and all practitioners are members. His stated goal was to bring forth the gold of the Dharma through practice-realization, and his wish was that we be sustained by the cream of this Dharmic river.

He offers a similar sentiment in "Hotsu Bodai Shin" (Bringing Forth the Mind of Bodhi): "This mind is not ours, not another's, not coming from elsewhere; yet after we bring forth this mind, when we take up the whole earth, it turns entirely to gold, when we stir up the great oceans, they turn immediately to ambrosia."[13]

As the genius work of a remarkable mind, "Genjōkōan" represents the beginning of Dōgen's teaching career yet also, somehow, the mature blossoming of his life's expression. Because of its concise and clear description of what realization is and how we practice and develop the mind of a buddha, "Genjōkōan" establishes Dōgen's place in the family of the buddhas and ancestors. We are all invited to drink deeply from the cream of this long river and mine the gold of Dōgen's teachings.

Appendix 1

Dharma Position: *Jū Hōi*

Jū hōi (住法位), or abiding in a dharma position, is one of the most important aspects of Dōgen's teaching, because it pertains to understanding the nature of our relationships to and interconnection with all other dharmas and our immediate present practice as the Dharma. All aspects of reality arise and fall within the context of a dharma position. All manifestations of awakened action or delusional pitfalls are dharma positions. Comprehending Dōgen's teaching on the nature of the self and all beings as dharma positions will give us a conceptual framework to better apprehend his view of Dharmic enactment. Furthermore, if we can integrate and act upon these teachings, we will be manifesting suchness, our true Dharma nature.

In this appendix, I will briefly discuss the similarities between Dōgen's concept of a dharma position in Shōbōgenzō "Genjōkōan" (Realized Kōan) and "Uji" (Being-Time). Then I move on to an exploration of the origins of the phrase "to abide in a dharma position" (jū hōi). But the major topic of this appendix is an in-depth examination of each aspect of a dharma position and its relationship to realizing and manifesting the Buddha Dharma.

In some ways "Genjōkōan" (written in 1233) and "Uji" (written in 1240) are complementary fascicles. "Uji" discusses practice through the lens of being-time, which is synonymous with a dharma position. Since actualization happens within the context of a dharma position, "Genjōkōan" describes how we must understand our dharma position (self's practice) and that of others as it relates to enacting the bodhisattva path.

"Genjōkōan" investigates our understanding of the actualization of enlightenment: what it is, what it looks like, and learning to manifest it through the activity of the self. This self is a dharma position abiding in time-being with all of a dharma position's various aspects presencing, as the "now" of our practice experience. Dōgen comments in "Genjōkōan," "When we intimately practice and return right here, it is clear that all things have no [fixed] self."[1] This "no [fixed] self" is not different from jū hōi, to abide in suchness.

The opening words in "Genjōkōan," "When all dharmas . . .," locate our practice within the context of a dharma position or a being-time. "When" is time, and "dharmas" is being. The next sentence begins with the same frame of reference: "When the ten thousand dharmas. . . ." And later in "Genjōkōan," "to forget the self" is the dharma position of the self functioning in suchness. It is "to let the body and mind of the self and the body and mind of others drop off," thus manifesting our continuous practice (gyōji) and presencing with all beings as the dharma position of actualizing the Buddha Dharma.[2] Continuous practice and presencing both imply the time of meeting and the inter-are-ing of dharmas. This is not different from abiding in suchness or abiding in a dharma position. Dōgen specifically refers to hōi (dharma position) in "Genjōkōan" when he uses the dharma positions of firewood and ash to discuss the independent aspect of a dharma position, which we often mistake as a separate self.

Firewood becomes ash. Ash cannot become firewood again. However, we should not view ash as after and firewood as before. We should know that firewood dwells in the dharma position [hōi] of firewood and has its own before and after. Although before and after exist, past and future are cut off. Ash stays in the position [hōi] of ash, with its own before and after.

Firewood and ash having "[their] own before and after" yet at the same time their "past and future is cut off" are just two aspects of totality of a dharma position's multiplicity and their implications in practice. Knowing the full scope of a dharma position is key to understanding how we reside in and live the time and form of our current experience as it relates to a no-inherently-existing-self and enacting realization. A dharma position has several aspects, a few of which Dōgen mentions in the passage above from "Genjōkōan." Whether specifically named or implied, all dharma positions share multiple characteristics, even as they may be discussed (as in "Genjōkōan") from only one or two aspects.

Meaning of Jū Hōi

Jū hōi refers to abiding a dharma position, such as "firewood dwells (*jū*, 住) in the dharma (*hō*, 法) position (*i*, 位) of firewood." Since all things are dharmas, a dharma position is any place, time, position, being, thing, or person that has particularity. Because firewood is a dharma position, it is a recognizable being-time that holds a specific position in time and has certain characteristics or being-ness. The word *firewood* itself is also a dharma position separate from what it describes. The word and the thing named are each particular and are different dharma positions.

Jū is to dwell, live, be at home; but in this context it is usually translated as "abiding." The phrase *jū hōi* comes from the Lotus Sutra: "The dharmas abide in their dharma positions; the marks of the world constantly abide."[3] The Lotus Sutra is the foundational text of the Tendai school of Buddhism, and Dōgen, as a former student of Tendai, often referred to the teachings found in the Lotus Sutra.

The scholar Jacqueline Stone traces the genesis of the term *dharma position* to medieval Tendai oral teachings.[4] "Constantly abide" has the connotation of constantly abiding in suchness.[5] One might ask, "How does an impermanent dharma abide constantly or eternally in suchness?" Saichō (767–822), who founded the Japanese Tendai school (based upon the Chinese Tiantai school), answered this question with a theory called "suchness according with conditions."

"Suchness according with conditions" has its roots in the Chinese Huayan school and was described by its Third Ancestor, Fazang (643–712). This view can be defined as:

> Myriad dharmas (all existents) are precisely Suchness. As principle, Suchness is unchanging; that is to say, no matter how much the phenomena of the actual world may shift and change, their essential nature, which is Suchness, never changes.[6] But at the same time, Suchness is precisely all dharmas, because it responds to conditions, manifesting the diverse forms of the phenomenal world.[7]

Because our world of form is always coexisting, cocreating and subject to causal conditions, it is impermanence personified. And because each dharma position is itself suchness or buddha nature, each dharma is both the essential nature of suchness and constantly in flux. Combined, we have the unchanging situation of a dharma's unfolding, which is not different from suchness's constant abiding.

Returning to the quotation from the Lotus Sutra on jū hōi, "The dharmas abide in their dharma positions; the marks of the world constantly abide." Dōgen makes a statement remarkably similar in "Uji": "The horses and sheep now arrayed throughout the world are each dharma stages dwelling in their suchness and moving endlessly up and down."[8] These dharmas, (horses and sheep) abiding in suchness are impermanent, coproduced entities while simultaneously an integral aspect of suchness's functioning. Considered from Saichō's view, they are dwelling in suchness (unchanging essential nature) while moving constantly up and down (responding to conditions). All dharma positions (which include the self) are dwelling as and in reality's is-ness. This is our home, the abode of all being(s) we call the world—the universe's activity. There is nothing outside these ten thousand dharmas.

In "Hotsu Bodai Shin" (Bringing Forth the Mind of Bodhi), Dōgen discusses the all-pervasive nature of "dharmas abiding in their dharma positions":

> All the worlds in the ten directions, the buddha nature of true suchness, are all the "dharmas abiding in their dharma positions [*jū hōi*]." How could grass, trees, and the like be within the buddha nature of true suchness? How could grass, trees, and the like not be the buddha nature of true suchness? The dharmas are not conditioned, not unconditioned; they are the real marks. The real marks are the real marks of suchness; suchness is the present body and mind.[9]

This passage is Dōgen's poetic and enigmatic way of restating Saichō's "suchness according with conditions."

While Dōgen only refers specifically to the phrase *dharma position* a few times in Shōbōgenzō,[10] there are numerous times that he refers to the concept of dharma positions. For example, in Shōbōgenzō "Shōji" (Birth and Death) he writes, "Birth is one position in time and clearly has a before and after."[11] In this passage "birth is one position in time" in Japanese is not *jū hōi* but rather *shō wa, hitotoki no kurai nite*, yet it clearly conveys the same teaching as the section from "Genjōkōan" on firewood and ash.[12]

Based on my reading of "Uji," Dōgen describes seven primary simultaneous states or aspects of a dharma position. They are characterized as: (1) particular independent moments of being-time, (2) having their own before and after, (3) all time(s) and being(s) presencing, (4) having no fixed identity or outcome, (5) a dharma's passage or passageless passage, (6) the eternal now, and (7) the locus of practice-realization.[13] Like many of Dōgen's teachings, when exploring one aspect of a dharma position, all the other characteristics will also be in play even when he does not necessarily discuss them. At other times, it is difficult to discuss one aspect without including the others.

Dharma Position as an Independent Moment of Being-Time

The quotations above from "Genjōkōan" and "Shōji" are illustrative of dharmas occupying a specific position, time, and state of being. Dōgen states, for example, that firewood and ash should be related to only in the context of their particularity as firewood or ash at that time. Since firewood and ash are Dōgen's metaphors for the self occupying a particular dharma position, we can understand these examples as they pertain to our practice of the Buddha Way. Within the context of a dharma position's arising as our present moment, it is also the place and time of practice-realization.

Shohaku Okumura wonderfully describes this state as "100 percent":

> No matter how seriously sick one may be, for example, one's life is still 100 percent life.[14] [And], . . . [a] seed's nature includes the potential to become a plant, the seed is nonetheless 100 percent seed when in the dharma position of a seed. This is why, for example, we don't call a seed an "underdeveloped plant" and we don't call a plant a "grown seed."[15]

No matter how ill a person may be, they are still living their life completely. As a healthy person who is unaware of this teaching, I might approach a dying person only from my perception that they are close to death. In a way, I am perceiving them as already dead. But, for that person, they are 100 percent alive.

Dōgen does not deny causal progressions, but his focus when giving the example of firewood and ash in "Genjōkōan" is on a dharma position's particularity or independent nature. This place of 100 percent engagement is the where and how of our life unfolding. From the perspective of awakening, the state of being "completely cut off" allows us a chance to free ourselves when we are trapped by karmic attachments or previous views. If a dharma position did not have this independent aspect, we would be forever caught by our delusional actions and desires, and we could not attain liberation.

Enacting realization is dependent upon our total and complete engagement with "just this" or our current dharma position. As Dōgen said in "Uji," "If in speaking of 'passage' [as one's practice life] you imagine that the place of passage lies somewhere outside [of the present moment or present life] . . . that is the result of not giving total devotion to the single-minded practice of the Buddha Way."[16]

By paying attention to each dharma position's presencing, we have the best possibility to completely respond to our current situation rather than what we imagine or wish were happening. Understanding that each dharma position is complete in and of itself allows us to pay particular attention to each encounter and action. We can only meet our life within the context of this moment and at this place.

Considering the present moment as time's expression and our mental perception of the self at that time, no matter what we may think about the past or future we cannot help but be physically in the present moment. The past is gone, the future has not yet arrived; therefore we (physical mind-body) are firmly in the present moment. Delusion arises when we are caught or blinded by preconceived ideas or emotions from past experiences or future mental projections that block us from responding to what is happening right now. This mentally constructed wall results in not being able to connect with a person or situation. Yet even when caught by delusion, we are still fully in the present moment.

Unfortunately, we can also get caught by the idea of 100 percent this or that. When we reify the nature of the self, we only experience the independent aspect of a dharma position and mistake it for the whole of our experience. Furthermore, we may think this teaching means we should live in the moment and not plan for the future or atone for past mistakes. This too is an incorrect or incomplete understanding.

Dharma Positions Have Their Own Before and After

As Dōgen said in "Genjōkōan," the dharma positions of ash and firewood both have their "own before and after." As mentioned earlier, Dōgen does not deny that we experience sequential time: past, present, and future. He wrote something similar in "Shōji": "Birth is one position in time and clearly has a before and after. . . . Cessation is also one position in time and also has a before and after."[17]

These examples from "Shōji" and "Genjōkōan" only make passing references to sequential time. This is true for almost all the comments Dōgen makes concerning chronological time in Shōbōgenzō. Although this is true, is there a function for examining before and after or past and future in practice? Does history have a place in the Buddha Dharma?

For Dōgen, looking back at the past often has to do with studying the examples of our Buddhist ancestors. In "Bendōwa," Dōgen says zazen "carries out the constant work of the way of buddha conversion within inexhaustible dharma realms in the past, present, and future."[18] And this activity's "echo has a wondrous sound that continues on and on both before and after the strike. How could it be limited only to this time?"[19] When Dōgen is speaking of sequential time, he is often using it to illustrate the vast and boundless power of the Dharma's reverberation throughout all time and space as practiced by the buddhas and ancestors of the lineage. It is his purpose to inspire us by the Buddha Dharma's "wondrous sound" and the unceasing practice of those who have carried this practice in the past.

These references reoccur throughout Dōgen's writing as he continuously uses examples of the practice wisdom of past Zen masters, bodhisattvas, and buddhas. In Zen, lineage is the history of those who made effort in practice and became our mentors on the path.

But how does our personal history affect our current practice of Buddhism? We made mistakes in the past, make them now in the present, and hopefully we learn from these mistakes and transform our behavior. Traditionally in Buddhism, the karmic stream we develop in our lifetime will affect our rebirth.[20]

In Zen we are taught that it is only within our current being-time-place (the independent aspect of a dharma position) that we can break from our karmic fetters. Conversely, it is within this being-time-place that we may become caught in our delusion. Either way, we are reminded that in each moment, we have the possibility of immediately transforming our response because we are already endowed as buddha nature.

For this reason, sequential being-time's function in practice is the unfolding of a learning curve leading to awakening our buddha mind. This is the activity of repenting, learning, and maturing from unskillful actions. In "Shizen Biku" (Monk of the Fourth-Stage Meditation), Dōgen observes, "Now those who know buddha dharma realize their faults in this way and quickly cast off their mistakes. Those who don't know it remain ignorant for the rest of their lives."[21]

We measure our own activity based upon the Buddhist teachings. We pay attention to how others respond to our actions. This process, whose function is never outside the Dharma, is perceived by the self as learning from one's mistakes within the context of our life as sequential passage.

Dharma Position as All Time(s) and Being(s) Presencing

Within each particular independent dharma position, all time-being is simultaneously presencing as and in that dharma position. This is the nondual, universal aspect of the particular.

Everything is the result and expression of all things, processes, events inter-being, rising and falling. Nonduality is another word for impermanence. Impermanence is the result of inter-being processes; it is nonduality presencing and interacting with, through, and as all dharmas. Thus, impermanence is the morphing from one action or thing to another based upon causal conditions.

A dharma, such as a piece of firewood, is both universal and particular at the same time. Things are not only individual or particular, nor are they only nondual or universal. Both aspects are present in each and all dharma positions. Firewood's particular position is the result of all of the activity of the world's functioning. This is true for everything we can name and see and what we cannot name or see.

In "Uji," Dōgen writes, "We must study and learn that myriad phenomena and numberless grasses *exist over* the entire earth, and each of the grasses and each of the forms *exists as* the entire earth."[22] This goes back to the idea of a dharma "abiding in suchness" while having a kind of autonomy—but not self-sufficiency. Self-sufficiency, for example, would be having no need to rely upon air, food, water, and so on for one's substance. The whole world's activity supports the life of each and every dharma position. This is the basis of abiding in suchness.

All dharmas are also part of the support system of all other dharmas. That system becomes the universal aspect of a dharma's cofunctioning as and with other dharma positions in support of the whole and the parts simultaneously. In the quotation above, Dōgen expresses ideas from Huayan Buddhism. One blade of grass is the entire earth because (1) all things share common traits that create sameness and unity, and (2) all things inter-are with one another.[23] Therefore this one blade of grass is both particular and, at the same time, is not apart from the whole of universal functioning. From this perspective, we can say it is the whole universal functioning.

Dōgen writes in "Gyōji" (Continuous Practice), "[The power of this continuous practice] affects the entire earth and the entire sky in the ten directions. Although not noticed by others or by yourself, it is so." And,

> Because of this practice, there are the sun, the moon and stars. Because of this practice, there are the great earth and the open sky. Because of this practice, there are body, mind, and their environs. Because of this practice, there are the four great elements and the five skandhas. Continuous practice is not necessarily

something people in the world love, but it should be the true place of return for everyone. Because of the continuous practice of all buddhas of the past, present, and future, all buddhas of the past, present, and future are actualized.[24]

Continuous practice is the practice of enacting inter-being, cofunctioning, and realizing nonobstruction. Fully engaging each moment's arising is predicated upon realizing our mutual identity and inter-are-ing.

These principles apply to all times, places, and beings arising as each moment's presencing. Thus, everything's being-time or dharma position is simultaneously making the world through their mutual identity and inter-being. In these nondualistic causal relationships, nothing is obstructing anything else because they are essentially one process—this includes time as well as being. In "Uji," Dōgen also says, "As the time right now is all there ever is, each being-time is without exception entire being time. . . . Entire being, the entire world, exists in the time of each and every now. Just reflect: right now, is there any entire being or an entire world missing from your present time, or not?"[25]

Viewing relationships by focusing on our sameness, not our differences, is transformative. Conflict arises when we view the "other" as obstructing our misperceived inherently-existing-self. If our actions toward others reflected the teaching that all dharma positions are foundationally codependent and inter-are-ing, perhaps we could alleviate some suffering for self and others in our personal, cultural, international, and political relationships. This is foundational to actualizing the bodhisattva's path.

Dharma Positions Have Particularity but No Fixed Identity or Outcome

A bodhisattva responds to each situation (a particular dharma position) in a way that will manifest and result in a buddha's understanding, which means responding to and including both the particular and universal. This understanding is based upon knowing that we are interconnected–inter-being with others (not clinging to outcome and/or fixed identity) and recognizing the intrinsic value of the independent dharma position of all beings.

An example of a failure in this regard is the destruction of our environment. It has become clear to us that our selfishness and one-sided, fixed view that humanity's needs are of greater importance than the rest of nature has created and continues to create huge problems. The bodhisattva response would include knowing that there is a problem, acknowledging the problem, "hearing the cries" of the problem, investigating the problem, but most importantly responding to the problem without attachment to one's own preferences. When we do not acknowledge that humans have a great deal to do with changing weather and a dying ecosystem, we are caught in trying to make a problem disappear by forcing it into the box of our delusional ideas in service of absolving humanity of any responsibility.

In "Uji," Dōgen admonishes us, "The sharp, vital quick of dharmas dwelling in their dharma positions is itself being-time. You must not by your own maneuvering make it into nothingness; you must not force it into being."[26] "The sharp, vital quick" refers to an immediate, spontaneous, vital, and flexible response to what is happening around us. If we want to make a skillful response, we cannot reify a dharma position (person, situation) with preconceived notions of what is happening. Nor can we hold on to ways that may be comfortable or known to us when the result is causing suffering for others. Helpful action only happens when we act through being inclusive, flexible, and without a fixed view of the outcome. The solution we desire is the one that includes the needs of everyone involved, not just our own.

Dōgen instructs us not to concretize anything based upon some desire to negate ("make it into nothingness") or create an idea ("force it into being"). This fluidity, combined with the simultaneous specificity and universality of our situation, can be understood as a kind of virtue. If we can incorporate this flexibility, combined with compassion and knowledge, we will express practice-realization. This is the immediate response that goes beyond this or that and becomes "the sharp, vital quick of dharmas dwelling in their dharma positions."

Dharma Positions' Passage[27]

How time passes or beings transform (essentially not different events) is what the Zen scholar Masao Abe termed "passageless passage."[28] By translating the Japanese *kyōryaku* (經) as "passageless passage," instead of the usual translation of "passage," Abe emphasizes the permeability between boundaries in the transition of one dharma position into another. Likewise, Hee-Jin Kim comments that *kyōryaku* has the meaning of "passing through." He observes, "Passage in the conventional view denotes the continuity of temporal units. . . . Dōgen is highly critical of this view."[29]

Kim continues, "Passage infers the dynamics of the 'intra-epochal' reality of the absolute present moment (*nikon*)."[30] Kim's comments relay Dōgen's understanding that passage is not defined as sequential (chronological time); rather, it is passage that must include a dharma position's universal (intra-epochal) passage within its presencing moment. A dharma position's passage happens as a particularity of universal nonduality functioning simultaneously through and as the present moment.

Time-being's passage or transformation (impermanence) has no beginning or end as it is making a transition because all dharma positions hold the qualities of inter-being and codependence, as well as particularity. From this perspective, a dharma position's passage is nonsequential and nondual while appearing to be dualistic and often seen as sequential. What we identify as a certain period of time, such as an epoch, which in this case would be a defining moment in history or a designated period of time such as a geological epoch, is dynamically morphing within itself.

In "Uji," Dōgen writes, "Even when the time of their reaching is not yet over, the time of their not-reaching has arrived. . . . 'Reaching' is not coming; 'not-reaching' is not yet. This is how being-time is."[31]

Before a situation, person, dharma, or time has completely arrived, there is within that arrival, the departure. What Dōgen is calling reaching and what he is calling not-reaching are just the time-being making passage. There is "reaching" in "not-reaching" and "not-reaching" in "reaching." Yet we can't forget that there are the specific dharma positions of "reaching" and "not-reaching."

These states of "reaching" and "not reaching," in Dōgen's example, can be viewed as overlapping sequential passages, but this horizontal view leaves out the vertical and holistic quality of the inter-being of realities as transformation and passage. Consequently Dōgen must say, "Even when the time of their reaching is not yet over, the time of their not-reaching has arrived."

Not labeling a dharma position's passage as "reaching" or "not-reaching" reflects a dharma position's fluidity. It is always in a state of impermanence, interconnection, process, and inter-being. Therefore we cannot just say it is this or that. As passage occurs, there is passage that must "pass through" as a particular independent aspect of a dharma position. That is why Dōgen wrote in "Uji," "[S]pringtime's passage invariably passes through spring. The passage is not spring, but as it is the springtime's passage, passing attains the Way now in the time of spring."[32]

How can we understand this? If we think of spring, how do we define spring? Is it the day of the vernal equinox, or is it a robin appearing on our lawn? Spring can be defined by weather patterns in our area. Perhaps it is the blossoming of a certain flower or snow melting. Regardless of how we determine the dharma position called "spring," the various elements that determine spring arrive at different times and from different causal conditions. All of those signs of spring are the result of eons of causal conditions inter-are-ing. If we could know them all, that knowing would reveal the totality of the world's history, function, and passage(s) without end.

From this perspective, what is "reaching" and what is "not-reaching"? How can we definitively say "This is spring"? Yet we do. We say "This is spring" because, as I quoted Dōgen from "Uji" above, "[s]pringtime's passage invariably passes through spring. The passage is not spring, but as it is the springtime's passage, passing attains the Way now in the time of spring." Springtime is 100 percent spring, although the elements we associate with spring do not necessarily arise simultaneously.

Having this understanding of nonsequential, completely intimate comingling while making one's appearance as an independent unique dharma is the fulcrum point of practice-realization or verification. It is at this time, at this place, that we must fully engage our life through the Dharma. That engagement has to include passageless passage as total intimate causality because without it, we could not respond to our position fully. This total engagement includes everything seen and unseen. This inclusive, fluid is-ness of right now in the midst of impermanence is the how of skillful response or realized activity. And that how can only be manifest in the presencing moment as we immediately respond to our life as it is. The knowledge that all aspects of a dharma position essentialize a moment's occurrence and response allows us to respond with wise discernment and flexibility. This is the bodhi mind at work.

The Eternal Now, Nikon

Can we directly experience any other time or place than this time-being-place? The past is remembered and thus it is now; the future is thought about in the present, thus it too is now. We can only experience this particular present moment as our being-time. This is the eternal now (*nikon*, 而今). From this perspective, while there is a past and future, what we directly experience is only the present.

In "Uji," Dōgen writes,

> As long as time is not a modality of going and coming, that time on the mountain is the immediate present—right now—of "the time being" (being-time). Yet as long as time takes upon itself a modality of going and coming, the being in me in the immediate now [*nikon*] of 'the time being' is being-time.[33]

Dōgen calls linear sequential time the "modality of going and coming." This is a conventional way to talk about time passing or progressing. Dōgen does not deny this aspect of causation. This is the progression of being-time, or our self's dharma position that seems to progress in a straight timeline from birth to death. But if we are not viewing our life or current experience's presencing as "going and coming," then it must be viewed as "right now or the immediate present." Even if we do view it as "going and coming" or as time's passage, it is still happening "right now."

From a practice perspective, everything (all stages or responses) is fully present or within the current now. Whatever stage of practice you may be expressing, all stages are still presencing simultaneously. In "Hotsu Bodai Shin," Dōgen comments,

> The Buddha Śākyamuni said, "When the dawn star appeared, I, together with the whole earth and sentient beings, simultaneously attained the way." Thus, bringing forth the mind [of bodhi], practice, bodhi, and nirvāṇa must be a "simultaneous" bringing forth the mind, practice, bodhi, and nirvāṇa.[34]

Shākyamuni Buddha's awakening is the now of his experience that also includes the now of our experience. This present moment includes the awakening present moment of what we may consider a historical past, but from the perspective of nikon, this moment's awakening must include Shākyamuni's awakening along with our own or others. This is universal nondual being-time. From this perspective, the Buddha's awakening is our awakening. Our buddha-nature is the buddha-nature of all beings, simultaneous presencing. This is true as well for all "stages" of practice, which are functioning simultaneously as our now, regardless of our labeling that moment as lacking or manifesting these stages: "[bodhi] mind, practice, bodhi, and nirvāṇa."

Our spiritual journey can be talked about as a sequential passage, but each stage is still all stages presencing as the eternal present moment. In classic Dōgen style, he expresses the same idea in "Uji":

> Entirely worlding the entire world with the whole world is thus called penetrating exhaustively. To immediately manifest the bodying of the tall golden Buddha with the body of the tall golden Buddha as the arising of the religious mind, as practice, as enlightenment, as nirvana—that is being, that is time.[35]

This is the time

> when you go directly into the mountains and look at the myriad peaks around you . . . there is no passing away. So even that three-headed, eight-armed creature makes a passage as my being time. Although it might seem as if it were somewhere else far away, it is the time right now. The sixteen-foot Buddha-body also makes a passage as my being-time. Although it might seem as if it were somewhere else over there, it is the time right now.[36]

Each immediate moment of our spiritual journey contains all the moments of climbing and crossing as this very time. This is true even when we define passage as coming and going (sequential stages); it is still inclusive of all stages of our journey. Each now holds all nows yet can only be right now, thus it is called "the eternal now."

In the quotation above, Dōgen also expresses the idea that delusion ("three-headed, eight-armed creature") and realization ("sixteen-foot Buddha-body") are "mak[ing] passage as my being-time" and therefore are not disconnected events. You might ask yourself, "When I do something unskillful, where has my bodhi mind gone? And when I am skillful, where has my delusional mind gone?" Both are still an aspect of yourself and are present in the dharma position called self. One aspect comes forth, and the other recedes, thus making passage. But both aspects are possible since they are still presencing in and as this dharma position.

Practicing with Jū Hōi

Dōgen's understanding of a dharma position explains to us how the self is the self yet is also not the self. As we incorporate this teaching, we see that the person we experience as a solid and settled self is actually a vast permeable entity. Fortunately, this means we are not trapped by past mistakes, and we have the innate capacity to integrate our life with the lives of others. Furthermore, we can see that others possessing the same virtues are also capable of transformation.

Taken in its totality, the concept of a dharma position gives us an overview of how we can describe to ourselves the nature of our experience. By breaking down the various aspects of our present time, we may be able to take this broader view of being-time and open ourselves to the freedom and variety of the Buddha Dharma, thus skillfully manifesting practice-realization.

Appendix 2

Practice-Enlightenment or Practice-Verification?

You may notice in Shohaku Okumura's translation of "Genjōkōan" (page xiii) the term *shushō* is translated as "practice-enlightenment" or "practice-realization," while in the commentary by Kyōgō and Senne, the *Okikigakishō* or *Goshō* (appendix 4), it is translated as "practice-verification." It is worthwhile to discuss the distinctions between the two translations of this term. As you'll see, each translation has its pluses and minuses. Sometimes "practice-realization" seems to best reflect Dōgen's meaning; at other times, "practice-verification" might be the better option.[1]

The Japanese kanji characters for *shushō* are 修證. *Shu* (修) refers to discipline, conduct, study, master, or practice and is usually translated as "practice." *Shō* (證) is most often translated as "enlightenment," but the dictionary definition is "proof, evidence, certify, verify, testify, guarantee, or witness." This discrepancy has arisen because the character 證 in Chinese means enlightenment; in Japanese kanji, it is translated as "verification."[2] Most of the English translations of Dōgen translate *shō* as "enlightenment" rather than "verification."

Hee-Jin Kim attributes the translation of *shō* as "enlightenment" to the translator and religious scholar D. T. Suzuki's influence on English translations of *satori*. Kim writes, "The word *satori*, translated as 'enlightenment,' has become a household word in the West, thanks to D. T. Suzuki."[3] Francis H. Cook writes that Dōgen didn't necessarily like using the word *satori* and preferred various expressions, in particular *shō* as "verification."[4] Cook wrote in defense of the translation "verification," which he also called "authentication": "Perhaps Dōgen also had in mind the idea that awakening is also a process of becoming an authentic or genuine self, which is our essential nature or Buddha nature. Awakening is thus both the process of proving, certifying, or authenticating, and the process of becoming genuine or authentic."[5]

In the supplementary notes of the Sōtōshu translation of Shōbō-genzō, another explanation of this term is that *shushō* is "an abbreviation of two terms that when combined become 'practice' (*shugyō*) and 'verification of awakening' (*shōgo*)."[6] Perhaps, using the logic presented above, practice-awakening or practice-verification are interchangeable.

Okumura writes that he originally translated *shushō* as "practice and enlightenment" but lately has felt a better translation would be "practice-verification." Okumura says in part,

> *Shu* (修) is practice. . . . *Shō* (証) translated here as "enlightenment," but a more literal translation is "verification." . . . *Shushō* is an abbreviation of a longer expression, *mon shi shu shō* (聞思修証). *Mon* (聞) is to listen or hear; *shi* (思) is to think; *shu* (修) is to practice; and *shō* (証) is verification. When we hear a teaching from someone, directly from a teacher or by reading some texts, we think about it; we try to understand what the teaching means. . . . After we practice for a certain period of time, we verify that the teaching is true. That is the common understanding of the process of our study and practice. But Dogen says that practice and verification are *ichinyo* (一如): *ichi* is "one," and *nyo* means "suchness"—one suchness, one reality.[7]

The phrase *mon shi shu shō* (聞思修証) occurs once in Shōbō-genzō, in the fascicle "Hachi Dainin Gaku" (The Eight Understandings of a Great Person), in Dōgen's consideration of the seventh attribute. He writes, "The arousing of hearing, considering, practicing, and realizing is wisdom."[8] A more common list used by Dōgen

is seeing, hearing, perceiving, and knowing (*ken mon kaku chi*, 見
聞覺知).⁹ An example of the use of this phrase is found in "Busshō"
(Buddha-Nature), wherein Dōgen discusses buddha-nature's manifesting: "Not understanding this principle is not clarifying, seeing,
or hearing the attainment of buddhahood."¹⁰

Dōgen views these kinds of lists not as sequential but as each
element simultaneously arising. Each aspect informs and drives
the response of the other aspects. In "Hotsu Mujō Shin" (Arousing
the Aspiration for the Unsurpassable), Dōgen clearly states that all
apparent stages of practice-realization or practice-verification are
presencing simultaneously.¹¹ "Thus aspiration, practice, enlightenment, and nirvana must be *simultaneously* aspiration, practice,
enlightenment, and nirvana [with all sentient beings]." He ends this
train of thought with, "This is practice and realization."¹² Okumura
makes a similar point in his definition of verification quoted above:
"But Dōgen says that practice and verification are *ichinyo* (一如):
ichi is 'one,' and *nyo* means 'suchness'—one suchness, one reality."

Dōgen expresses the teaching of the simultaneity of practice-
realization and designated stages in the opening lines of "Genjōkōan": "There is delusion and realization, practice, life and death,
buddhas and living beings"; and "there is no delusion and no realization, no buddhas and no living beings, no birth and death."
"There is" and the "There is no" function together. When our need
is to focus on one step, it is this or that. But essentially all bifurca-
tions are manifestations of "not this" or suchness, the simultaneity
of all dharmas arising together.

It is important to note that these praxis lists also depend upon a
relationship with a living teacher. In Shōbōgenzō "Menju" (Face-
to-Face Conferral), Dōgen emphasizes the importance of directly
interacting with, learning from, and realizing the Dharma through
an awakened teacher. He writes, "One who never in a lifetime meets
a master is not a disciple, and one who never meets a disciple is
not a master."¹³

Just understanding practice-verification as hearing, thinking,
practicing, and verifying (or any other list) outside the container

of the student-teacher relationship is not, according to Dōgen, a viable way to enact the Dharma.

Can we reconcile the translations of *shō* as "enlightenment," "realization," or "verification?"

As a teacher, I find the word *enlightenment* problematic because of all the baggage it carries; it seems to indicate a state of being rather than a process of relating. For this reason alone, I think it is misleading. Sōtō Zen understands enlightenment as a cooperative, codependent, and interactive state of mind and action between self and others. It is not something one attains outside the context of relational response. For this reason, I prefer the words *actualization* or *realization*.

What is one actualizing? What is one realizing? We are actualizing and realizing our simultaneous, interdependent, cooperative functioning with self and others. Unlike enlightenment, actualizing and realizing are verbs that by definition contain movement and connection. They communicate action by and between self, others, and the Dharma, as well as placing those responses within time. Realization or actualization happens at a specific time within a certain situation enacted with particular persons, beings, or things.

There is also the translation of *shushō* as "practice-verification," and I think that presents its own problems. We may ask, "Who is verifying? What is verified? And how do we know verification?" If we understand verification strictly as *mon shi shu shō* (listening, knowing, practice, and verification), then we might think that we can attain awakening within the context of our individual effort divorced from the practice with a teacher and with all being(s). As we have seen, this runs counter to Dōgen's understanding of how we awaken.

This listening, thinking, practicing, and verifying is not steps-and-stages practice. As mentioned earlier, it is the simultaneous arising of all aspects functioning and manifesting as awakening. Taking a moment to reflect on the various meanings of *mon* (聞 listen) and *shi* (思 thinking) is instructive. Both Japanese characters have components that give them emotional depth. *Mon* is not only to listen to something but also learning and inquiry. *Shi* incorporates belief, realization, regard, yearning, and caring for—all of which are aspects of our emotional engagement with practice-verification. If we just understand *shi* as thinking, then we may mistake this for intellectual understanding—it is not. It is the inter-being of yearning for connection and caring for something (in this case, the Dharma).

In Okumura's commentary on Dōgen's "Sansui Kyō" (The Sutra of Mountains and Water), he asks, "Who is studying? Who is inquiring? In the case of Buddhadharma, Buddha studies Buddha's way through our practice. Or Dharma studies Dharma itself through us, through this person, because this person is part of the Dharma."[14]

Since all of us are buddhas (all dharmas are buddha-nature), we verify not just our faith in Buddhist teachings but our inter-are-ing with reality's suchness. Therefore, we are buddhas studying with buddhas (all dharmas) and affirming our original nature.

Our verification of the Buddha Dharma is a kind of reciprocity between self, Dharma, and other, all manifesting within the context of our active participation in formal training and as enacted in our life. As I said earlier, Dōgen believed that our ability to verify the truth of the Dharma is predicated and validated by the transmitted Dharma through face-to-face encounters with a teacher.

In "Genjōkōan," Dōgen writes, "Conveying the self to the myriad things to authenticate [verify] them is delusion; the myriad things advancing to authenticate [verify] the self is enlightenment."[15] An alternative translation that does not use *authenticate* or *verify* is, "To carry the self forward and illuminate myriad things is delusion. That myriad things come forth and illuminate the self is awakening."[16] But, when authentication or verification is used, it is natural to ask the questions, "Who is verifying whom? And how do I know that I am verified?"

In the second example, we are less likely to ask those questions because there is a sense of reciprocity between self, myriad things, and awakening. Myriad things "illuminate" or shine a light upon our original self or buddha-nature. Here the question of who or what is verifying/verified is avoided.

This practice is always predicated upon practicing with all being(s), thus having avoided self-imposing our will upon any given situation. Whether this is understood through our being illuminated by our inter-beingness or by being verified, ultimately both point to the same thing. One is never awakened outside the context of the totality of arising dharmas—whether we know it or not. From this perspective, knowing or not knowing who or what is irrelevant. As Dōgen writes in "Genjōkōan," "When Buddhas are truly Buddhas, there is no need for the self to understand that it is Buddha."[17] In *Eihei Kōroku (Dōgen's Extensive Record)*, Dōgen asks,

> The teaching is already thus, the practice is also thus, and verification is also thus. As such, we cannot control whether or not we ourselves can control the teaching, the practice, and verification. Wherever they have penetrated, how could there not be Buddha Dharma?[18]

Another use of practice-verification in "Genjōkōan" comes in this passage:

> When a person practices and verifies the way of the buddhas, it is to *get one dharma is to penetrate one dharma; to meet practice is to cultivate one practice.* Since, in this, the place exists, and the way penetrates [everywhere], the fact that the known limits are not conspicuous is so because this knowing is born together with and studies together with the exhaustive investigation of the buddha dharma.[19]

Here practice-verification seems to serve the meaning more clearly than practice-realization would. In this case, it is the occasion of our verification of the practice for ourselves that we clearly understand that each moment, action, and dharma position is the locus of our actualization of the Buddha Dharma. Verification, knowing, studying, and exhaustive investigation all support *shō*'s definition as proof, verification, or evidence rather than enlightenment.

Cook points out that in a text like "Bendōwa" (On the Endeavor of the Way), "practice-realization" or "enlightenment" seem to fit the meaning of Dōgen's teaching better than "practice-verification." He writes, "The special suitability of the term *shō* in referring to enlightenment is particularly evident when seen in connection with Dōgen's well-known insistence that meditation and enlightenment are identical (*shushō ittō*)."[20] In his discussion of shushō, Francis H. Cook integrates both translations in his summary. He writes Dōgen's "central teachings" are

> that everything, including ourselves, is already a Buddha right from the beginning, and consequently what we call "awakening" or "enlightenment" can really be only a process of proving to ourselves this fact. In other words, to awaken to one's essential nature is the process of *authenticating* what the scriptures have told us is a fact and I have chosen to translate *shō* as "authentication" for that reason.[21]

From a doctrinal point of view, this reconciliation of the two translations seems to be valid, yet Cook ultimately lands on "verification." Other contemporary translators use "enlightenment." Consequently, from a practitioner's perspective, it is difficult to definitively state one translation is better than another. Is there a way that we can benefit from this ambiguity?

Perhaps just knowing the fluidity of the translation of *shushō* will deepen our understanding of Dōgen's teachings. As we explore substituting one translation for the other, we can ask, "Which translation fits best? Can I realize a more nuanced understanding by examining a passage using both translations?" We should feel free to interchange translations and perhaps come to a new understanding of the complexity and depth of Dōgen's Dharma.

Appendix 3

Introduction to *Okikigakishō* (御聴書抄) by Zuiko Redding

Okikigakishō (御聴書抄), usually known as *Goshō*, is the oldest of the commentaries on the seventy-five-fascicle version of Shōbō-genzō. It is actually two commentaries: one by Yōkō Senne 永興詮慧 (n.d.), and the other by his disciple Kyōgō 経豪 (n.d.).

The title expresses the titles of both the commentaries. *Kikigaki* is the title of Senne's manuscript. Kyōgō placed the honorific *go* before it to show his respect for his master. *Kikigaki* literally means "transcription," but Senne used it to express his intention to communicate an accurate understanding of Shōbō-genzō.[1] *Shō* refers to Kyōgō's commentary and means "summary" or "annotation."

Senne and Kyōgō wrote independently of each other. Each commentary is a freestanding, coequal expression of ideas. In the final manuscript, Kyōgō organized them as pairs of comments on each Shōbōgenzō passage. Kyōgō placed his comments first and followed them with those of his teacher. In his comments, Senne expressed his thoughts using "bullet points" to delineate each point, while Kyōgō wrote his observations as a basic narrative.

Who are Senne and Kyōgō? First of all, they are the least well-known among Dōgen's great disciples. Ejō, Jakuen, Giin, and other disciples built temples, trained their own disciples, and developed sanghas. They became celebrated ancestors in the Sōtō Zen school. Senne and Kyōgō were scholars whose temple is gone but who left us crucial insight into Dōgen's thought. We in the twenty-first century are fortunate to have both lines of ancestors.

Senne, who had originally ordained as a Tendai monk, became Dōgen's disciple and *jisha* (primary attendant) at Kōshōji. He, along with Ejō and Sōkai, received Dharma transmission from Dōgen there as well. Sōkai died at Kōshōji in 1242, but Ejō and Senne accompanied Dōgen and the sangha to Echizen, where Dōgen founded Eiheiji, in 1243. Some say that Senne was only second to Ejō in his closeness to Dōgen.

Kyōgō was Senne's student. He was born in Kyoto to an aristocratic family and, like Senne, originally ordained as a Tendai monk before entering the sangha at Kōshōji and following Senne to Echizen.[2]

Both Senne and Kyōgō remained at Eiheiji after Dōgen's death. Senne compiled volume 1 of *Eihei Kōroku*, along with many of the kōans in volume 9 and the poetry in volume 10. However, in the early 1260s, he and Kyōgō returned to Kyoto where they founded Yōkōji near Dōgen's cremation site. Senne also penned a commentary on Dōgen's writing on the precepts. We don't know when either monk died, but we know that Yōkōji continued for at least five more generations of abbots.

Senne's and Kyōgō's purpose in writing was to anticipate objections to some of Dōgen's bewildering and confusing assertions and explain Dōgen's meaning and intention in making them. They address the work line by line, often noting that Dōgen's statements might seem strange, then setting out to explain what he meant. They are concerned with showing Dōgen's work as a consistent whole, and they refer to other parts of his work in order to clarify a perplexing passage or phrase. They also strive to clearly differentiate Dōgen's teaching from that of other Japanese and Chinese masters. Their criticism of those teachings, like Dōgen's own such criticism, is often harsh.

Goshō has an interesting history. Senne began *Kikigaki* in 1263, ten years after Dōgen's death, and completed it in 1283. Kyōgō began *Shō* in 1303, fifty years after Dōgen's death, and finished it in 1308. Kyōgō, who gave the manuscript its final structure, wove Dōgen's work together with the two commentaries.

After its compilation, there is evidence that *Goshō* was studied at Yōkōji, Senne and Kyōgō's temple in Kyoto, for at least five generations of abbots. But Yōkōji did not last. When Daichi Sokei (大智祖継, 1290–1366), the Kyushu monk and poet, visited sometime before 1340, he described Yōkōji's "desolate, moss-covered, empty buildings."[3] Today even its location has been lost.

Goshō disappeared with Yōkōji and was missing for around two hundred years. It reappeared in 1586 when it was included in a record of items saved from a fire at Senpukuji in Kyushu. It continued to exist in obscurity until modern study of Shōbōgenzō began in the late 1600s.

Goshō is critically important to our understanding of Shōbōgenzō. Manzan Dōhaku (卍山道白, 1635–1715), Menzan Zuihō (面山瑞方, 1683–1769), Banjin Dōtan (萬仞道坦, 1698–1775), and other Soto Zen scholars who studied and commented on Shōbōgenzō in the early Edo period depended on it for insight into Dōgen's rewording of the language of the Chinese masters and keys to understanding his views, which often diverged radically from those of Chinese and Japanese Buddhist masters. *Goshō* also helped establish the authenticity of Dōgen's writings, which had been hidden and dispersed for many centuries, their authorship having fallen into doubt. Senne's and Kyōgō's line-by-line comments and their explanations of Dōgen's strange use of language helped scholars understand Dōgen's revolutionary interpretation of Chinese writings. *Goshō*'s importance was further heightened by the fact that it had been written by close disciples of Dōgen who had intimate access to his teachings and thought processes.[4]

This was the beginning of our modern understanding of Dōgen. Without Manzan, Menzan, and *Goshō*, we would likely not be studying and practicing as we do today.

Nishiari Bokusan (西有穆山, 1821–1910), who popularized Dōgen in the early twentieth century and is another important influence on our practice today, relied on *Goshō* in his Dharma talks and commentaries. Though they have unfortunately not been translated into English, Nishiari's writings are a foundation for present-day interpretation of Dōgen. Nishiari sought to make Shōbōgenzō widely available and accessible to both clergy and laity, emphasizing its practice aspects. Though he endorsed Dōgen's viewpoint, he took a scholarly rather than hagiographic approach. He also encouraged the use of Western philosophical methods in analyzing Dōgen. Nishiari's work shaped the way in which Shōbōgenzō is read, interpreted, and practiced in our times, and it is based in part on *Goshō*.

Acknowledgments

I want to thank Shinshu Roberts for giving me the opportunity to edit this chapter of *Goshō*. It was a joy and a privilege to be able to work with this material, and to work with Shinshu. Her questions about the text kept me on my toes and kept me focused in the midst of the duties of being a temple pastor. Our collaboration helped me clarify the material so I could present it more accessibly.

I'm deeply grateful to Shohaku Okumura, whose translation is presented here, for his help with understanding just what it is Senne and Kyōgō were saying, and for his kind corrections of my sometimes misguided expressions of their thoughts, and for his encouragement of and gratitude for my work. Working with him was a great honor.

I'd also like to thank my dear friend Tonen O'Connor for her constant encouragement, and for her reading of and comments on the manuscript. She caught awkward phrases and suggested more felicitous expressions, and she pointed out the typos that I'd missed.

William Bodiford and Steven Heine both graciously answered my inquiries for whatever unpublished information they might have about *Goshō*, Senne, or Kyōgō. They reassured me that I'd left no stone unturned in researching the pertinent history, at least in the material available in English. Finally, David Thompson of the Dōgen Institute was helpful with his interest and with reading through the final draft and making suggestions.

Zuiko Redding
Jikyōji, Cedar Rapids, Iowa, October 2023

Appendix 4

Okikigakishō (御聴書抄) "Genjokōan"

TRANSCRIBED COMMENTS AND NOTES BY YŌKŌ
SENNE (永興詮慧) AND KYŌGŌ (経豪)
TRANSLATED BY SHOHAKU OKUMURA
EDITED BY ZUIKO REDDING

The First Chapter of Shōbōgenzō: "Genjōkōan" (Actualization of Reality)

Gen (現) is being neither concealed nor revealed.

Jō (成) is not becoming through study.

Kō (公) is equalizing inequality.

An (按) is keeping one's lot.

About the Title

Kyōgō

Titles of Buddhist sutras express the essential meaning of the Buddha Dharma, are metaphors [of the Dharma], or are named after a significant person. [In] *Hannya-kyō* (Prajñāpāramitā Sutra), *hannya* (prajñā) is another name for the Buddha Dharma. The lotus flower in *Myōhōrenge-kyō* (Wondrous Dharma Lotus Flower Sutra) is a metaphor [for the Dharma]. Shōman (Śrīmālā) in the title of *Shōman-gyō* (Śrīmālādevī Siṃhanāda Sutra) is the name of the person who expounded the Dharma in the sutra.

Now [the title of this writing] Shōbōgenzō (The True Dharma Eye Treasury) points to the Buddha Dharma. When the Buddha transmitted the Dharma to Mahākāśyapa, he said, "I have the *shōbōgenzō nehan-myōshin* (the true dharma eye treasury, wondrous mind of nirvana, 正法眼蔵涅槃妙心). I entrust this to Mahākāśyapa." This is the expression of the essential truth transmitted through this tradition.

The title of each chapter in this [collection of] writings should be called *Shōbōgenzō Nehan-myōshin*, chapter 1, chapter 2, and so forth. However, the last four characters (*nehan myō shin*, 涅槃妙心) are left out, and [it] is simply called Shōbōgenzō.

Since this writing does not depend on any particular sutras, we cannot base the name of our school on the title of a particular sutra. Though the Parinirvāṇa (Nehan) Sutra [has the word *nehan* in its title], we do not call our school Nehan (Nirvana) school. The Buddha did not say [he had] *nehan-kyō* but *nehan-myōshin*. Instead of the [name of the] sutra, the Buddha said *nehan-myōshin*. The word *shōbōgenzō* can be used together with everything [Dōgen Zenji expounded]. Since the Buddha held up the flower and blinked his eyes, we may call our school the Nenge (Holding Flower) school, or [because Mahākāśyapa responded to the Buddha with a smile,] we may call our tradition the Hagan (Smiling) school. We don't call our school by these names.

Senne

- Some people call our school *Daruma-shū* (Dharma school) after the founding ancestor, Bodhidharma. Others call our school *Busshin-shū* (Buddha-Mind school) because we study mind-nature [instead of the Buddha's recorded words]. Neither is right. The Buddha said, "I have the true dharma eye treasury." We should not use our own words.

   Of the Buddha's words, what shall we keep and what shall we discard? We may say *Butsugen-shū* (Buddha Eye school). We may say *Nenge-shū* (Flower-Holding school). Why should we take only the word *mind*? People do such a thing because they do not understand the word *mind*. Since the Buddha said, "I have the true dharma eye treasury, the wondrous mind of nirvana," if we take the ten characters (吾有正法眼蔵涅槃妙心) there will be no mistake.

• The title Shōbōgenzō (The True Dharma Eye Treasury) is not a metaphor. It does not mean to follow other people's ideas. It means to follow one's own intention. Even though we say "following the intention of one's self," this is not the self that we compare to others. The Buddha said, "I have the true dharma eye treasury, wondrous mind of nirvana," and it has been correctly transmitted [until today]. Why do we have to make a name for our school? [We should simply call it the correctly transmitted Buddha Dharma].

• The word *genjōkōan* can be used together with any term. When we expound the dharma of "being" (*u*, 有), we can say, *genjōkōan* of being (*u*). When we talk about the dharma of nonbeing (*mu*, 無), we can say *genjōkōan* of nonbeing (*mu*). When we explain the dharma of neither being nor nonbeing (*hi u hi mu*, 非有非無), we can speak in the same way. The title of each of the seventy-five chapters of this writing can be called *genjōkōan* [for example, Shōbōgenzō Genjōkōan "Busshō" (Buddha-Nature)].

There can be the *genjō* of delusion, the *genjō* of realization, or the *genjō* of a whisk or a monk's staff, because the reality of each thing is manifested (*genjō*) [within each thing]. This delusion is the delusion at the time when all dharmas are the Buddha Dharma. After all, this expression (*genjōkōan*) is used to convey the meaning [that has been transmitted in] this tradition.

Kōan refers to this Shōbōgenzō (The True Dharma Eye Treasury). However, *genjō* (manifestation) does not mean that something that has been concealed is now being revealed. We should not consider this *genjō* (manifestation) to be the opposite of being hidden or concealed. If we dislike *genjō*, we should avoid using words. If we avoid using words, it is not right to use the Buddha's words, "I have the true dharma eye treasury." It is wrong.

- We should carefully consider this word *jō* (成). In discussing the meaning of *sokushin-jōbutsu* (即身成仏, this body itself becomes buddha), a scholar said, "The expression *sokushin-jōbutsu* is not [in accord with] Buddha Dharma because such a buddha [one that becomes a buddha at a certain time] cannot be revered because it is very inferior." Although this criticism sounds as if it is really transcending common understanding, when we say "this body itself," it refers to the perfect buddha. This should not be understood as people commonly understand the meaning of *jō* (to become). We should understand this *jō* on the [ground of] buddha. In a commentary on the Lotus Sutra it is said, "By practicing according to the teaching, living beings naturally accomplish the buddha way." It sounds as if "practicing according to the teaching" and "naturally" are contradicting each other. And it does not define how extensively this "practice according to teaching" should be done. Therefore, what the sutra says is very profound. Although it says "naturally," it is not what non-Buddhists mean when they discuss "naturalness." Also, practicing according to the teaching is not practicing in order to attain some result. We should understand this *jō* of *genjō* (to become, 成) as *jō* in *jōbutsu* (to become a buddha).
- This word *kōan* (公按) came from the everyday world. This should be understood in both worldly and supra-worldly meaning. To equalize an unequal condition (*heifuhei*, 平不平) is called "to be public" (*ko*, 公). Certainly, to equalize inequality when conditions are unfair is most public. To rule over people with benevolence is to equalize unequal conditions. To keep one's lot is called *an* (按, investigate). Doing anything to keep one's lot and not create confusion is most *an*. The non-Buddhist teachings should be considered on this level. Even in the practice of śrāvaka, pratyeka-buddha, and bodhisattva, at each rank we should practice in a way that equalizes inequality and keeps our lot. Because of this, these seventy-five chapters are all genjōkōan (manifestation of reality), though the titles and wordings are different. We should understand and interpret these dharma phrases as having

one (absolute) meaning. [Dōgen Zenji] is talking only about the principle of total function (*zenki*, 全機) that has no separation between subject and object, this and that. From the first chapter, "Genjōkōan," through to the seventy-fifth or final chapter of Shōbōgenzō, "Shukke" (Leaving Home), [Dōgen Zenji] expounds the same meaning.

• First of all, if we understand the expressions "equalizing inequality" and "keeping one's lot" in terms of worldly meaning, they are not in accordance with [Dōgen Zenji's] original meaning. It is difficult to determine what inequality is. What criterion can we use to define the equalizing of inequality? Once we understand that to be equal and to be unequal are one, it is not possible to say that we equalize inequality. If we use the expression "keeping one's lot," as if there is a fixed distinction in our lots, it cannot be the Buddha Dharma we are discussing now. What *kōan* means should be inequality and keeping one's lot within the total function (*zenki*).

(1) When all dharmas are the Buddha Dharma, there is delusion and realization, practice, life and death, buddhas and living beings.

Kyōgō

"When all dharmas are the Buddha Dharma" refers to the time when we point out that all phenomenal beings are without exception the Buddha Dharma. [Dōgen Zenji] mentions seven kinds of dharmas, from "delusion and realization" to "living beings" [in this sentence]. Although all dharmas should be listed, it is impossible to enumerate them all, so the remainder are omitted. Although the examples of dharmas [Dōgen Zenji] gave are few, we should not say they are insufficient. Simply, when we penetrate (*gūjin*, 究尽) the one dharma (*ippō*, 一法) of "delusion," though we don't discuss the myriad other dharmas, we are not in conflict with reality. This is because we are not caught up in [the dichotomy of] one and many. The truth of Buddha Dharma is like this. When [Dōgen Zenji] says that there is "delusion and realization" and so forth until "living beings," this "being" (*u*, 有) is not the "being" that is separate, as in "being" (*u*, 有) and "nonbeing" (*mu*, 無). When we simply discuss "delusion and realization," "buddhas and living beings," it is not mistaken to say "there is (*u*). . . ."

When he says, "When all dharmas are the Buddha Dharma," [Dōgen Zenji] is discussing dharmas (beings) when they are Buddha Dharma. If we interpret this with our worldly view, it is like trying to put a square peg into a round hole.

Senne

- "All dharmas" is "What is the thing that has thus come? (*ze jūmo butsu inmo rai*, 是什麼物恁麼来)." The sentence "When the ten thousand dharmas are without [fixed] self" points to "If I point out one thing, I am off the mark." Therefore, these two sentences' meanings are one and the same.
- To say all dharmas "are" (*u*, 有) is [the same as], for example, "The mind is itself buddha." To say all beings "are not" (*mu*, 無) is [the same as] "neither mind nor buddha."
- To say "There is life" is [the same as saying] "Life is the manifestation of total function." To say "There is death" is [the same as saying] "Death is the manifestation of total function."

(2) When the ten thousand dharmas are without [fixed] self, there is no delusion and no realization, no buddhas and no living beings, no birth and no death.

Kyōgō

This "self" is the "self" of all beings. This is not [a person's] "ego." The phrase "there is no . . ." (*mu*) is not "nonbeing" that is part of the dichotomy between "being" (*u*) and "nonbeing" (*mu*). This is "being" and "nonbeing" discussed in terms of the buddha-nature. Or this refers to "neither mind nor buddha" on top of "mind itself is buddha." This is comparable to expressions such as "understanding" and "not understanding" (beyond understanding) or "seeing buddha" and "not seeing buddha" (because of intimacy with buddha). However, when we penetrate the oneness of all dharmas (things), since there is no boundary that separates buddhas from living beings, it is not a mistake to say "There is not . . ." (*mu*).

Senne

- We can say that when all dharmas are the Buddha Dharma, there is no delusion and no realization, no buddhas and no living beings, no birth and no perishing.

  There are some people who have a mistaken view and insist that good and bad are the same thing, because in the Buddha Dharma, ignorance is itself dharma-nature and dharma-nature is itself ignorance. We must be very careful and fear having such a mistaken view.

- For example, there is fire in the world. This fire burns people's houses and kills people and animals. This fire may also burn temple buildings, stupas, buddha images, or sutras. Yet the same fire can be used to build temple buildings or make buddha images. We offer candlelight to buddhas. When we offer incense, we burn it. Yet good and bad are as completely different as heaven and earth. We should understand this even with these examples before our eyes. The delusion and realization [Dōgen Zenji] is discussing now is on the ground of the Buddha Dharma. We should not say that good and bad, delusion and realization, are the same thing. It is clear with the example of fire.

- This sentence is simply the continuation of the first sentence. The same thing is expressed again. "When all dharmas are the Buddha Dharma" is when all things "are without [fixed] self." In the previous sentence, it is said that there are delusion and realization, practice, life and death, buddhas and living beings. This is not the common, worldly understanding. If myriad dharmas are the Buddha Dharma, there is nothing to be called delusion and realization, buddhas and living beings, birth and perishing. To say "there is no A, no B, no C" is the same as saying "there is A, B, and C." The words "there is" (being, *u*) and "there is not" (not being, *mu*) should not be used in the worldly, ordinary sense. When all things are not the Buddha Dharma, how can we say we are deluded? We can see that we are deluded only when all things are the Buddha Dharma. When there is only delusion, who can name it as delusion?

In the Lotus Sutra, there is a chapter entitled "Skillful Means" (*Hōben-hon*). This is strange. Since this chapter expresses the true form [of all beings] (*shohō-jissō*, 諸法実相), it should be called the "True Form" chapter. Or it should be called the chapter of "Skillful Means and the True Form." Yet the sutras before the Lotus Sutra are called sutras of skillful means. Also, people who practice the two vehicles do not know that the teachings of the two vehicles are skillful means [to lead inferior people to the Dharma]. Now, at the time of the Lotus Sutra, we know those teachings were true form, (*jissōhin*, 實相品)and we say they are [taught as] skillful means. That is how the true form is revealed. When true form is revealed, the words *skillful means* (appropriate/suitable teachings) appear. We should understand that the word *delusion* can be used only when all dharmas are the Buddha Dharma. Both "delusion" and "realization" [here] are not understood as we commonly understand them. This is why it is said that there is "delusion and realization" (*mei-go*, 迷悟 as a compound). We do not understand this realization as realization in comparison with delusion. "Buddhas" and "living beings" are the same. This "living beings" refers to the human body in the expression "the ten-direction world is the true human body." When we say "buddhas," there is no living being that remains. When we say "realization," there is no delusion that remains. This is also a truth. But when we are intimate [with the reality of all beings], we call that time "when all dharmas are the Buddha Dharma." There is no obstacle to saying it both ways at the same time.

(3) Since the Buddha Way by nature goes beyond [the dichotomy of] abundance and deficiency, there is arising and perishing, delusion and realization, living beings and buddhas. Therefore flowers fall even though we love them; weeds grow even though we dislike them.

Kyōgō

This paragraph has nothing special to discuss. Here [Dōgen Zenji] again says that there is "arising and perishing," "delusion and realization." This "there is" (being, *u*, 有) refers to arising and perishing, delusion and realization, living beings and buddhas discussed [on the ground of] all dharmas are the Buddha Dharma. [Dōgen Zenji] says that there are those things. There is a [significant] reason to say so. "To love them is to begrudge them to others." "To dislike" means to hate them. [Dōgen Zenji] writes this as a caution for his later students. [Dōgen Zenji] says "There is . . ." in the first sentence and "There is no . . ." in the second sentence. It is all right to understand that there is the existence (*u*) of "delusion" and "living beings" and the nonexistence (*mu*) of "buddhas and living beings."

Senne

- We commonly think delusion is bad and realization is good and that these two are completely different things. But in the Buddha Dharma, we go beyond the dichotomy of abundance and deficiency and yet we use [the dichotomies of] arising and perishing, delusion and realization, living beings and buddhas. [Dōgen Zenji] expresses this clearly by saying these are only caused by our like and dislike, love and hatred.

(4) Conveying oneself toward all things to carry out practice-verification is delusion. All things coming and carrying out practice-verification through the self is realization.

Kyōgō

[Dōgen Zenji] says, "conveying oneself." This self is the self of "when all things are the Buddha Dharma." Carrying the self and carrying the buddha are the same thing. "Conveying" points to the reality of "the whole ten-direction world is the self." For now, it says "to convey" because the self completely penetrates the dharma world. Also, "living beings" and "self" refer to the same thing. For now, temporarily, we should understand this self as the single self on the ground of "All dharmas are the Buddha Dharma." "Self," "myriad things," and "delusion" are simply the same thing. The understanding of the phrase "practice-verification" is also different from our usual understanding. After all, the reality of the self is called practice-verification. Commonly speaking, it seems [Dōgen Zenji is saying] that to practice-verify the myriad things using the self is delusion, and that the myriad things coming toward the self and carrying out practice-verification is realization. Such understanding is not right. If we understand in such a way, "self" and "myriad things," and "delusion" and "realization," become separate things. This [interpretation] is not correct. Such understanding is contrary to the truth of Dharma. Yet when we want to understand in the ordinary way, "carrying out practice-verification by the self" should thus be delusion. "The myriad things come toward the self to carry out practice-verification" should not be understood according to the common meaning. We should understand these sentences [on the ground of] all things being the buddha dharma. "Conveying one's self toward all things to practice and verify all things" is "conveying one's self toward the self to practice and verify the self." "The myriad things come toward the self to practice and verify the self" is "the myriad things come toward myriad things to practice and realize the myriad things."

Senne

• Both "delusion" and "realization" are the total realization (*zengo*, 全悟) and the total delusion (*zennmei*, 全迷). We should understand that these are not relative to each other and are not two separate things. Delusion is not the opposite of realization; realization is not the opposite of delusion.

- In order to expound (the relationship between) "the self" and "the myriad things," "conveying" and "coming forward," "delusion" and "realization," Seppō 雪峰義存 (C. Xuefeng Yicun, 822-908) said, "All buddhas in the three times (past, present, and future) dwell in the fire and turn the great Dharma wheel." (Seppō spoke of the relation between the place and expounding the Dharma.)
- Gensha 玄沙師備 (C. Xuansha Shibei, 835-908) said, "The fire expounds the Dharma for the sake of all buddhas in the three times and all buddhas in the three times stand on the ground and listen to it." (Gensha spoke of the relationship between those who were listening and what was listened to.)
- Engo 圜悟克勤 (C. Yuanwu Keqin, 1063-1135) said, "I thought it was a white monkey but there is a black monkey too. Good spirits and evil spirits are appearing and disappearing in turn and exchanging their functions. The powerful flame spreads in the entire sky, the Buddha expounds the Dharma; the entire sky becomes the powerful flame, the Dharma expounds the Buddha." Engo spoke of the white and black monkeys, good and evil spirits appearing and disappearing in turn and exchanging their functions, and the powerful flame permeating the entire sky and the entire sky becoming the flame in order to express that the Buddha and the Dharma are one and the same. Now the relation between "self" and "myriad things," "delusion" and "realization," should be understood in the same way.

(5) Those who greatly realize delusion are buddhas. Those who are greatly deluded in realization are living beings. Furthermore, there are those who attain realization beyond realization and those who are deluded within delusion.

Kyōgō

Those who greatly realize delusion are called buddhas. Those who are greatly deluded in realization are called living beings. If we are careless, we understand these sentences in the same way as common people. However, it is not the case. "Delusion," "realization," "all buddhas," and "living beings" are simply the same things. Because there should not be any discrimination, [Dōgen Zenji] concludes that there are people who attain realization beyond realization and who are deluded within delusion. [Dōgen Zenji] wrote, changing the order of "delusion," "realization," "all buddhas," and "living beings" at the time when all dharmas are Buddha Dharma. *Kan* (漢, those) means "person." It seems the person appears specifically and abruptly, but this person refers to the person of "the entire ten-direction world is the true human body." We should understand that being [on the ground of] realization is called a "person," and being within delusion is called a "person."

(6) When buddhas are truly buddhas, they don't need to perceive that they are buddhas; however, they are verified buddhas and they continue verifying buddha.

Kyōgō

When buddhas are buddhas, they don't say, "I am a buddha." All buddhas are simply all buddhas. In buddhahood, there is no one who perceives that they are a buddha. Because it is the principle of "beginningless original awakening," perception is not used. [Dōgen Zenji] concludes, "However, they are verified buddhas." Also, it is not mistaken even if we say that all buddhas are awakening (perception, *kakuchi*, 覚知). In this paragraph, [Dōgen Zenji] does not write reversing the order of the words. He simply describes the way all buddhas are truly all buddhas.

When all buddhas are truly all buddhas, the ten-direction world is the entire buddha (*zenbutsu*, 全仏). At that time, perception is not used. To the extent that there is separation between the "self" as the subject and "a buddha" as the object (the self is a buddha), how can we depart from perception?

This word "perception" (*kakuchi*, 覚知) is commonly used [as an action of the subject] upon objects. However, when all buddhas are truly all buddhas, there is neither self nor perception. [Dōgen Zenji] continues, "However, they are verified buddhas, and they continue verifying buddha." This "verification" has no separation between subject and object. Though it is said that "they continue verifying," there is no one who verifies. Buddha's verification is like this. "To continue verifying" is called verification.

Senne

This verification is not relative to practice. This is simply buddha. Therefore, "to continue verifying" is also buddha. "All buddhas" and "verified buddhas" are the same words.

(7) In seeing color and hearing sound with body and mind, although we perceive them intimately, [the perception] is not like reflections in a mirror or the moon in water. When one side is verified, the other is dark.

Kyōgō

"Seeing color . . . with body and mind." This body/mind is [on the ground] that all things are the Buddha Dharma. This body/mind is itself color or sound. That is why it is said that we perceive them intimately. Body/mind and color, body/mind and sound, are not relative to each other. If two things are separate from each other, we cannot say "to perceive them intimately." It is different from the analogy of "reflections in a mirror or the moon in water." When we say "body/mind," there is nothing outside of the body/mind. When we say "color" or "sound," there is nothing outside the color or the sound. This is the meaning of "when one side is verified, the other is dark." "Mirror" and "reflections," or "water" and "moon," must be two separate things. This is not the Buddha Dharma.

Senne

- We should just say that the moon is reflected in the moon and the mirror is reflected in the mirror. Therefore, it is said that "when one side is verified, the other is dark."
- The Lotus Sutra says, "If people listen to the Dharma, none fail to become buddha." This is exactly the same as what is said here. What the Lotus Sutra says is that since there are no living beings outside the Dharma, there is no one who fails to become a buddha. "Hearing the sound" and "listening to the Dharma" are the same.

(8) To study the Buddha Way is to study the self. To study the self is to forget the self. To forget the self is to be verified by all things. To be verified by all things is to let the body and mind of the self and the body and mind of others drop off. There is a trace of realization that cannot be grasped. We endlessly express the ungraspable trace of realization.

Kyōgō

There is nothing particular to discuss here. We should simply understand as it is said in this paragraph: "A trace of realization that cannot be grasped." When we consider this from the perspective of duality between "delusion" and "realization," there is a boundary. There is nothing that can be called the trace of realization. Since the "trace of realization that cannot be grasped" has no boundary, it is stated, "endlessly keep expressing [this ungraspable trace of realization]." "The trace of realization that cannot be grasped" should be understood as the trace of original realization without beginning.

Senne

- There is nothing particular to discuss here. Being verified by all things is dropping off. This self is not the self as ego (*goga*, 吾我). To forget means to know without touching things (*fushokujijichi*, 不触事而知). The reason why [Dōgen Zenji] uses the expressions "trace of realization that cannot be grasped" and "ungraspable trace of realization" is not to say that there is "not grasping" after realization, but that "not grasping" is itself realization. As long as we make a distinction between "trace of realization" and "realization itself," we "see" the "trace" of "realization." Also, there is no time that "realization" is "not grasped." This is why [Dōgen Zenji] says that "trace of realization that cannot be grasped" is being endlessly express[ed] (*chōchō shutsu*, 長長出)." This "endlessly" does not mean a long period of time but rather "excellently." For example, it is like calling a person of virtue a *chōja* (長者). (The Chinese character 長 means both "long" and "superior.")
- Also, we should understand, [as Dōgen Zenji said in Shōbōgenzō "Shoaku-makusa" (Not Doing Evil Deeds)] that evil deeds are not doing, not doing is evil deeds; good deeds are doing, doing is good deeds. The entirety of the "ungraspable trace of realization" is called "endlessly express[ing]."

(9) When one first seeks the Dharma, one strays far from the boundary of the Dharma. When the Dharma is correctly transmitted to the self, one is immediately an original person.

Kyōgō

We should understand these sentences as they are written. This truth is really clear without any question. "Original person (*honbun nin*, 本分人)" means something like the principle of original enlightenment (*hongaku*, 本覚). The expression "to stray far from" that when the Dharma has been correctly transmitted, [the Dharma] never separates from the person's body and mind.

Senne

To seek after the Dharma is "to stray far from." We may think that we should not vainly seek after the Dharma. However, without seeking, there is no Dharma that has been correctly transmitted. We should seek after it as the most important thing. Yet there is a reason to say that when we seek, we become far from it. The correct transmission means "You attain my skin, flesh, bones, and marrow" or "I am thus, you are also thus." At that time, the person can be called an original person. There are two ways to interpret the expression "to stray far from the boundary of the Dharma."

- First, in order to point out that there is no way to seek after the Dharma, we say that "seeking" is "straying far from." Second, the expression "straying far from" is used in the meaning of "when one side is verified, the other is dark."
- Someone has said, "There are the words 'to stray far from' beside [the words] 'when one first seeks the Dharma.' This 'straying far from' should be understood as enlightenment because the person seeks after the Dharma."

  I don't agree with this. This opinion arises because one is not clear about the essential meaning of this writing. In order to determine true meaning by showing a mistaken understanding, it is said that the person strays far from the boundary of the Dharma. This is based on the common meaning in the world. "When the Dharma is correctly transmitted to the self, a person is immediately an original person." This is to settle down in the Buddha Dharma. We should choose this interpretation.
- Another person says, "*Hon* (本, original, true) in *honbun-nin* (本分人, original person) should be understood as *Hō* (法, Dharma). We should say that when the Dharma is correctly transmitted to

the self, one is immediately a Dharma person (*hōbun-nin*, 法分
人). *Hon* (original) should be changed to *Hō* (Dharma)." I don't
agree with this opinion. "Original person" is the best expression,
since when Dharma has been correctly transmitted, the Dharma
and the person are intimate. The expression "original person"
is in accord with the meaning that Dharma is the same as the
person. We should take this interpretation.

(10) If one riding in a boat watches the coast, one mistakenly perceives
the coast as moving. If one watches the boat [in relation to the surface
of the water], then one notices that the boat is moving. Similarly,
when we perceive the body and mind in a confused way and grasp
all things with discriminating mind, we mistakenly think that the
self-nature of the mind is permanent. When we intimately practice
and return right here, it is clear that all things have no [fixed] self.

Kyōgō

This is an analogy. Even in actuality, when we see the coast, it seems
that the coast is moving. However, the coast is not moving, but the
boat is moving. In the same way, to see that "body is impermanent"
and "the self-nature of the mind is permanent" is a mistaken view
in the same way as to see the coast moving though it is not moving.
[Dōgen Zenji] uses this analogy to show this [reality]. After all, we
should not think that body and mind are two separate things. When
we discuss permanence, both body and mind are permanent. Body
and mind are not two separate things. [Dōgen Zenji] discusses this
point in this section.

Senne

When we form a conception of our body and mind in confusion
and discriminate all myriad things, we mistakenly think that the
self-nature of our mind is permanent. It is clear that myriad things

have no [fixed] self. If we grasp self-mind and call it self-nature, we cannot say, "To forget the self," "to be verified by all things," or "dropping off body and mind."

Also, when we conceive of our body and mind without confusion, is the self-nature of our mind actually permanent? [If we say so,] it is like saying that discussing mind-nature is the Buddha Dharma even though we dislike discussing mind-nature.

It is said, "When myriad things are without [fixed] self, there is no delusion and no realization, no buddhas and no living beings, no birth and no death." What can be permanent? After all, this section does not mean that we should avoid confused conceptualization and grasp permanence because it is said that such is a mistaken view. This analogy does not mean that the boat is self-nature and the coast is body and mind. Since this simply says that it is a mistake [to have such a view], it is also said that the coast is moving. Right here in "return right here" is not a particular place. "Right here" refers to the Buddha Dharma. The principle that "all things have no [fixed] self" refers to, for example, "when the Triple World is only one mind, all dharmas are true form."

• [Dōgen Zenji used] the analogy of the boat and the coast to point out the matter of conceptualizing in confusion. It does not refer to any particular phenomenon.

(11) Firewood becomes ash. Ash cannot become firewood again. However, we should not view ash as after and firewood as before. We should know that firewood dwells in the dharma position of firewood, and it has its own before and after. Although before and after exist, past and future are cut off. Ash stays in the position of ash, and it has its own before and after. As firewood never becomes firewood again after it is burned to ash, there is no return to living after a person dies. However, in Buddha Dharma, it is an unchanged tradition not to say that life becomes death. Therefore we call it no-arising. It is the established way of buddhas' turning the Dharma wheel not to say that death becomes life. Therefore, we call it no-perishing. Life is

a position in time; death is also a position in time. This is like winter and spring. We don't think that winter becomes spring, and we don't say that spring becomes summer.

Kyōgō

This is also an analogy. In actuality too, after firewood becomes ash, it cannot become firewood again. In the same way, we commonly think that life is before and death is after. Also, to think that we will not be reborn after death is a non-Buddhist view of extinction (*danken*, 断見). To think that we should make our body into ash to eliminate our wisdom (mind) and that they both come out of ash is the view of the two vehicles. Here it is said that firewood dwells at the dharma position of firewood, and firewood has its own before and after. Although there are before and after, the boundary between before and after is cut off. This refers to the principle of "Life is manifestation of the total function; death is manifestation of the total function." After a person dies, there is no return to living. Death does not become life. This is the unchangeable way of turning the Dharma wheel. When people hear such words, those who do not receive the oral transmission may mistakenly interpret this in the same way as the non-Buddhist view of extinction. This is not right. Since death is a manifestation of the total function, after death a person does not become alive again. This makes sense. Since life is a manifestation of the total function, life does not become death. If we read this sentence without understanding this principle, we surely make a mistake. We should consider this point thoroughly. Because of this principle, life is a position at one time; death is also a position at one time. This corresponds well with the principle of life and death as the total function. This is also like winter and spring. We don't think that winter becomes spring or spring becomes summer. This refers to the same principle. We should not say that life is before and death is after by considering life and death in a dualistic way. We should say that life has its own before and after; death has its own before and after. This is what is meant by saying, "Although there is before and after, past and future are cut off." This life and death is not the same as life and death in the conventional world. Life and death are that of "When all things are Buddha Dharma, there is life and death" in the very beginning of this writing.

When we discuss life and death in transmission, we don't say no-life, no-death. When we say no-life, this doesn't mean that nothing is alive. We don't say death becomes life, but this does not mean there is no death. Since we don't say life becomes death, we may understand that the principle of no-life is the same as the Small Vehicle idea of no-later-karma. Certainly there is death. However, death is used as extinction (cessation) as a principle of the Small Vehicle. Furthermore, when a person has become a great arhat with three wisdoms and six divine powers, the person has been released from death as worldly people think of it. "Firewood never becomes firewood again after it has burned to ash." It is a mistaken view to think of this as extinction in the Small Vehicle. Before and after is used with both life and death.

Senne

Before and after exist both with firewood and ash. This discussion is not about "firewood is before, and ash is after." This is why it is said that past and future are cut off. We see the principle that there is no before and after in the Buddha Dharma. Since to say that life does not become death is the custom of the Buddha Dharma, we say no-life (fushō, 不生). Since death does not become life, we say no-extinction (fumetsu, 不滅).

There is no before and after in firewood or ash. When firewood verifies firewood itself, how we can say before and after? On hearing the analogy of firewood and ash, and saying that after firewood becomes ash it never returns to living again, in the non-Buddhist view we may think that after we die, we will not have rebirth. This is a distorted view. This analogy is used just as the evidence of the one-time of ash and one-time of firewood. It is a mistaken view to think of this as life and death.

- We don't understand that firewood is before and ash is after. We just say total firewood and total ash in the same way as life is manifestation of the total function, and death is manifestation of the total function. Therefore, now we should understand that both firewood and ash are the total life and the total death.
- Someone says, "After a person dies, that person never returns to living. However, in the Buddha Dharma, it is an unchanging tradition not to say that life becomes death. Therefore we call it no-arising (*fushō*, 不生). What does this mean? If life does not become death, we should say no-birth. We cannot say no-arising."
- Reply: "There are two meanings. There is a principle of no-arising, no-perishing in life; and there is a principle of no-arising, no-perishing in death too. [This is the first]. Next, in the world, we say life and death is a dharma of transmigration [in samsara]. In the Buddha Dharma, we say life is manifestation of the total function, death is manifestation of the total function, the mind of total function is no-arising (*fushō*). Why is it a problem to say no-arising (*fushō*)?
- We should deeply understand this principle. When we say that since life does not die, there is no-death, and since death does not become life, there is no-life, we are completely in darkness without understanding life and death. Since life is "life of no-life," we call it no-death. Since death is "death of no-death," we call it no-life. Although we say this life is no-death, if we say we don't die, it is against the reality of life. Although we say this death is no-life, if we say there is no life, we don't understand the reality of death.
- We should not argue on the basis of vertical (time) and horizontal (space) logic. When we say spring, the whole ten-direction world is spring. When we say summer, the whole ten-direction world is summer.

(12) When a person attains realization, it is like the moon's reflection in water. The moon never becomes wet; the water is never disturbed.

Although the moon is a vast and great light, it is reflected in a drop of water. The whole moon and even the whole sky are reflected in a drop of dew on a blade of grass. Realization does not destroy the person, as the moon does not make a hole in the water. The person does not obstruct realization, as a drop of dew does not obstruct the moon in the sky. The depth is the same as the height. [To investigate the significance of] the length and brevity of time, we should consider whether the water is great or small and understand the size of the moon in the sky.

Kyōgō

In this section, [Dōgen Zenji] uses another analogy to show that realization does not obstruct a person. In the previous section, [Dōgen Zenji] said, "[The perception] is not like reflections in a mirror or the moon in water." In this section he says, "It is like the moon's reflection in water." It sounds as if these two very much contradict each other. However, in the previous section, [Dōgen Zenji] uses this analogy simply to show that the principle that the two separate things (sound and hearer; color and seer) correspond to each other; they are not like a mirror and its reflections or water and the moon. Here, [Dōgen Zenji] uses the same analogy to show that the moon does not destroy the water, and that even though the moon is like a huge palace, fifty yojana square and four thousand yojana high, the moon reflects itself "in a drop of dew on a blade of grass." This section and the previous section do not contradict each other. [Dōgen Zenji] uses this analogy to teach us the principle that Dharma and our body-mind do not obstruct each other. The "height" and the "depth" are simply the same length. "Length and shortness of this time" and "greatness and smallness of water" should be examined in order to grasp the vastness or narrowness of the moon in the sky. This means that we should examine the principle that we do not argue about greatness and smallness of water to understand the vastness and narrowness of the moon in the sky.

Although I argue in this way, we should not abandon the coast, boat, and the moon and water just as mere analogies. Within the principle of the Buddha Dharma, there is no extra thing at all.

When we consider time on the basis of the Buddha Dharma, we should not be caught up in its length and shortness. The three great kalpas are not long. Also, one moment (*kṣaṇa*) is not short. Raising one's fist is the three great kalpas, and putting a monk's staff down is one moment. Therefore we don't need to discuss length and shortness of time. The moon in the sky stays in a drop of dew on a blade of grass. The fifty-yojana-square palace of the moon can be reflected in a single drop of dew on a blade of grass, so it has nothing to do with vastness and narrowness. [Dōgen Zenji] shows this reality.

This is only an analogy to show that even though the moon reflects itself on water, it does not destroy the water. This is a partial analogy. "The depth is the same as the height." This means that realization and the practitioner are two, and yet there is no discrimination. [The height of the moon and depth of realization of the person are thus.] When we point to depth, it shows height. When we point to height, it shows depth. Height and depth are the same.

"[In order to investigate the significance of] the length and brevity of time, we should consider whether the water is great or small and understand the size of the moon in the sky." This is the evidence that greatness and smallness of water and [length of] time are one. That is the time when a person attains realization. That which is important is not time.

Senne

- [In this section, Dōgen Zenji] says that when a person attains realization, there is no difference between great water and small water.
- "We should consider whether the water is great or small and understand the size of the moon in the sky" means that we should clarify that "the whole moon and even the whole sky are reflected in even a drop of dew on a blade of grass."
- Therefore it seems that there are length and shortness, greatness

and smallness, in the water, but heavenly moon and the entire sky reflect themselves on the water whether or not they are long or short and great or small. Since there is no length or shortness, greatness or smallness, in the heavenly moon and the whole sky, how can we measure length or shortness and greatness or smallness of the water? For example, when all things are the Buddha Dharma, delusion and realization, life and death, are all equally the Buddha Dharma, and there is neither superiority nor inferiority between them.

- "Hearing sound with body and mind, although we perceive them intimately, [the perception] is not like reflections in a mirror or the moon in water." [In this sentence, Dōgen Zenji] uses the analogy of the water and the moon in a negative sense because he wants to point out that there is no dichotomy between subject and object. In this section, [Dōgen Zenji] discusses the time when a person attains realization, using the analogy of water and the moon. This shows that the water and the moon do not destroy or obstruct each other.

(13) When the Dharma has not yet fully penetrated body and mind, one thinks one is already filled with it. When the Dharma fills the body and mind, one thinks that something is [still] lacking. For example, when we sail a boat into the ocean beyond sight of land and our eyes scan [the horizon in] the four directions, it simply looks like a circle. No other shape appears. This great ocean, however, is neither round nor square. It has inexhaustible characteristics. [To a fish] it looks like a palace; [to a heavenly being] a jeweled necklace. [To us] as far as our eyes can see, it looks like a circle. All the myriad things are like this. Within the dusty world and beyond, there are innumerable aspects and characteristics; we only see or grasp as far as the power of our eye of study and practice can see. When we listen to the reality of myriad things, we must know that there are inexhaustible characteristics in both ocean and mountains, and there are many other worlds in the four directions. This is true not only in the external world but also right under our feet or within a single drop of water.

Kyōgō

This "body and mind" refers to living beings in delusion. Even when we think that someone has already attained realization, though that person has not yet gotten it, we think that the Dharma fills [that person's body and mind]. When the Dharma completely fills a person's body and mind, that person would feel that it is not yet enough. The words "not enough" may sound strange. However, in the world there is an expression: "When we practice the Way with sincere heart, [when we are cutting a tree,] the more we cut, the harder the tree becomes; [when we climb a mountain,] the more we look up, the higher [the mountain becomes]." First of all, [Dōgen Zenji] wrote this point. Also, the principle of "one dharma completely penetrating all dharmas" is expressed with the words "not enough." This does not deviate from the truth. Also, the case of the boat is very clear. This is an example from the world. From the sentence "All the myriad things are like this," [Dōgen Zenji] examines the truth in the Buddha Dharma [rather than in a worldly example]. "This is true not only in the external world but also right under our feet or within a single drop of water." This means that we should not cling to our views that see only the objects within the sphere where our eyesight reaches. "Right under our feet or within a single drop of water" means that at the bottom of water or in one drop of water, what kind of truth lies there?

Senne

- "For example, when we sail a boat into the ocean beyond sight of land and our eyes scan [the horizon in] the four directions, it simply looks like a circle. No other shape appears. This great ocean, however, is neither round nor square. It has inexhaustible characteristics." Also, "[to a fish], it looks like a palace; [to a heavenly being], a jeweled necklace." These are mentioned as examples of the Dharma not yet fully penetrating one's body and mind. When the Dharma fills us, we feel something lacking.

These examples are not in accord with when we are filled. In the former section, [Dōgen Zenji] says, "In seeing color and hearing sounds with body and mind, although we perceive them intimately, [the perception] is not like reflections in a mirror or the moon in water. When one side is verified, the other is dark." This is an example of the time when Dharma is filled. These words are never different. When we are filled with life, death, realization, or delusion (this delusion is within the Buddha Dharma), always the other side is dark.

- When we are filled with zazen, we can say that we are killing Buddha.
- To see the ocean beyond sight of land as a circle is about our eyes. As for the virtues of the ocean, to be seen as circle is one of the virtues of the ocean. Yet the virtues of the ocean are inexhaustible.
- "When we listen to the reality of the myriad things, we must know that there are inexhaustible characteristics in both ocean and mountains" besides being seen as "round or square." This "besides" is not clear. Does this mean that it is all right to see the ocean as round or square, but we should know the qualities of the ocean besides those characteristics? Or does this mean that to see the ocean as a square or a circle is also a deluded view? Should we know the many other worlds in the four directions? Since it is said that though it can be seen as round or square, it sounds like the ocean is neither a square nor a circle, but when we know the rest of the virtues of the ocean and mountains above [being] a square or a circle, it is clear that neither the ocean nor mountains are square or round.
- For example, it is like saying that outside delusion and realization, we should know that there are practice, life and death, all buddhas and living beings.
- "The Triple World is only one mind; there is nothing outside the mind." "Is nothing" (*mu*) and "outside" in this sentence are the same, because we know the limitless virtues of the ocean through the form of a square or a circle.

• "Nothing besides the mind" is on the ground of mind. This means that the Triple World is only one mind. There is nothing outside the mind. At the time, nothingness is on the ground of the mind. "We must know that there are inexhaustible characteristics in both ocean and mountains" besides a circle or a square. This means that the virtues [or characteristics, (*toku*, 徳)] are neither one nor more than one.

(14) When a fish swims, no matter how far it swims, it doesn't reach the end of the water. When a bird flies, no matter how high it flies, it cannot reach the end of the sky. Therefore, since ancient times, no fish has ever left water and no bird has ever left the sky. When a bird's need or a fish's need is great, the range is large. When the need is small, the range is small. In this way, each fish and each bird uses the whole of space and vigorously acts in every place. However, if a bird departs from the sky or a fish leaves the water, it immediately dies. We should know that [for a fish] water is life, [for a bird] sky is life. A bird is life; a fish is life. Life is a bird; life is a fish. And we should go beyond this. There is practice-verification—this is the way of living beings.

Therefore, if there are fish that would swim or birds that would fly only after investigating the entire ocean or sky, they would find neither path nor place. When we make this very place our own, our practice becomes the actualization of reality [*genjōkōan*]. When we make this path our own, our activity naturally becomes actualized reality [*genjōkōan*]. This path, this place, is neither big nor small, neither self nor others. It has not existed before this moment nor has it come into existence now. Therefore, [the reality of all things] is thus.

In the same way, when a person engages in practice-verification in the Buddha Way, as the person realizes one dharma, the person permeates that dharma; as the person encounters one practice, the person [fully] practices that practice. [For this] there is a place and a path. The boundary of the known is not clear; this is because the known [which appears limited] is born and practiced simultaneously with the complete penetration of the Buddha Dharma. We should not think that what we have attained is conceived by ourselves and known by our discriminating mind. Although complete verification is immediately actualized, its intimacy is such that it does not necessarily form as a view. [In fact] viewing is not something fixed.

Kyōgō

In this section, [Dōgen Zenji] again uses the examples of water and fish, and bird and sky. What he wants to say is that although we tend to think that fish and water, bird and sky, are separate things, if a bird leaves the sky, it dies; if the fish leaves the water, it dies. This is obvious. We should know that the water is life to the fish; the sky is life to the bird. From this reality, we can say that a bird is life, a fish is life; and life is a bird, and life is a fish. Using examples from the world, [Dōgen Zenji] tries to show the relationship between a person and Buddha Dharma. At this time, [he says], "As the person attains one dharma, the person penetrates that dharma; as the person encounters one practice, the person [fully] practices that practice." We have never learned that the Buddha Dharma can be conceived by discriminating mind. The reason the boundary to be known is not clear is because knowing is born and practiced together with the complete penetration of the Buddha Dharma. We should not think that we perceive what we have attained and that it is known by our discriminating mind. "Although complete verification is immediately actualized" means that the attainment of one dharma is penetration into one dharma; encountering one practice is practicing one practice. This "intimate" [being] is "not necessarily form[ed] as a view." "Intimate" [being] (*mitsu u*, 密有) is the original principle of each and every being. Human beings cannot create it. Therefore, it is said that intimate being is "not necessarily form[ed] as a view." "Not something fixed" (*kahitsu*, 何必) means, for example, as it is said that when all dharmas are the Buddha Dharma, there is delusion and realization, life and death, buddhas and living beings. This is also the same principle as "If you point out one thing and try to explain it, you are off the mark." We should not be caught up even in the one dharma.

Senne

- We should go beyond this. There is practice-verification. A bird should use the sky as its own legs or wings without being limited in its life.
- And we should go beyond this. There is practice-verification— this is the way of living beings.
- "Going beyond," and "practice-verification" mean our body and mind. They are not limited in the water, the sky, and life. "Going beyond" and "practice-verification" mean that we should not put the sky and the water outside our body. Appearing in various ways is called "going beyond" or "practice-verification." These various ways are not limited in living beings; it can be said that our mind and body are the same because it is said that we should go beyond this.
- Living beings (*jusha myōsha*, 寿者命者) are discussed in the Small Vehicle teachings. Now it means that not only "going beyond" practice-verification but [all things] appear in various ways.
- "When a person engages in practice-verification in the Buddha Way, as the person realizes one dharma, the person permeates that dharma; as the person encounters one practice, the person [fully] practices that practice." In order to express this, [Dōgen Zenji] uses the examples of a fish and water, and a bird and sky.
- "Attaining one dharma is penetrating one dharma" is the same as "attaining zazen is penetrating becoming-buddha." When one is sitting, one does not know the merits [of zazen]. Yet this is zazen. Zazen is becoming buddha. Therefore, it is said that "we should not think that what we have attained is conceived by ourselves and known by our discriminating mind." Also, it is said that there is a place for us to do so and a path on which we can travel. The boundary to be known is not clear.

- "To be known" and "not clear" show that unless we are apart from the boundary of the Dharma, there is no intimacy with the Dharma. This is the meaning of "When Dharma fills [body and mind], one side is dark."
- "To know" in "knowing is born and practiced" is not knowing with discriminating mind. This is knowing that knows that zazen is sitting buddha.
- "Not something fixed" (*kahitsu*, 何必) means there is no way to define it.
- This "intimate being" is "being" in "All living beings entirely are buddha-nature" (*shitsu-u busshō*, 悉有仏性).
- "Not something fixed" (*kahitsu*, 何必) is the principle of the Buddha Dharma.

There are some people who think everything is the same when they hear good and evil are not two; right and wrong are one; relative and absolute are not two; form and essence are one. Also, sometimes it is said that the Triple World is not peaceful, like a burning house, so we should dislike it. Sometimes it is said that the Triple World is only one mind; there is nothing outside the one mind. Sometimes it is said that [the Triple World] is the body and the land of Vairocana Buddha. Sometimes it is said that there is no *saha* world outside the calm and bright buddha land. (This world is called the *saha* world, which literally means "the world where we need patience.") People use these expressions based on their own views. Also, it is said that though the Buddha preached the Dharma with one sound, living beings hear it various ways depending upon their capacity. So, people's understandings vary. Therefore, they speak whatever they feel is in accord with their minds. When the Buddha was alive, he knew people's capacities and taught the Dharma depending on those capacities, and yet by admonishing and advising, the Buddha caused them to have one perfect function. We must clearly think about "to be filled" or "not to be filled." When one side is verified, the other is dark. "Not filled" means "completely filled." "Not something fixed" (*kahitsu*, 何必), "forming as a view" (*kenjō*, 見成) means whether we say being (*u*, 有) or nonbeing (*mu*, 無), either is "not something fixed." We should not think that there is something fixed as "not-fixed."

(15) [The] Zen master of Mt. Magu was waving a fan. A monk approached him and asked, "The nature of wind is ever present and permeates everywhere. Why are you waving a fan?"

The master said, "You know only that wind's nature is ever present—you don't know that it permeates everywhere." The monk said, "How does wind permeate everywhere?" The master just continued waving the fan. The monk bowed deeply.

The genuine experience of Buddha Dharma and the vital path that has been correctly transmitted are like this. To say we should not wave a fan because the nature of wind is ever present, and that we should feel the wind even when we don't wave a fan, is to know neither ever-presence nor the wind's nature. Since wind's nature is ever present, the wind of the Buddha's family enables us to actualize the gold of the great earth and to transform [the water of] the long river into cream.

Kyōgō

The wind's nature is ever-present. If so, even when we don't use a fan, the eternal wind must exist. Why did the master use a fan? It seems that the monk did not understand this. His question is really off the mark. Therefore, the master criticized the monk and said, "You only know that wind's nature is ever present—you don't know that it permeates everywhere." The master used a fan on the principle of ever-presence. His action was not against the principle of ever-presence at all. If using a fan is against the principle, where should we put the fan when we do not use it? We should question this. On this point, whether the monk understood or not is not clear in the context of this writing. However, since he made a prostration, he certainly got the meaning [of the master's teaching].

Also, about the wind of Buddha's family. The whole ten-direction world is entirely the wind. Even plain water and ordinary earth become gold or cream when we discuss the Buddha's wind.

Also, when [the monk] asked, "How does wind permeate everywhere?" by lifting a fist or hitting with a monk's staff, the principle can be revealed without making a mistake. However, if the teacher acted in this way, it seems the teacher would negate using a fan. By using the fan continuously, the master showed that he was intimate with the principle of "the wind's nature permeates everywhere."

Senne

- The monk asked the meaning of the wind in the conventional world. The Zen master answered with the wind of Buddha's family.

  For example, it actualizes "the Triple World is only one mind" and enables "the reality of all beings" to mature (*sanjuku*, 参熟) into cream.

- If we discuss the distinction between the fan and wind, it is not discussion of the wind of Buddha's family.

- It is said that when [Emperor Wu, 武帝] gave a lecture on the Mahāparinirvāṇa Sutra, because of his merits, the earth became gold and water became cream. (When the Emperor Wu of Liang dynasty gave a lecture on the Mahāparinirvāṇa Sutra, it is said that heavenly flowers rained and the earth became gold.) This is not different from the worldly view because something valueless became something valuable. When we question [the original self] before our father and mother were born, sometimes we use a fan. This is really the pleasant wind of Buddha. If we understand with this meaning, it is more difficult to show the wind's nature by using a fan. And we don't question the wind. Also, the original face before father and mother were born is not the wind. There is no special reason to use the fan. [The master] only showed [the reality] with a thing that was at hand at that moment.

- If we use the example of a fan in order to discuss the wind, the understanding of the wind becomes a delusion in the world. Even if it is ever present or it permeates everywhere, the Buddha Dharma is not limited in either the wind that blows in the world, or the wind caused by a fan. We should use the gold as the wind, also the cream as the wind. The earth and gold, the water and cream, are still used in a relative (conventional) sense. It cannot be thought to be the Buddha's wind.
- Although the monk knew the principle of ever-presence of the wind's nature, he did not know the principle of the wind's nature permeating everywhere.
- For example, he knew the principle that the Triple World is one mind, yet he did not know that there is no dharma outside of the mind.
- We should say that "all buddhas are ever-present and they penetrate everywhere."
- We should say that "living beings are ever-present and they penetrate everywhere."
- When you use it, just use it. When you put it down, just put it down. This means that when it is needed, we use it; when it is not needed, we put it down. If it really penetrates everywhere, whether we use a fan or not should be at our will. This attitude is in accord with the principle of ever-presence. When needed, just use it; when not needed, just leave it alone.
- Although Master (Dōgen Zenji) seemed to agree that the wind's nature is ever present, actually he did not. It is like, "Although even a three-year-old infant can say it." After all, we should understand that the ever-presence of the wind's nature and ubiquitousness of it are the same. Therefore, my late teacher (Dōgen Zenji) talked about the ever-presence of the wind's nature but did not discuss omnipresence because it is included in ever-presence.
- When [Dōgen Zenji] quotes from sayings of ancestors in Shōbō-genzō, there are reasons to do so. For example, in the chapter of "Shoaku-makusa," there is a question and answer between

Chōka Dōrin (鳥巢道林, C. Niaoke Daolin, 741–824) and Haku Kyoi (白居易, C. Bai Juyi , 772–846). [Dōgen Zenji] quotes the story because the story is about the expression "Not doing evil deeds, practice all good deeds." It is questionable why Dōgen Zenji quotes the kōan of the ever-presence and omnipresence of the wind's nature.

• The answer: This is truly questionable. However, if living beings and buddhas, delusion and realization, and a fan are all equal, it is in accord with the principle of omnipresence. The great earth is itself gold and the long river is itself cream. If the buddha wind is like this, when all things are the Buddha Dharma, nothing is the principle of omnipresence. This is why this kōan is quoted.

The End of "Genjōkōan" Kikigakishō

Notes

Introduction

1. William Bodiford and T. Griffith Foulk, contribs., *Treasury of the True Dharma Eye: Dōgen's Shōbōgenzō; An Annotated Translation by the Sōtō Zen Text Project* (Tokyo: Sōtōshu Shumachō, 2023), vol. 8 [240, table 8]. The seventy-five-chapter version was a later revision of the sixty-chapter compilation.

2. Since Dōgen's death, there have been various compilations of Shōbōgenzō. Most of us in the United States are familiar with the ninety-five-fascicle collection, an official version created by the Japanese Sōtō school in the late eighteenth century, commonly referred to as the *Honzan* editions. Since that time, there have been several revisions. See Bodiford and Foulk, *Treasury of the True Dharma Eye*. vol. 8, suppl. 2, 184-96.

3. Appendix 4, "*Okikigakishō* 'Genjōkōan,'" "About the Title," Senne.

4. Appendix 4, "*Okikigakishō* 'Genjōkōan,'" "About the Title," Senne.

5. J. Tendo Nyojō, C. Tiantong Rujing (1163-1228).

6. The following timeline is from Kazuaki Tanahashi, ed., *Treasury of the True Dharma Eye: Zen Master Dogen's Shobo Genzo* (Boston: Shambhala Publications, 2010), vol. 1, lii-lv.

7. Steven Heine, *Dogen: Japan's Original Zen Teacher* (Boulder, CO: Shambhala Publications, 2021), 112.

8. For a discussion of the meaning of "compiled and arranged," which appears in the colophon of "Genjōkōan" and is basis of the question of whether Dōgen continued to edit or just arranged the placement of "Genjōkōan" in Shōbōgenzō, see William M. Bodiford, "Rewriting Dogen," *International Zen Studies*, vol. 12, no. 4 (2019): 278-79.

9. Steven Heine, *Readings of Dōgen's Treasury of the True Dharma Eye* (New York: Columbia University Press, 2020), 72.

10. Carl Bielefeldt, ed., *Treasury of the True Dharma Eye: Dōgen's Shōbōgenzō* (Tokyo: Sōtōshu Shumachō, 2023), vol. 1, Introduction to "Genjōkōan."

11. See Shohaku Okumura, *Dōgen's Shōbōgenzō Zuimonki: The New Annotated Edition* (Somerville, MA: Wisdom Publications, 2022), 17-18.

12. To further investigate Dōgen's writing career, see Heine, *Dogen*; Heine, *Readings of Dōgen's Treasury of the True Dharma Eye*; and the introductory volume of the Sōtō Zen Text Project written by Bodiford and Foulk, *Treasury of the True Dharma Eye: Dōgen's Shōbōgenzō*, vol. 8.

13. Heine, *Dogen*, 12-13. *The Record of Kenzei* was published in 1472 by the fourteenth abbot of Eiheiji, Kenzei.

14. Heine, *Dogen*, 48.

15. Heine, *Dogen*, 48.

16. Thomas P. Kasulis engages in a lively discussion of the genesis, meaning, and result of this question in Dōgen's teaching. See "Dōgen (1200-1253) Nothing Doing; Everything Counts," chap. 6, in *Engaging Japanese Philosophy: A Short History* (Honolulu: University of Hawai'i Press, 2018), 213-18.

17. Taigen Daniel Leighton and Shohaku Okumura, trans., *Dōgen's Pure Standards for the Zen Community: A Translation of Eihei Shingi* (Albany: State University of New York Press, 1996), 41-42. Brackets added by this author. One of my favorite commentaries on Dōgen's "Tenzo Kyokun" is Dōgen and Kōshō Uchiyama, *How to Cook Your Life: From the Zen Kitchen to Enlightenment* (Boulder, CO: Shambhala Publications, 2005). Kōshō Uchiyama's insights are deep and at times funny and surprising.

18. Kasulis, "Dōgen (1200-1253) Nothing Doing; Everything Counts," 213.

19. In other schools of Buddhism, such as the Theravada, the goal is to stop rebirth and to enter a state referred to as nirvana separate from rebirth. But this is not the goal of the bodhisattva practice of Mahayana Buddhism. Specifically, Dōgen locates nirvana as part of our life, not some state outside this life. He wrote in SBGZ "Shōji" (Birth and Death), "Just understand that birth-and-death itself is nirvana, and you will neither hate one as being birth-and-death, nor cherish the other as being nirvana." Norman Waddell and Masao Abe, trans., *The Heart of Dōgen's Shōbōgenzō* (Albany: State University of New York Press, 2002), 106.

20. Leighton and Okumura, *Dōgen's Pure Standards for the Zen Community*, 42.

21. *Shushō* (修證), "practice-realization" (also translated as "practice-verification"), is discussed in appendix 2, "Practice-Enlightenment or Practice Verification?" An easy way to understand this word is that we do not practice to attain realization; realization is expressed through practice. Or we verify the veracity of realizing the Dharma through the practice of the Dharma.

22. Leighton and Okumura, *Dōgen's Pure Standards for the Zen Community*, 43. Bracketed sections (added by this author) are from note 35 (p. 54). In

note 36 (p. 55), one-flavor Zen is defined as a "genuine practice free from attachment to, or desire for, fame and profit."

23. Waddell and Abe, *Heart of Dōgen's Shōbōgenzō*, 5.

24. Gudo Nishijima and Chodo Cross, trans., *Master Dogen's Shobogenzo* (London: Windbell Publications, 1994), bk. 2, 75.

25. Nishijima and Cross, *Master Dogen's Shobogenzo*, bk. 2, 75.

26. "Fukanzazengi" is found in *Eihei Kōroku* (*Dōgen's Extensive Record*), a compilation of Dōgen's sermons and other teachings by his disciples. See Taigen Dan Leighton and Shohaku Okumura, *Dōgen's Extensive Record: A Translation of the Eihei Kōroku* (Somerville, MA: Wisdom Publications, 2004), 532. Dōgen included two important fascicles on zazen in Shōbōgenzō: "Zazengi" (Principles of Seated Meditation) and "Zazen Shin" (Lancet of Seated Meditation).

27. My comments are in part a response to the American Sōtō Zen priests and practitioners who believe Dōgen's teachings were only focused on seated meditation. Dōgen's instruction encompasses far more than formal training. If our understanding of zazen includes all aspects of our life, then, yes, Dōgen's primary teaching can be understood as the practice of "just sitting." To "just sit" in the middle of our lives is the practice of fully responding to the presencing moment. Dōgen continued to write about the importance of formal zazen throughout his life. Three years before his death he wrote, "The essence of patch-robed monks' study of the way is meditation." Leighton and Okumura, *Dōgen's Extensive Record*, Dharma Hall Discourse 175, 329.

28. Throughout this commentary I have most often commented on *shushō* as "practice-realization" because that is Okamura's translation in "Genjōkōan." Nevertheless, it can be useful to interchange the two translations as a way to explore nuances in Dōgen's teachings. For an essay-length consideration of translations of this crucial term, please consult appendix 1, "Dharma Position."

29. Waddell and Abe, *Heart of Dōgen's Shōbōgenzō*, 53.

30. Waddell and Abe, *Heart of Dōgen's Shōbōgenzō*, 106.

31. Kazuaki Tanahashi, ed., *Moon in a Dewdrop: Writings of Zen Master Dōgen* (San Francisco: North Point Press, 1985), 163–64.

32. Waddell and Abe, *Heart of Dōgen's Shōbōgenzō*, 51.

33. Waddell and Abe, *Heart of Dōgen's Shōbōgenzō*, 54.

34. Waddell and Abe, *Heart of Dōgen's Shōbōgenzō*, 54. In this translation, Waddell and Abe translate the pronoun as "we" and "our." But Japanese does not specify pronouns. For this reason, we can understand this passage to mean both self and other. The Buddhist scholar Hee-Jin Kim translates this passage as "The deva kings and hosts of heaven—now manifested on

the right now on the left—are the 'existence-time' which, even now, they continue to exert through their utmost efforts. . . . Unless it is a passage of its own utmost efforts at this moment, not a dharma, not a thing, can ever realize itself or pass through itself. This we should study." Hee-Jin Kim, trans., *Flowers of Emptiness: Selections from Dōgen's Shōbōgenzō*, Studies in Asian Thought and Religion vol. 2 (Lewiston, NY: Edwin Mellen Press, 1985), 228. Bracketed words added by this author.

35. Kōshō Uchiyama and Thomas Wright, trans., *Refining Your Life: From the Zen Kitchen to Enlightenment* (New York: Weatherhill Press, 1983), 7–8.

36. Hee-Jin Kim, *Dōgen on Meditation and Thinking: A Reflection on His View of Zen* (Albany: State University of New York Press, 2007), 84.

37. Kim, *Dōgen on Meditation and Thinking*, 84.

38. *Datsuraku* (脱落), "dropped off," is also translated as "sloughing off." It refers to a state of mind in which one is functioning from a place of knowing the emptiness or inter-being of all dharmas while at the same time engaging in action or response. Dropping off body and mind of self and other is to engage in the skillful means of inclusivity. This intimate inter-being with self and other is "to forget the self." It does not mean one enters a meditative jhana state or that one literally disappears or loses consciousness of one's surroundings.

39. Bielefeldt, *Treasury of the True Dharma Eye*, vol. 5, [63:17]. Brackets added by this author.

40. Waddell and Abe, *Heart of Dōgen's Shōbōgenzō*, 50.

41. Waddell and Abe, *Heart of Dōgen's Shōbōgenzō*, 48–49.

42. See John Daido Loori, *The True Dharma Eye: Zen Master Dōgen's 300 Kōans* (Boston: Shambhala Publications, 2009); and Gudo Nishijima and Chodo Cross, trans., "Kannon," *Master Dōgen's Shōbōgenzō*, bk. 2 (London: Windbell Publications, 1996), 211.

43. Waddell and Abe, *Heart of Dōgen's Shōbōgenzō*, 57.

44. Bielefeldt, *Treasury of the True Dharma Eye*, vol. 2, [20:16], n56.

45. For more on this section of "Uji," see Shinshu Roberts, *Being-Time: A Practitioner's Guide to Dōgen's Shōbōgenzō Uji* (Somerville, MA: Wisdom Publications, 2018), 210–15.

1. "Genjōkōan": The Realized Koan

1. Appendix 4, "*Okikigakishō* 'Genjōkōan,'" "About the Title," Senne.

2. Appendix 4, "*Okikigakishō* 'Genjōkōan,'" "About the Title." For an in-depth discussion of each character's meaning, see Shohaku Okumura, *Realizing Genjokoan: The Key to Dogen's Shobogenzo* (Boston: Wisdom Publications, 2010), 13–17.

3. This is a description from SBGZ "Uji." Dōgen wrote, "The sharp, vital quick of dharmas dwelling in their dharma positions is itself being-time. You must not by our own maneuvering make it into nothingness; you must not force it into being." The word Dōgen used for "sharp, vital quick" is *kappatsupatchi*, an onomatopoeic word for a fish leaping free of and then splashing down into water. We don't want to (or need to) force our practice or ideas about realization into a particular shape based upon those ideas. Realization is a response grounded in an understanding in concert with the totality of our life as a particular situation. See Norman Waddell and Masao Abe, trans., *The Heart of Dōgen's Shōbōgenzō* (Albany: State University of New York Press, 2002), 53n32.

4. Okumura, *Realizing Genjokoan*, 13–14.

5. Waddell and Abe, *Heart of Dōgen's Shōbōgenzō*, 39.

6. Appendix 4, "*Okikigakishō* 'Genjōkōan,'" "About the Title," Senne.

7. These are the three Buddhist marks of existence (Skt. *lakṣaṇa*; J. *sō*). These marks define the qualities of all conditioned things: (1) impermanence, (2) a state of dissatisfaction, and (3) no-inherently-existing-self. A fourth mark, nirvana, is sometimes added. See Robert Buswell Jr. and Donald Lopez Jr., s.v. "*lakṣaṇa*," *The Princeton Dictionary of Buddhism* (Princeton, NJ: Princeton University Press, 2014), 463.

8. The character for *an* (按) specifically refers to "keeping one's lot"; see Okumura, *Realizing Genjokoan*, 15. "One's own original lot" (original lot, *honbun*, 本分), another Japanese phrase, refers to one's buddha-nature, or true nature. As you can see *an* in *kōan* is a different character then used in *honbun*. *Hon* (本) means "true" or "original." *Honbun* is used in "Genjōkōan" in the line, "When the Dharma is correctly transmitted to the self, one is immediately an original [*honbun*] person." See Carl Bielefeldt, ed., *Treasury of the True Dharma Eye: Dōgen's Shōbōgenzō; An Annotated Translation by the Sōtō Zen Text Project* (Tokyo: Sōtōshu Shumachō, 2023), vol. 1, [1:8].

9. *Jū hōi* (法位), "abiding in a dharma position." See appendix 1 for an in-depth discussion of the meaning of this phrase.

10. Appendix 4, "*Okikigakishō* 'Genjōkōan,'" "About the Title," Senne, bullet points 5 and 6.

11. Expressing the nondual aspect of life should never be understood to be nihilistic. Referring to nonduality or emptiness is a way to say that all things are inter-being and interconnected. If everything lacks inherent existence, then all things must be expressing as part of a unified process. Dōgen tends to emphasize the nondual inter-being aspect of reality. But we should never forget, nor does he, that this is just another way to discuss connection, community with all beings, and compassion. We could say the Buddhist

precepts are based in emptiness because if we are aware of the intrinsic value of each thing or person, and we are aware of each being's connection with others, then we would not, for example, steal from another. It would not occur to us. Furthermore, we would understand the devastation of the harm we may be causing through our actions and empathize with those who might suffer as a result.

12. Appendix 4, "*Okikigakishō* 'Genjōkōan,'" "About the Title," Senne, bullet point 6.

13. Okumura, *Realizing Genjokoan*, 17.

14. Okumura, *Realizing Genjokoan*, 18.

15. Bielefeldt, *Treasury of the True Dharma Eye*, vol. 3, [34:25]. Brackets in the original quotation.

16. Appendix 4, "*Okikigakishō* 'Genjōkōan,'" "About the Title," Senne, bullet point 3. Brackets in original quotation.

17. The idea of realization as metaphorically crossing from one shore to another has several interpretations depending upon the school of Buddhism in question.

2. Buddhist Study, Reality, and Human Experience

1. *Shōji* (生死) can be translated as either life or birth. Okumura has used both words in his translation of the opening lines.

2. When Dōgen went to China, he left Japan from the island of Kyushu.

3. "Genjōkōan," written in 1233 (continuously edited until 1255), is the first fascicle of Dōgen's compilation of both the sixty- and seventy-five-fascicle Shōbōgenzō. See Steven Heine, ed., *Dōgen: Textural and Historical Studies* (New York: Oxford University Press, 2021), 25.

4. The first four sentences of "Genjōkōan" are rather like a Rorschach test—there are many interpretations. The most obvious and common understanding is that the first sentence refers to relative practice and the second to nondualistic practice. In *Realizing Genjokoan*, Shohaku Okumura makes a connection between these opening sentences and early Buddhist teachings, Mahayana teachings, and Dōgen's understanding. See Shohaku Okumura, *Realizing Genjokoan: The Key to Dogen's Shobogenzo* (Boston: Wisdom Publications, 2010), 24. For the Western Zen master Albert Low, this first sentence identifies a delusory view. It is a delusion to think that delusion, realization, practice, etc., are unique states. See Albert Low, *Genjokoan by Zen Master Dogen* (self-pub., 2014), 21-22. Others have connected these lines to Tendai teachings. These are just three examples.

5. See Carl Bielefeldt, ed., *Treasury of the True Dharma Eye: Dōgen's Shōbōgenzō; An Annotated Translation by the Sōtō Zen Text Project* (Tokyo:

Sōtōshu Shumachō, 2023), vol. 1, [1:1], n1: "'At times when the dharmas are the buddha dharma' (*shohō no buppō naru jisetsu* . . .) Probably to be taken in the sense 'when everything is seen in terms of the Buddhist teachings.'" Japanese characters omitted.

6. Norman Waddell and Masao Abe, trans., *The Heart of Dōgen's Shōbōgenzō* (Albany: State University of New York Press, 2002), 106.

7. "The sixteen-foot golden Buddha-body is time; because it is time, it has time's glorious golden radiance. You must learn to see this glorious radiance in the twelve hours of your day. The [demonic asura with] three heads and eight arms is time; because it is time, it can be in no way different from the twelve hours of your day." Waddell and Abe, *Heart of Dōgen's Shōbōgenzō*, 48. In Dōgen's time, a day was divided into twelve periods, instead of the Western twenty-four hours. For this reason, when he writes "the twelve hours of your day" we should understand this to mean the twenty-four hours of our day.

8. Going beyond (*chōshutsu*, 跳出) means to jump beyond or to escape or transcend. See Bielefeldt, *Treasury of the True Dharma Eye*, vol. 1, [04:15], n63.

9. "Complicated"—*kattō* in Japanese—specifically refers to having problems or complications that stem from relationships. *Kattō* 葛藤 usually refers to vines that are intertwined, often the kudzu vine and wisteria.

10. Gudo Nishijima and Chodo Cross, trans., *Master Dogen's Shobogenzo* (London: Windbell Publications, 1997), bk. 3, 35–36.

11. "Genjo Koan, 1–3: Sesshin Lecture: Genjo-Koan, Paragraphs 1–3, Sunday Morning, March 13, 1966, Lecture A, Sokoji, San Francisco," ShunryuSuzuki .com. I have edited this passage by deleting repeated passages and adding linking words.

3. What Does Realization Look Like?

1. These are a few of the practices that Shantideva presents in his book. There are many English translations of this text. For example, see Shantideva, *The Way of the Bodhisattva: (Bodhicaryavatara)*, rev. ed., trans. Padmakara Translation Group (Boulder, CO: Shambhala Publications, 2006).

2. This is the definition of *shinjin-datusuraku* (casting off or dropping body and mind). The religion scholar Masao Abe wrote in his commentary on this section, "The self must be emptied, for all things to advance and confirm the self. Accordingly, 'to forget one's self' is critical. To forget one's self is nothing other than body-mind casting off. And when body-mind are cast off, the world and history are also cast off." Masao Abe, *A Study of Dōgen: His Philosophy and Religion* (Albany: State University of New York Press,

1992), 33. One is able to completely respond to the totality of an arising situation without the baggage of history or self-centered clinging.

3. Norman Waddell and Masao Abe, trans., *The Heart of Dōgen's Shōbōgenzō* (Albany: State University of New York Press, 2002), 40n2. A more recent translation and commentary on *Gakudō Yōjinshū* is Gien Inoue, *A Blueprint of Enlightenment: A Contemporary Commentary on Dōgen Zenji's Gakudō Yōjinshū Guidelines for Studying the Way* (Olympia, WA: Temple Ground Press, 2020). *Gakudō Yōjinshū* was written in 1234, and Dōgen wrote the first draft of "Genjōkōan" in 1233. *Points to Watch in Practicing the Way* is a stand-alone text, not part of Dōgen's Shōbōgenzō or *Eihei Kōroku*.

4. Gudo Nishijima and Chodo Cross, trans., *Master Dogen's Shobogenzo* (London: Windbell Publications, 1994), bk. 3, 10.

5. Appendix 4, "*Okikigakishō* 'Genjōkōan,'" sec. 4, Kyōgō, opening paragraph.

6. The Japanese for this sentence is *issai shujō, shitsu u busshō* (一切衆生、悉有佛性). Here, as in "Genjōkōan," "living beings" is *shujō* (衆生). My source is Carl Bielefeldt, ed., *Treasury of the True Dharma Eye: Dōgen's Shōbōgenzō; An Annotated Translation by the Sōtō Zen Text Project* (Tokyo: Sōtōshu Shumachō, 2023), vol. 1, [3:1], n1. Italicized font indicates that Dōgen wrote this section in Chinese, possibly indicating that he is quoting a Chinese source.

7. Waddell and Abe, *Heart of Dōgen's Shōbōgenzō*, 60–61.

8. Waddell and Abe, *Heart of Dōgen's Shōbōgenzō*, 106.

9. Waddell and Abe, *Heart of Dōgen's Shōbōgenzō*, 106.

10. "Delusion within delusion" (*meichū yūmei*, 迷中又迷) is defined by Dōgen in SBGZ "Keisei Sanshoku" (Sound of the Stream, Form of the Mountain) as a person who does not see the "real thing." He wrote, "Because it is rare for them to seek the real thing, people today, though their bodies lack practice and their minds lack insight, when they get praise from another, seem to look for the people who will tell them that their practice and understanding are in accord. Delusion within delusion—this is it." Bielefeldt, *Treasury of the True Dharma Eye*, vol. 2, [25:19].

11. In a conversation with Paula Arai, she points out that this sentence, "Furthermore, there are those who attain realization beyond realization and those who are deluded within delusion," is ambiguous in Japanese. In Japanese there is no subject or pronoun. Therefore, this could translate this sentence as "Realizing beyond realization is, delusion throughout delusion is," which is just stating that there is delusion throughout delusion and there is realizing beyond realization. Paula Arai, personal communication, April 2020.

12. Calligrapher, Zen teacher, and translator Kazuaki Tanahashi, ed., *Treasury of the True Dharma Eye: Zen Master Dogen's Shobo Genzo* (Boston: Shambhala, 2010), vol. 1, 29.

13. Mel Weitsman, Shohaku Okumura, and Michael Wenger, trans., "Commentary by Nishiari Bokusan," in *Dōgen's Genjo Koan: Three Commentaries* (Berkeley, CA: Counterpoint, 2011), 47.
14. Appendix 4, "*Okikigakishō* 'Genjōkōan,'" sec. 5, Kyōgō.
15. Another translation using "verify" rather than "carry out practice-enlightenment": "Bringing the self to practice and verify the myriad dharmas represent delusion; the myriad dharmas proceeding to practice and verify the self is awakening." Bielefeldt, *Treasury of the True Dharma Eye*, vol. 1, [1:4].
16. Appendix 4, "*Okikigakishō* 'Genjōkōan,'" sec. 6, Kyōgō.
17. Appendix 4, "*Okikigakishō* 'Genjōkōan,'" sec. 6, Kyōgō.
18. See appendix 2, "Practice-Enlightenment or Practice-Verification?"

4. Perceptions and Verification

1. Dai-I Daien, C. Dayuan of Dawei, a.k.a Weishan Lingyou Dayuan (771–853).
2. This seems to be a variant spelling used by Nishijima and Cross for SBGZ "Keisei Sanshoku."
3. Dates are unknown. C. Lingyun Zhiqin. Brackets added by this author for clarity.
4. This is from a Chinese story about a man who, while sailing in a boat, dropped his sword into the water. He marks the side of the moving boat to indicate where he had lost the sword, with the intention of retrieving it again later.
5. SBGZ "Keisei Sanshiki" (Sound of the Stream, Form of the Mountain) in Gudo Nishijima and Chodo Cross, trans., *Master Dogen's Shobogenzo* (London: Windbell Publications, 1997), bk. 1, 89. The koan related to this story can also be found in Dōgen's *Shinji Shōbōgenzō*, a collection of three hundred koans. There are two English translations that I am aware of: Gudo Nishijima, *Master Dogen's Shinji Shobogenzo: 301 Kōan Stories* (Guildford, UK: Windbell Publications, 2003), bk. 2, 205, case 55; and John Daido Loori, *The True Dharma Eye: Zen Master Dōgen's Three Hundred Kōans* (Boston: Shambhala Publications, 2005), 207, case 155.
6. Kyōgen Chikan, C. Xiangyan Zhixian, d. 898.
7. SBGZ "Keisei Sanshiki" (Sound of the Stream, Form of the Mountain), in Nishijima and Cross, *Master Dogen's Shobogenzo*, bk. 1, 88. Also see Gudo Nishijima, *Master Dogen's Shinji Shobogenzo: 301 Kōan Stories* (Guildford, UK: Windbell Publications, 2003), bk. 1, 205, case 17; and Loori, *True Dharma Eye*, 23, case 17. Italics in original quotation.
8. Hee-Jin Kim, trans., *Eihei Dōgen: Mystical Realist* (Boston: Wisdom Publications, 2004), 105.

9. Hee-Jin Kim, trans., *Flowers of Emptiness: Selections from Dōgen's Shōbō-genzō*, Studies in Asian Thought and Religion, vol. 2 (Lewiston, NY: Edwin Mellen Press, 1985), 57n7. This footnote continues, "The 'principle of simultaneous establishment of concealment and disclosure,' one of the 'ten mysteries' (*jūgen*; *shih-hsüan*) of Hua-yen Buddhism. In this connection consider the following illustration by Ch'eng-kuan (738–840), the fourth ancestor of the Hua-yen sect in China: 'On the eighth day of the [lunar] month, half of the moon is bright and the other half dark; the very appearance of the bright part, [the disclosed] affirms but does not negate the existence of the hidden part. Likewise, the manifestation of something always implies the existence of the unmanifested or concealed part of the same thing. At the moment when the bright part of the moon is disclosed, the dark part also "secretly" establishes itself.'" Quoted from Garma C. C. Chang, *The Buddhist Teaching of Totality: The Philosophy of Hwa Yen Buddhism* (University Park: Pennsylvania State University Press, 1977), 162.

10. Appendix 4, "*Okikigakishō* 'Genjōkōan,'" sec. 7, Senne.

11. Appendix 4, "*Okikigakishō* 'Genjōkōan,'" sec. 7, Kyōgō.

12. These ideas are expressed in the Huayan as Indra's Net. Fazang's "The Golden Lion" describes Indra's Net as follows:

> The infinite interpenetration [of all things], the unimpeded identity [of all things], . . . [is] shown in the symbol of the net of Indra. When these concepts are manifested [in the mind of the Bodhisattva], then when one of the many obstacles is overcome, all are overcome, and one acquires the destruction of [moral and intellectual faults]. . . . In practicing the virtues, when one is perfected, all are perfected, and with regard to reality, when one [part] is revealed, everything is revealed. All things are endowed with universality and particularity, beginning and end are the same, and when one first arouses the aspiration for enlightenment [bodhicittotpāda], one also becomes perfectly enlightened. . . . The goal is inherent in causal practice.

Francis H. Cook, *Hua-Yen Buddhism: The Jewel Net of Indra* (University Park: Pennsylvania State University Press, 1977), 77. Brackets in original text.

13. This translation is from Hee-Jin Kim, *Eihei Dōgen: Mystical Realist* (Boston: Wisdom Publications, 2004), 66. A similar translation can also be found in Francis H. Cook, *Sounds of Valley Streams: Enlightenment in Dōgen's Zen* (Albany: State University of New York Press, 1989), 77–78.

5. Dropping Body and Mind

1. "Getting rid of the self" is *datsuraku* (脱落), the same characters used in *shinjin-datsuraku* (身心脱落), "to drop off body-mind." *Shinjin-datsuraku*

refers to experiencing liberation through dropping off one's self-sided views. This doesn't mean eradicating the self. A fuller explanation of this term is offered later in this chapter.

2. Nishijima and Cross translate *shōkai* (證契) as "accordance." *Shōkai* refers to verification, or in accordance with teachings of the Buddha. Gudo Nishijima and Chodo Cross, trans., *Master Dogen's Shobogenzo* (London: Windbell Publications, 1994), bk. 4, 33n16.

3. Nishijima and Cross, *Master Dogen's Shobogenzo*, bk. 4, 33, 35.

4. Francis H. Cook, trans., *Sounds of Valley Streams: Enlightenment in Dōgen's Zen* (Albany: State University of New York Press, 1989), 77–78. Yunju Daoying (d. 902).

5. In his book *Realizing Genjokoan*, Shohaku Okumura explains the meaning of the Japanese word for study: *narau* (習). *Narau* means to become "accustomed," "familiar," "used to," or "intimate with" something—in this case, the Buddha Way. Okumura separates the upper and lower parts of the character that make up this word; one refers to the wings of a bird, and the other to the self. He comments, "So *narau* means to study something in the way a baby bird 'studies' flying with its parents." In this way, the activity of study becomes about imitation and a kind of innate ability to learn the how of this activity as well as intellectual understanding. See Shohaku Okumura, *Realizing Genjokoan: The Key to Dogen's Shobogenzo* (Boston: Wisdom Publications, 2010), 76.

6. Okumura, *Realizing Genjokoan*, 76–77.

7. Norman Waddell and Masao Abe, trans., *The Heart of Dōgen's Shōbōgenzō* (Albany: State University of New York Press, 2002), 57.

8. Appendix 4, "*Okikigakishō* 'Genjōkōan,'" sec. 8, Senne.

9. San Francisco Zen Center, *Shōbōgenzō Genjō Kōan: An Analytic Study* (San Francisco: San Francisco Zen Center, n.d.), 8.

10. See appendix 2, "Practice-Enlightenment or Practice-Verification?"

11. Nishijima and Cross, *Master Dogen's Shobogenzo*, bk. 4, 217.

12. Nishijima and Cross, *Master Dogen's Shobogenzo*, bk. 4, 218.

13. Taigen Dan Leighton and Shohaku Okumura, trans., *Dōgen's Extensive Record: A Translation of the Eihei Kōroku* (Boston: Wisdom Publications 2004), 386.

14. Both the four formless absorptions (P. ārūpya-samāpatti) and the four dhyana are attainment stages of meditative practice that result in "a shift in attention from the sensory world to another, subtler realm. Essentially they are a training in increasing introversion, achieved by progressively diminishing the impact of external stimuli." Edward Conze, *Buddhist Thought in India* (Ann Arbor: University of Michigan Press, 1987), 53.

15. Taigen Dan Leighton and Shohaku Okumura, trans., "Removing Poison Arrows in Vigorous Sitting," *Dōgen's Extensive Record: A Translation of the Eihei Kōroku* (Boston: Wisdom Publications, 2004), 389.

16. Taigen Dan Leighton and Shohaku Okumura, trans., "The Practice of Thusness," *Dōgen's Extensive Record: A Translation of the Eihei Kōroku* (Boston: Wisdom Publications, 2004), 91.

17. Taigen Dan Leighton and Shohaku Okumura, trans., "A Breakfast for Dropping Off Body and Mind," *Dōgen's Extensive Record: A Translation of the Eihei Kōroku* (Boston: Wisdom Publications, 2004), 285.

18. Taigen Dan Leighton and Shohaku Okumura, trans., "The Practice of Thusness," *Dōgen's Extensive Record: A Translation of the Eihei Kōroku* (Boston: Wisdom Publications 2004), 91n102.

19. Leighton and Okumura, "The Practice of Thusness," 91.

20. Appendix 4, "*Okikigakishō* 'Genjōkōan,'" sec. 8, Kyōgō.

21. Nishijima and Cross, *Master Dogen's Shobogenzo*, bk. 4, 213.

22. Nishijima and Cross, *Master Dogen's Shobogenzo*, bk. 4, 213.

23. Appendix 4, "*Okikigakishō* 'Genjōkōan,'" sec. 8, Senne.

24. Gudo Nishijima and Chodo Cross, trans., *Master Dogen's Shobogenzo* (London: Windbell Publications, 1994), bk. 1, 97.

25. Carl Bielefeldt, ed., *Treasury of the True Dharma Eye: Dōgen's Shōbōgenzō; An Annotated Translation by the Sōtō Zen Text Project* (Tokyo: Sōtōshu Shumachō, 2023), vol. 3, [31:3].

26. Bielefeldt, *Treasury of the True Dharma Eye*, vol. 3, [31:3].

6. Looking for the Path of the Authentic Self

1. The character 人 can be understood as *nin* or *hito*. *Nin* is a technical term in Buddhism, meaning in Sanskrit *manuṣya*, *pudgala*, or *puruṣa*. These Sanskrit terms respectively have to do with rebirth, person as the five aggregates, and person as the product of rebirth through karmic causes and subject to impermanence. See Robert Buswell Jr., and Donald Lopez Jr., *The Princeton Dictionary of Buddhism* (Princeton, NJ: Princeton University Press, 2014). *Hito* simply refers to a person or people in general: one who is involved in day-to-day affairs. See T. P. Kasulis, *Zen Action, Zen Person* (Honolulu: University of Hawai'i Press, 1985), 5. The Japanese speakers I consulted about whether one could put any emphasis on Dōgen's use of *nin* as a technical term felt that would be stretching the meaning of this sentence. Nevertheless, I wonder if Dōgen's use of *nin* is in counterpose to *honbun nin* (original person) used in the second sentence.

2. Carl Bielefeldt, ed., *Treasury of the True Dharma Eye: Dōgen's Shōbōgenzō;*

An Annotated Translation by the Sōtō Zen Text Project (Tokyo: Sōtōshu Shumachō, 2023), vol. 1, [1:9].

3. William Bodiford and T. Griffith Foulk, contribs., *Treasury of the True Dharma Eye: Dōgen's Shōbōgenzō; An Annotated Translation by the Sōtō Zen Text Project* (Tokyo: Sōtōshu Shumachō, 2023), vol. 8, 370. *Honbun* is defined as "buddha-nature."

4. Appendix 4, "*Okikigakishō* 'Genjōkōan,'" sec. 9, Kyōgō.

5. Norman Waddell and Masao Abe, trans., *The Heart of Dōgen's Shōbōgenzō* (Albany: State University of New York Press, 2002), 52.

6. Appendix 4, "*Okikigakishō* 'Genjōkōan,'" sec. 9, Senne.

7. Bielefeldt, *Treasury of the True Dharma Eye*, vol. 4, [51:10], n24 indicates that the characters for "realization" are the same as *genjō* in *genjōkōan*.

8. Bielefeldt, *Treasury of the True Dharma Eye*, vol. 4, [51:10].

9. Gudo Nishijima and Chodo Cross, trans., *Master Dogen's Shobogenzo* (London: Windbell Publications, 1994), bk. 2, 11.

10. Hee-Jin Kim, trans., *Flowers of Emptiness: Selections from Dōgen's Shōbōgenzō*, Studies in Asian Thought and Religion, vol. 2 (Lewiston, NY: Edwin Mellen Press, 1985), 71.

11. Shohaku Okumura, trans., *Shōbōgenzō-zuimonki: Sayings of Eihei Dōgen Zenji Recorded by Loun Ejō* (Tokyo, Japan: Soto-shu Shumucho, 2004), 139–40.

7. Riding in a Boat

1. In "Bendōwa" (On the Endeavor of the Way), Dōgen strongly refutes the Senika theory, which is the belief that we have some kind of eternal soul that continues through rebirths. See "Bendōwa," question 10. There are various translations of this text in English. One such translation is Gudo Nishijima and Chodo Cross, trans., *Master Dogen's Shobogenzo* (London: Windbell Publications, 1994), bk. 1, 13–14. The question begins, "[Someone] asks, 'It has been said that we should not regret our life and death, for there is a very quick way to get free of life and death. That is, to know the truth that the mental essence is eternal.'" Dōgen's source for this theory may be the Mahaparinirvana Sutra, chapter 39, in which the Buddha debunks this theory.

2. Appendix 4, "*Okikigakishō* 'Genjōkōan,'" sec. 10, Senne.

3. In SBGZ "Sangai-yuishin" (The Triple World Is Only the Mind—or Tanahashi's translation, Three Worlds Are Inseparable from Mind), Dōgen defines the Triple World as "the whole world is the triple world. Because the triple world is the whole Universe, here and now is the past, present,

and future. The reality of past, present, and future does not obstruct the here and now. The reality of the here and now blocks off past, present, and future," (Gudo Nishijima and Chodo Cross, trans., *Master Dogen's Shobogenzo* [London: Windbell, Publications, 1997], bk. 3, 45), and later Dōgen defines the mind as "The coming and going of birth and death are mind. Year, month, day, and hour are mind. Dream, phantom, and empty flower are mind. Water, foam, splash, and flame are mind. Spring flowers and autumn moon are mind. All things that arise and fall are mind," (Kazuaki Tanahashi, ed., *Treasury of the True Dharma Eye: Zen Master Dogen's Shobo Genzo*, [Boston: Shambhala Publications, 2010], vol. 2, 490). I understand this to mean that the "mind" is both a particular time, place, entity (self), as well as all time(s), being(s) as now's presencing. What Dōgen is *not* saying is that all things are fabrications of our minds. Forms are real, the mind is real, the self is real. See for example, SBGZ "Sesshin Sesshō" (Speaking of Mind, Speaking of Essence) and "Sangai-yuishin" (Three Worlds Are Inseparable from Mind). "Mind" for Dōgen is both a universal mind and the minds of particular dharmas which are simultaneous functioning or continuously practicing together.

4. Appendix 4, "*Okikigakishō* 'Genjōkōan,'" sec. 10, Senne.
5. Tanahashi, *Treasury of the True Dharma Eye*, 490. This author added bracketed [universal].
6. Appendix 4, "*Okikigakishō* 'Genjōkōan,'" sec. 10, Senne.

8. What Do I Experience as a Particular Self?

1. I discuss the full ramifications of dharma position and practice in appendix 1 of this book. Also see my book-length commentary on SBGZ "Uji": Shinshu Roberts, *Being-Time: A Practitioner's Guide to Dōgen's Shōbōgenzō* (Somerville, MA: Wisdom Publications, 2018). Throughout my commentary on *Being-Time* I discuss the importance and full implications of the meaning and function of dharma position(s). Two other fascicles in Shōbōgenzō that parallel this section of "Genjōkōan" are "Shōji" (Birth and Death) and "Zenki" (The Whole Works).
2. Norman Waddell and Masao Abe, trans., *The Heart of Dōgen's Shōbōgenzō* (Albany: State University of New York Press, 2002), 52.
3. Waddell and Abe, *Heart of Dōgen's Shōbōgenzō*, 53.
4. Appendix 4, "*Okikigakishō* 'Genjōkōan,'" sec. 11, Kyōgō. "Life is a manifestation of total-function; death is a manifestation of total-function" is a quote from SBGZ "Zenki" (The Whole Works), attributed to Yuanwu Kequin (1063–1135).

9. Who Dies, Who Lives?

1. In "Shōji" (Birth and Death), Dōgen offers a passage almost identical to this passage in "Genjōkōan":

> It is a mistake to think you pass from life into death. Being one stage of time, life is possessed of before and after. For this reason, the Buddha Dharma teaches that life itself is as such unborn. Being one stage of time as well, cessation of life also is possessed of before and after. Thus it is said that extinction itself is undying. When there is life, there is nothing at all apart from life. When there is death, there is nothing at all apart from death. Therefore, when life comes you should just give yourself to life; when death comes, you should give yourself to death. You should neither desire them, nor hate them.

Norman Waddell and Masao Abe, trans., *The Heart of Dōgen's Shōbōgenzō* (Albany: State University of New York Press, 2002), 106.

2. Appendix 4, "*Okikigakishō* 'Genjōkōan,'" sec. 11, Kyōgō. *Danken* (断見) (Skt. *uccheda-dṛṣṭi*) is a term that refers to a teaching that death is the final end of a person without any kind of continuation at all, including rebirth. Richard Gard and Stanley Weinstein, eds., s.v. "Danken," *Japanese-English Buddhist Dictionary*, rev. ed. (Tokyo: Daitō Shuppansha, 1991), 48.

3. What is reborn lifetime to lifetime is like the shorter strands that make up a rope. Since the strands are woven together, they have continuity, but the beginning of the rope is not the same strands at the end of the rope. Each strand is like a lifetime. It affects the strands on each side of it, but over time the lifetimes morph into completely different causal conditions. Consequently there is no permanent rebirth of the current skandhas. Briefly, skandhas refer to an aggregate of five aspects that, taken together, make up a being (persons or other creatures subject to rebirth) in the form realm. They are: form, sensation, perception, mental formations, and consciousness.

4. In Mahayana Buddhism, the goal of a bodhisattva's practice is not to exit the wheel of birth and death. The desire of the bodhisattva to alleviate the suffering of others (a vow to save all beings) pulls them into the next rebirth. A bodhisattva continues rebirth after rebirth with this aim in mind. Therefore, it is not necessarily the goal of Mahayana practice to cease rebirths. In *An Introduction to Buddhism: Teaching, History, and Practices* (Cambridge: Cambridge University Press, 1990), Peter Harvey discusses the stages of the bodhisattva path. Harvey comments that in the sixth stage, a bodhisattva "*could* leave the round of rebirth and enter nirvāna, but his Mahāyāna 'great compassion' prevents him for doing so" (123). It is perhaps important to

add here that there are many schools of Mahayana Buddhism with various versions of the bodhisattva's goal in practice.

5. Appendix 4, "*Okikigakishō* 'Genjōkōan,'" sec. 11, Senne.

6. Carl Bielefeldt, ed., *Treasury of the True Dharma Eye: Dōgen's Shōbōgenzo; An Annotated Translation by the Sōtō Zen Text Project* (Tokyo: Sōtōshu Shumachō, 2023), vol. 2, [22:6].

7. Also known as Dōgo Enchi (C. Daowu Yuanzhi, 769–835) and Zengen Chūkō (C. Jianyuan Zhongxing, n.d.). Dōgo was Daowu's disciple.

8. John Daido Loori, *The True Dharma Eye: Zen Master Dōgen's Three Hundred Kōans* (Boston: Shambhala Publications, 2005), case 298, 394. Also found as case 55 of the *Blue Cliff Record* and Randolph Whitfield, *Records of the Transmission of Lamp* (pub. by author, 2017), vol. 4 (C. *Jingde Chunadeng Lu*), 103.

9. Dōgen does not refute the Buddhist doctrine of rebirth. It is mentioned in Shōbōgenzō. But since the focus of practice is to locate ourselves fully in our present circumstances, focusing on our future rebirth is not productive. To dwell on something that has not happened pulls us away from the immediacy of allowing myriad things to meet us, as Dōgen said earlier in the text. Furthermore, in SBGZ "Shōji" (Birth and Death), Dōgen writes, "Birth-and-death itself is nirvana." From this perspective, one need not exit samsara to find nirvana.

10. When Dōgen wrote "We don't think that winter becomes spring, and we don't say that spring becomes summer," he may also be thinking about how we perceive the passage of winter to spring to summer. He addresses this concept in SBGZ "Uji" (Being-Time): "You should learn in practice that passing takes place without anything extraneous. For example, springtime's passage invariably passes through spring The passage is not spring, but as it is the springtime's passage, passing attains the Way now in the time of spring." Waddell and Abe, *Heart of Dōgen's Shōbōgenzō*, 54–55. If we apply passage to our perception of aging, we might say, "Aging is, for example, like a person. A person has a great many features, all of which are aging (making passage) at different times." We should learn that a person ages without anything "extra." This means that the aging of a person always passes through a person's present age (dharma position or present moment). Aging is not the person, but because aging is happening to a particular person, that person's aging is included in the immediate time of their passage. The use of the phrase "100 percent" is from Shohaku Okumura, *Realizing Genjokoan: The Key to Dogen's Shobogenzo* (Boston: Wisdom Publications, 2010), 17.

11. Xuansha Shibei, 835-908. Also in Dōgen, *Mana Shōbōgenzō;* see Loori, *True Dharma Eye*, case 241.

12. Kazuaki Tanahashi, ed., *Treasury of the True Dharma Eye: Zen Master Dogen's Shobo Genzo* (Boston: Shambhala Publications, 2010), vol. 2 , 529.

13. Tanahashi, *Treasury of the True Dharma Eye*, vol. 2, 529.

14. Tanahashi, *Treasury of the True Dharma Eye*, vol. 2, 530.

10. Enlightenment: The Long and Short of It

1. When Dōgen used the analogy of the moon reflected in water earlier in "Genjōkōan," Dōgen wrote, "[the perception] is not like reflections in a mirror or the moon in water. When one side is illuminated, the other is dark." Please don't compare these two references to the moon and wonder why one says "is not" and the other says "is." Dōgen is using the same example to make two different points. Kyōgō discusses this in *Goshō*:

> In this section [Dōgen Zenji] uses another analogy to show that realization does not obstruct a person. . . . In this section he says, "It is like the moon's reflection in the water." It sounds as if these two very much contradict each other. However, in the previous section, [Dōgen Zenji] uses this analogy simply to show that the principle that the two separate things (sound and hearer; color and seer) correspond to each other; they are not like a mirror and reflections or water and the moon. Here, [Dōgen Zenji] uses the same analogy to show that the moon does not destroy the water.

Appendix 4, "*Okikigakishō* 'Genjōkōan,'" sec. 12, Kyōgō.

2. Michael Wenger, Mel Weitsman, and Shohaku Okamura, trans. "Shunryu Suzuki Commentary on Genjo Koan," in *Dōgen's Genjo Koan: Three Commentaries* (Berkeley, CA: Counterpoint Press, 2011), 114.

3. Hee-Jin Kim translates *kyakumei* as "illusion." Most translators use "delusion." I have changed Kim's use of "illusion" to "delusion" in this quotation. Brackets are Kim's addition.

4. Hee-Jin Kim, trans., *Flowers of Emptiness: Selections from Dōgen's Shōbōgenzō*, Studies in Asian Thought and Religion, vol. 2 (Lewiston, NY: Edwin Mellen Press, 1985), 148. Much of "Daigo" resonates with sections of "Genjōkōan."

5. Kazuaki Tanahashi, ed., *Treasury of the True Dharma Eye: Zen Master Dogen's Shobo Genzo* (Boston: Shambhala Publications, 2010), vol. 1, 301. Brackets added by this author. Italicization by Tanahashi.

6. Carl Bielefeldt, ed., *Treasury of the True Dharma Eye: Dōgen's Shōbōgenzō; An Annotated Translation by the Sōtō Zen Text Project* (Tokyo: Sōtōshu Shumachō, 2023), vol. 1, [10:14].

7. *Sahā* world (S. *Sahāloka*) literally means "world of endurance." This world is the buddha field of Shākyamuni Buddha, characterized by the difficulties we endure caused by delusional behavior and that all beings are affected by interconnected causal conditions. "Unenlightened beings may perceive it as a world of suffering and desire, the sahā world is in reality his [Buddha's] pure buddha field, a fact that is fully perceived by those who have achieved enlightenment." Robert E. Buswell, Jr. and Donald S. Lopez, Jr., "Sahāloka," in *The Princeton Dictionary of Buddhism* (Princeton, NJ: Princeton University Press, 2014), 736. Brackets added by this author.

8. Kim explains his use of activity-unremitting as "one of the most important religio-philosophical notions, denoting not only spiritual discipline in the ordinary sense but the universal dynamics inherent in all reality. For this reason I have rendered it as 'activity-unremitting.'" Kim, *Flowers of Emptiness*, 197n1.

9. Nishijima and Cross parse the meaning of *gyōji* as *gyō*, meaning "deeds, actions, or conduct," and *ji* referring to "observance of precepts." They explain the logic of this translation as "Buddhism is a religion of action. . . . In sum, the solution to all problems relies upon the philosophy of action and therefore Master Dogen esteemed action highly." This action of Buddhism is conduct manifest through following the Buddhist precepts. Gudo Nishijima and Chodo Cross, trans., *Master Dogen's Shobogenzo* (London: Windbell Publications, 1994), bk. 2, 129. Nishijima and Cross's translation of the title is unusual.

10. Kim, *Flowers of Emptiness*, 192, 193. Bracket added by this author for clarity.

11. Kim, *Flowers of Emptiness*, 194.

12. Appendix 4, "*Okikigakishō* 'Genjōkōan,'" sec. 12, Kyōgō.

13. Appendix 4, "*Okikigakishō* 'Genjōkōan,'" sec. 12, Kyōgō.

14. Appendix 4, "*Okikigakishō* 'Genjōkōan,'" sec. 12, Senne.

15. Appendix 4, "*Okikigakishō* 'Genjōkōan,'" sec. 12, Kyōgō.

16. Norman Waddell and Masao Abe, trans., *The Heart of Dōgen's Shōbōgenzō* (Albany: State University of New York Press, 2002), 50.

17. Appendix 4, "*Okikigakishō* 'Genjōkōan,'" sec. 12, Senne.

11. There's Always Something

1. Taigen Dan Leighton and Shohaku Okumura, trans., "The Richness of Cultivation," in *Dōgen's Extensive Record: A Translation of the Eihei Kōroku* (Boston: Wisdom Publications, 2004), 306.

2. Appendix 4, "*Okikigakishō* 'Genjōkōan,'" sec. 13, Kyōgō.

3. I have defined *shō* in this section as "realization," and it can also (perhaps more correctly) be translated as "verification." For a full discussion of the differences and similarities of these translations, see appendix 2, "Practice-

Enlightenment or Practice-Verification?" In this chapter I have chosen to emphasize the translation "practice-enlightenment" or "practice-realization" over "practice-verification."

4. In appendix 4, "*Okikigakishō* 'Genjōkōan,'" sec. 13, both Kyōgō's and Senne's commentaries refer to Dōgen's line in "Genjōkōan," "When one side is illuminated, the other is dark," as a positive example of being filled with the Dharma. They cite this sentence as an example of *ippō-gūjin*, the total engagement with one thing. (See chapter 4 of this book, "Perceptions and Verification.") Senne's example is "When we are filled with zazen, we can say that we are killing buddha," a reference to Linji Yixuan's (J. Rinzai Gigen, d. 866) koan that upon meeting the Buddha, one should kill the Buddha, thereby avoiding getting caught in labels and preconceived ideas about the meaning of Buddha. For more on this, see Ruth Fuller Sasaki, trans., *The Record of Linji* (Honolulu: University of Hawai'i Press, 2009), 236. For Dōgen's commentary, see Shōbōgenzō "Zazen Shin" (Lancet of Seated Meditation) and "Butsu Kōjō Ji" (Beyond the Buddha).

5. Other translations of *oboyu* (おぼ) are "feel," "know," or "realize." See San Francisco Zen Center, *Shōbōgenzō Genjō Kōan: An Analytic Study* (San Francisco: San Francisco Zen Center, n.d.), 19.

6. Dōgen's use of this example is probably the result of his trip to China where he would have seen the ocean appearing to be a circle around the boat. At the same time, he would have known that the shore was not one continuous unbroken line. For a discussion of the importance of Dōgen's passage to China, see Steven Heine, "'When Mountains Can No Longer be Seen': A Critical History of Interpretations of an Ambiguous *Shōbōgenzō* Sentence," *Journal of Chan Buddhism* 2 (2020): 26–28.

7. Carl Bielefeldt, ed., *Treasury of the True Dharma Eye: Dōgen's Shōbōgenzō; An Annotated Translation by the Sōtō Zen Text Project* (Tokyo: Sōtōshu Shumachō, 2023), vol. 1, [1:13], n14.

8. Appendix 4, "*Okikigakishō* 'Genjōkōan,'" sec. 13, Senne.

9. The Japanese expression for this is *isshin-shiken* (一水四見), or the four appearances of water: celestial beings see jewels, humans see ordinary water, hungry ghosts see pus, and fish experience water as their home. This points to the subjective aspects of all things. *Japanese-English Buddhist Dictionary*, rev. ed. (Tokyo: Daitō Shuppansha, 1991), 145. For a modern scientific exploration of how other being's perceptions work, read Ed Yong, *An Immense World: How Animal Senses Reveal the Hidden Realms Around Us* (New York: Random House, 2022).

10. This is what Senne refers to briefly in his commentary as the Triple World is one mind. See appendix 4, "*Okikigakishō* 'Genjōkōan,'" sec. 13, Senne.

For Dōgen's extensive definition of this term, see SBGZ "Sangai-yuishin" (Three Worlds Are Inseparable from Mind), in Gudo Nishijima and Chodo Cross, trans., *Master Dogen's Shobogenzo* (London: Windbell Publications, 1997), bk. 3, 43-49.

11. Kazuaki Tanahashi, ed., *Treasury of the True Dharma Eye: Zen Master Dogen's Shobo Genzo* (Boston: Shambhala Publications, 2010), vol. 2, 555-56.

12. Shohaku Okumura, ed., *Dōgen's Shōbōgenzō Zuimonki: The New Annotated Translation* (Somerville, MA: Wisdom Publications, 2022), 59.

13. The character being translated is *toku* or *doku* (德), which can be translated as "characteristics" or "virtue." In a footnote to this section, Waddell and Abe write, "The word *virtue* is used here in its original sense of *virtus*, the inherent power in a person or thing." Norman Waddell and Masao Abe, trans., *The Heart of Dōgen's Shōbōgenzō* (Albany: State University of New York Press, 2002), 43n15. "Virtue" is used in the majority of translations rather than "characteristics."

14. Gudo Nishijima and Chodo Cross, trans., *Master Dōgen's Shōbōgenzō* (London: Windbell Publications, 1994), bk. 1, 167. This author has added the italicized Japanese.

15. Mel Weitsman, Michael Wenger, and Shohaku Okumura, ed., trans., Nishiari Bokusan, "Commentary on Genjo Koan," *Dōgen's Genjo Koan: Three Commentaries* (Berkeley, CA: Counterpoint, 2011), 82.

16. Tanahashi, *Treasury of the True Dharma Eye*, vol. 2, 538.

12. Fish, Birds, and Humans Practice

1. Thomas Cleary, trans., *Shōbōgenzō Zen Essays by Dōgen* (Honolulu: University of Hawai'i Press, 1986), 34. *Yō* (用) can be translated as "function," "use" "need," "demand," or "business." In this context, all of these definitions can be descriptions of a bodhisattva's or buddha's activity-response.

2. Hee-Jin Kim, trans., *Flowers of Emptiness: Selections from Dōgen's Shōbōgenzō*, Studies in Asian Thought and Religion, vol. 2 (Lewiston, NY: Edwin Mellen Press, 1985), 246. A koan associated with this quotation from the Buddha can be found in Dōgen's collection of three hundred kōans. See John Daido Loori, "Caoshan's Dharmakāya," in *The True Dharma Eye: Zen Master Dōgen's Three Hundred Kōans* (Boston: Shambhala Publications, 2005), case 125, 170.

> Caoshan asked Senior Monastic De, "Buddha's true dharma body is like empty sky. It reflects forms just like water. How do you express this principle?"

De said, "It is like a donkey looking at a well."

Caoshan said, "You have got the point, but you have said only 80 or 90 percent of it."

De said, "Master, how would you say it?"

Caoshan said, "It's just like a well looking at the donkey."

Dōgen refers to this kōan in SBGZ "Butsu Kōjō Ji" (Beyond the Buddha) and "Tsuki" (The Moon).

3. Bracketed characters added by author. "Realization" in this quotation is *genjō*, the same word Dōgen uses in *genjōkōan*. *Genjō* means "'manifestation', 'appearance', 'occurrence'—as in *genjō kōan* (現成公案 'realized kōan')." Carl Bielefeldt, ed., *Treasury of the True Dharma Eye: Dōgen's Shōbōgenzō; An Annotated Translation by the Sōtō Zen Text Project* (Tokyo: Sōtōshu Shumachō, 2023), vol. 2, [22:1], n. 3.

4. Gudo Nishijima and Chodo Cross, trans., *Master Dogen's Shobogenzo* (London: Windbell Publications, 1996), bk. 2, 285. *Kikan* (機關), translated here as "pivot-point," means the "central mechanism of a machine: a mainspring, a hinge, or a pivot. At the same time, *ki* (機) carries the meaning of a momentary opportunity for action. So, here *kikan*, 'the momentary pivot-state,' suggests the state that is total realization of life and death in each moment." Nishijima and Cross, *Master Dogen's Shobogenzo*, 285n3.

5. Norman Waddell and Masao Abe, trans., *The Heart of Dōgen's Shōbōgenzō* (Albany: State University of New York Press, 2002), 44.

6. Bielefeldt, *Treasury of the True Dharma Eye*, vol. 1, [1:14].

7. Kazuaki Tanahashi, ed., *Treasury of the True Dharma Eye: Zen Master Dogen's Shobo Genzo* (Boston: Shambhala Publications, 2010), vol. 1, 32.

8. Kim, *Flowers of Emptiness*, 54.

9. The Japanese for this section is *shushō ari, sono jusha myōsha aru koto, kaku no gotoshi* (修證あり、その壽者命者あること、かくのごとし). Bielefeldt, *Treasury of the True Dharma Eye*, vol. 1, [1:15], n27.

10. Kim, *Flowers of Emptiness*, 59n18. It is unclear what Kim means by "eternal" in this quotation. What it does not refer to is some kind of eternal soul or essence of a person that continues endlessly. Perhaps Kim is referring to *nikon*, the "eternal now," and the loci of practice-realization.

11. Mel Weitsman, Michael Wenger, and Shohaku Okumura, ed., trans., Nishiari Bokusan, "Commentary on Genjo Koan," in *Dōgen's Genjo Koan: Three Commentaries* (Berkeley, CA: Counterpoint, 2011), 84-85.

12. Appendix 4, "*Okikigakishō* 'Genjōkōan,'" sec. 14, Senne.

13. Bielefeldt, *Treasury of the True Dharma Eye*, vol. 2, [25:16-25:18].

13. Walking the Walk

1. Appendix 4, "*Okikigakishō* 'Genjōkōan,'" "About the Title," Senne. This is quite close to a tetralemma (fourfold negation) of there is being, there is nonbeing, there is both being and nonbeing, there is neither being nor nonbeing, used by Nagarjuna. In this case, Senne is saying that no matter which possibility presents, they are all within the sphere of genjōkōan, or the kōan realized.

2. Appendix 4, "*Okikigakishō* 'Genjōkōan,'" "About the Title," Senne.

3. Shohaku Okumura, *Realizing Genjokoan: The Key to Dogen's Shobogenzo* (Boston: Wisdom Publications, 2010), 16. For a full dissection of the meaning of both *genjō* and *kōan* in *Realizing Genjokoan*, see chapter 2, "The Meaning of 'Genjōkōan.'"

4. Okumura, *Realizing Genjokoan*, 16.

5. Taigen Dan Leighton and Shohaku Okumura, trans., *Dōgen's Extensive Record: A Translation of the Eihei Kōroku* (Boston: Wisdom Publications, 2004), 521.

6. Norman Waddell and Masao Abe, trans., *The Heart of Dōgen's Shōbōgenzō* (Albany: State University of New York Press, 2002), 49.

7. Hee-Jin Kim, trans., *Flowers of Emptiness: Selections from Dōgen's Shōbōgenzō*, Studies in Asian Thought and Religion, vol. 2 (Lewiston, NY: Edwin Mellen Press, 1985), 54.

8. "Just understand that birth-and-death is itself nirvana." SBGZ "Shōji" (Birth and Death). Kazuaki Tanahashi, ed., *Moon in a Dewdrop: Writings of Zen Master Dōgen* (San Francisco: North Point Press, 1985), 7.

9. The three pure precepts: To do no harm, to do good, and to benefit all beings. Ten precepts: (1) refrain from killing, (2) refrain from taking what is not given, (3) refrain from abusing sexuality, (4) refrain from false speech, (5) refrain from intoxicating self or others, (6) refrain from slander, (7) refrain from praising self at the expense of others, (8) refrain from being avaricious, (9) refrain from harboring ill will, and (10) refrain from abusing the Three Treasures: Buddha, Dharma, and Sangha.

10. In this case, "thus" does not refer to suchness. In Japanese it is *kaku no gotku*, which means "in this way." Another translation is "hence they exist like this." Carl Bielefeldt, ed., *Treasury of the True Dharma Eye: Dōgen's Shōbōgenzō; An Annotated Translation by the Sōtō Zen Text Project* (Tokyo: Sōtōshu Shumachō, 2023), vol. 1, [1:15].

11. I am not suggesting that Dōgen thought the buddhas and ancestors were hanging around in their bodily forms; rather, it is the energy and continuing

influence of their lives and understanding that support and inform our practice. When I say "literally," I mean that this influence and encouragement witnesses and supports us in a very real way.

12. Kazuaki Tanahashi, ed., *Treasury of the True Dharma Eye: Zen Master Dogen's Shobo Genzo* (Boston: Shambhala Publications, 2010), vol. 2, 880.

13. Tanahashi, *Treasury of the True Dharma Eye*, vol. 2, 880-81.

14. Leighton and Okumura, *Dōgen's Extensive Record*, 535.

15. Bielefeldt, *Treasury of the True Dharma Eye*, vol. 6, [T01:52].

16. Tanahashi, *Treasury of the True Dharma Eye*, vol. 2, 881.

14. Encountering, Practicing, Permeating, and Realizing Each Moment

1. Original translation is "patriarchs"; the author has substituted "ancestors."

2. Norman Waddell and Masao Abe, trans., *The Heart of Dōgen's Shōbōgenzō* (Albany: State University of New York Press, 2002), 20. The original text read "[practicers]" and was changed to "practitioners" to make the quotation more readable.

3. Masao Abe discusses the teaching of "The Oneness of Practice and Attainment" in *A Study of Dōgen: His Philosophy and Religion* (Albany: State University of New York Press, 1992), 16-33.

4. Daijaku Kinst, *Trust, Realization, and the Self in Sōtō Zen Practice* (Moranga, CA: Institute of Buddhist Studies and BDK America, 2015), 34. Brackets added by this author.

5. Carl Bielefeldt, ed., *Treasury of the True Dharma Eye: Dōgen's Shōbōgenzō; An Annotated Translation by the Sōtō Zen Text Project* (Tokyo: Sōtōshu Shumachō, 2023), vol. 3, [31:28].

6. Taigen Daniel Leighton and Shohaku Okumura, trans., *Dōgen's Pure Standards for the Zen Community: A Translation of Eihei Shingi* (Albany: State University of New York Press, 1996), 33.

7. Leighton and Okumura, *Dōgen's Pure Standards for the Zen Community*, 35. The three virtues (*santoku*, 三徳) are light and tender, clean and wholesome, and properly cooked. The six tastes (*rokumi*, 六味) are bitter, sour, sweet, spicy-hot, salty, and bland.

8. Leighton and Okumura, *Dōgen's Pure Standards for the Zen Community*, 37.

9. David Brooks, *How to Know a Person: The Art of Seeing Others Deeply and Being Deeply Seen* (New York: Penguin Random House, 2023).

10. See, for example, case 4, "The World Honored One Points to the Ground" in Thomas Cleary, trans., *Book of Serenity: One Hundred Zen Dialogues* (Boston: Shambhala Publications, 2005).

11. Appendix 4, "*Okikigakishō* 'Genjōkōan,'" sec. 14, Senne.

12. Kazuaki Tanahashi, ed., *Treasury of the True Dharma Eye: Zen Master Dogen's Shobo Genzo*, vol. 1 (Boston: Shambhala Publications, 2010), 307.

13. Tanahashi, *Treasury of the True Dharma Eye*, vol. 1, 308.

14. Taigen Dan Leighton and Shohaku Okumura, trans., *Dōgen's Extensive Record: A Translation of the Eihei Kōroku* (Boston: Wisdom Publications, 2004), 533. This instruction is attributed to Yakusan Gudō, whose Chinese name was Yuehsan Hungtao (745–828).

15. Waddell and Abe, *Heart of Dōgen's Shōbōgenzō*, 4. Japanese added by this author. I am using as the basis of my discussion T. P. Kasulis, *Zen Action Zen Person* (Honolulu: University Press of Hawai'i, 1981), 70–77.

16. Kosho Uchiyama, *Opening the Hand of Thought: Foundations of Zen Buddhist Practice* (Somerville, MA: Wisdom Publications, 2004), 16.

17. Bielefeldt, *Treasury of the True Dharma Eye*, vol. 5, [63:16].

18. Hee-Jin Kim, trans., *Flowers of Emptiness: Selections from Dōgen's Shōbōgenzō*, Studies in Asian Thought and Religion, vol. 2 (Lewiston, NY: Edwin Mellen Press, 1985), 228. In this translation of "Uji," bracket added by this author, Hee-Jin Kim translates those who are practicing as "they." For example, in the second line in this quotation, he writes, "They continue to exert through their utmost effort." But since pronouns are ambiguous in Japanese, this could also be translated as "Even now being-time that puts forth my total exertion." See Waddell and Abe, *Heart of Dōgen's Shōbōgenzō*, 54. This begs the question, Was Dōgen referring to my exertion or their exertion? Probably he meant both. All beings are engaged in their total exertion, which of course includes my (and your) total exertion. Both are necessary. As a practitioner and teacher, I prefer Kim's translation because it removes the possibility of someone thinking that their effort is somehow separate and more important than that of other beings. If this is the case, a person can misconstrue the meaning of this passage and miss the teaching that all beings in concert bring about reality's functioning. On the other hand, by translating the quotation as Waddell and Abe did, the responsibility for practicing is shifted to the individual, which is, of course, the only place and time a person can practice.

19. Tanahashi, *Treasury of the True Dharma Eye*, vol. 1, 332.

20. Tanahashi, *Treasury of the True Dharma Eye*, vol. 1, 333.

21. Thomas Cleary, trans., *Shōbōgenzō Zen Essays by Dōgen* (Honolulu: University of Hawai'i Press, 1986), 117.

15. Knowing Is Not Knowing

1. Kazuaki Tanahashi, ed., *Moon in a Dewdrop: Writings of Zen Master Dōgen* (San Francisco: North Point Press, 1985), 72.

2. Norman Waddell and Masao Abe, trans., *The Heart of Dōgen's Shōbōgenzō* (Albany: State University of New York Press, 2002), 57.

3. John Daido Loori, *The True Dharma Eye: Zen Master Dōgen's Three Hundred Kōans* (Boston: Shambhala Publications, 2005), case 156, 210. Also see Randolph Whitfield, *Records of the Transmission of the Lamp*, vol. 3 (pub. by author, 2016), 97.

4. Carl Bielefeldt, ed., *Treasury of the True Dharma Eye: Dōgen's Shōbōgenzō; An Annotated Translation by the Sōtō Zen Text Project* (Tokyo: Sōtōshu Shumachō, 2023), vol. 1, [1:15].

5. Appendix 4, "*Okikigakishō* 'Genjōkōan,'" sec. 14, Senne.

6. Hee-Jin Kim, *Dōgen on Meditation and Thinking: A Reflection on His View of Zen* (Albany: State University of New York Press, 2007), 54.

7. This example is from Shōbōgenzō "Maka Hannya Haramitsu" (Manifestation of Great Prajna). For a translation, see Gudo Nishijima and Chodo Cross, trans., *Master Dogen's Shobogenzo*, bk. 1 (London: Windbell Publications, 1994), 29-30. Dōgen quotes his master, Tiantong Rujing (1162-1227).
   Whole body like a mouth, hanging in space,
   Not asking if the wind is east, west, south, or north,
   For all others equally, it chatters prajñā:
   Chin Ten Ton Ryan Chin Ten Ton.

16. Intimacy

1. "Mutan" (無端): "(MU) expresses absence. (TAN) means end, limit, or origin. (MUTAN), 'limitless,' describes freedom or adaptability which can neither be pinned down by the intellect nor totally perceived by the senses." Gudo Nishijima and Chodo Cross, trans., *Master Dogen's Shobogenzo* (London: Windbell Publications, 1994), bk. 2, 261n14.

2. Nishijima and Cross, *Master Dogen's Shobogenzo*, bk. 2, 261. The phrase "matter which is it" refers to suchness or things as they are. See notes 12 and 14 associated with this citation. Bracketed sections in original translation. Parentheses added by this author.

3. There are two possible translations of the character 見: *ken* (view) or *gen* (manifestation or actualization). Okumura translates 見 as "does not necessarily form as a view [*ken*]" and "viewing [*ken*] is not something fixed." The Sōtō Zen Translation Project translates this character as *gen*. "While ultimate verification may be realized suddenly, a hidden existence is not necessarily the realization [*gen*]; the realization [*gen*] is, "why necessarily so?" See Carl Bielefeldt, ed., *Treasury of the True Dharma Eye: Dōgen's Shōbōgenzō; An Annotated Translation by the Sōtō Zen Text Project* (Tokyo: Sōtōshu Shumachō, 2023), vol. 1, [1:16]. Most translators use a variation of

the latter version. I asked Okumura why there seemed to be a discrepancy between these two translations. In a private email he wrote, "In「正法眼蔵要語索引」(*Shōbōgenzō Yogo Sakuin, Index of Important Words in Shōbōgenzō*) made by Shuko Katō and published in 1962, 見成 [*kenjō*] and 現成 [*genjō*] are considered as the same word." Consequently, this has become the norm in modern translations. Okumura is following the lead of his teacher Kōshō Uchiyama, who translates 見 as *ken*. As a practitioner, I find that the "view" is much more helpful than the rather enigmatic use of *gen*. Considering *gen*, the meaning could be paraphrased as "realization can happen suddenly, but one may not realize the fullness of that realization because what is realized is 'just this.'" This author added Japanese words in brackets.

4. Hee-Jin Kim, trans., "Mitsugo," in *Eihei Dōgen: Mystical Realist* (Boston: Wisdom Publications 2004), 86. Italics and brackets in original translation. For another translation, see Kazuaki Tanahashi, ed., *Treasury of the True Dharma Eye: Zen Master Dogen's Shobo Genzo* (Boston: Shambhala Publications, 2010), vol. 2, 535: "Intimate means close and inseparable. There is no gap. Intimacy embraces buddha ancestors. It embraces you. It embraces the self. It embraces action. It embraces generations. It embraces merit. It embraces intimacy."

5. Kim, *Eihei Dōgen*, 86.

6. Appendix 4, "*Okikigakishō* 'Genjōkōan,'" sec. 14, Senne.

7. Carl Bielefeldt, ed., *Treasury of the True Dharma Eye: Dōgen's Shōbōgenzō; An Annotated Translation by the Sōtō Zen Text Project* (Tokyo: Sōtōshu Shumachō, 2023), vol. 1, [1:16], n33.

17. The Student-Teacher Relationship

1. Master Baoche of Mt. Magu (a.k.a. Master Hotetsu of Mount Mayoku), an eighth-century Chinese Zen master (n.d.). He was a student of Mazu Daoyi (709–788). Author added bracket name. If you want to know more about Magu Baoche, read Shohaku Okumura, *Realizing Genjokoan: The Key to Dogen's Shobogenzo* (Boston: Wisdom Publications, 2010), 182–88.

2. This story can be found in Gudo Nishijima, *Master Dogen's Shinji Shobogenzo* (Guilford, UK: Windbell Publications, 2003), case 24, 173; and John Daido Loori, "Mayu's 'Nature of the Wind,'" *The True Dharma Eye: Zen Master Dōgen's Three Hundred Kōans* (Boston: Shambhala Publications, 2005), case 123, 168.

3. Hakuun Yasutani, *Flowers Fall: A Commentary on Zen Master Dōgen's Genjōkōan* (Boston: Shambhala Publications, 1996), 96, 97.

4. Gudo Nishijima and Chodo Cross, trans., *Master Dogen's Shobogenzo* (London: Windbell Publications, 1994) bk. 1, 29.

5. Master Baoche was male, and considering the tradition and time of this story from "Genjōkōan," the students were probably male too. In imagining the story in the present, I want to shift us out of this historical gender normativity. This assembly can be cis-gendered women or men, people who are trans, gender fluid, or any other identity. We can be brown, black, white, or any color of the rainbow. Asian, African, Middle Eastern. Perhaps devas and other form beings are also present. As a cis-gender lesbian, I will not deny myself the opportunity to be included at this occasion.

6. Steven Heine, *Dogen: Japan's Original Zen Teacher; Lives of the Masters* (Boulder, CO: Shambhala Publications, 2021), 48. Heine's biography of Dōgen in this book is one of the best I have read.

7. Kazuaki Tanahashi, ed., *Enlightenment Unfolds: The Essential Teachings of Zen Master Dogen* (Boston: Shambhala Publications, 1999), 32. Heine's discussion of Dōgen's question is in *Dogen: Japan's Original Zen Teacher; Lives of the Masters* (Boulder, CO: Shambhala Publications, 2021), 48-52. This kōan of Dōgen's can be found in texts on Dōgen's life and spiritual development. Thomas Kasulis discusses in depth the importance of this topic in *Engaging Japanese Philosophy: A Short History* (Honolulu: University of Hawai'i Press, 2018), 212-18.

18. What Does It All Mean?

1. Norman Waddell and Masao Abe, trans., *The Heart of Dōgen's Shōbōgenzō* (Albany: State University of New York Press, 2002), 3.

2. Appendix 4, "*Okikigakishō* 'Genjōkōan,'" sec. 15, Senne.

3. Appendix 4, "*Okikigakishō* 'Genjōkōan,'" sec. 15, Senne.

4. Hee-Jin Kim, *Flowers of Emptiness: Selections from Dōgen's Shōbōgenzō*, Studies in Asian Thought and Religion, vol. 2 (Lewiston, NY: Edwin Mellen Press, 1985), 193. This author has added "[gyōji]" for the convenience of the reader. Otherwise brackets are in the original quotation.

5. Waddell and Abe define *zenki* as "*zen* 全 means complete, a totality encompassing the entire universe with nothing excluded, and *ki* (機) covers such significances as motive power, spring, trigger, mechanism, opportunity. Thus for Dōgen, *zenki* indicates the total dynamic function of man and the world, in which total reality is disclosed." Norman Waddell and Masao Abe, "Dōgen's *Shōbōgenzō Zenki* 'Total Dynamic Working' and *Shōji* 'Birth and Death,'" *Eastern Buddhist*, n.s., 5, no. 1 (May 1972): 71.

6. Kim, *Flowers of Emptiness*, 198n5.

7. Michele Hall, producer, *Nature*, PBS, season 41, ep. 6, first aired January 5, 2023, 53:13 min.

8. Kazuaki Tanahashi, ed., *Treasury of the True Dharma Eye: Zen Master Dogen's Shobo Genzo* (Boston: Shambhala Publications, 2010), vol. 1, 265.

9. Carl Bielefeldt, ed., *Treasury of the True Dharma Eye: Dōgen's Shōbōgenzō; An Annotated Translation by the Sōtō Zen Text Project* (Tokyo: Sōtōshu Shumachō, 2023), vol. 3, [34:4].

10. Bielefeldt, *Treasury of the True Dharma Eye*, vol. 3, [35:4].

11. Bielefeldt, *Treasury of the True Dharma Eye*, vol. 7, [S1:33].

12. Tanahashi, *Treasury of the True Dharma Eye*, vol. 1, 4.

13. Bielefeldt, *Treasury of the True Dharma Eye*, vol. 6, [T4:10], n14. The note accompanying this paragraph is "When we take up the whole earth, it turns entirely to gold (*daichi o kosureba, mina ōgon to nari* 大地を擧すれば、みな黄金となり), perhaps recalling an expression used in reference to the powers of the advanced bodhisattva: "to churn the Long River [of the Milky Way] into butter and turn the whole earth into gold (*jiao changhe wei sulao bien dadi wei huangjin* 攪長河爲酥酪變大地爲黄金)."

Appendix 1: Dharma Position: *Jū Hōi*

1. Shohaku Okumura, *Realizing Genjokoan: The Key to Dogen's Shobogenzo* (Boston: Wisdom Publications, 2010), 2.

2. Okumura, *Realizing Genjokoan*, 2.

3. See for example, Carl Bielefeldt, ed., *Treasury of the True Dharma Eye: Dōgen's Shōbōgenzō; An Annotated Translation by the Sōtō Zen Text Project* (Tokyo: Sōtōshu Shumachō, 2023), vol. 1, [1:11], n12.

4. Jacqueline I. Stone, *Original Enlightenment and the Transformation of Medieval Japanese Buddhism* (Honolulu: University of Hawai'i Press, 1999), 201.

5. See Bunnō Katō, Yoshirō Tamura, and Kōjirō Miyasaki, trans., *The Three-fold Lotus Sūtra* (Tokyo: Kosei Publications, 1988), 70n34. Other words for suchness are: emptiness, *tathata* (Sanskrit), *shinnyo* (Japanese), reality itself, just this, the true form of things, buddha-nature, and real existence, among other expressions. Various Buddhist schools have different doctrines about how suchness functions or manifests.

6. Suchness without conditions was used as a rebuttal to the idea that a being only has the potential to become buddha, but before achieving their potential they must first attain or activate buddhahood through practice over many lifetimes. Once they have attained this state, it is said they have "activated" their buddha-nature. Saichō's position was that one is already endowed with buddha-nature. Dōgen also believed that all beings are buddha-nature, as he wrote in "Busshō" (Buddha-Nature):

    Entire being is the Buddha-nature. I call the whole integral entity of *entire being* "sentient beings." Just at the very time when things are thus, both inside and outside of sentient being are as such, the *entire being* of the Buddha-nature.

Norman Waddell and Masao Abe, trans., *The Heart of Dōgen's Shōbōgenzō* (Albany: State University of New York Press, 2002), 61.

7. Asia Endō, "The *Lotus Sūtra* as the Core of Japanese Buddhism: Shifts in Representations of Its Fundamental Principle," *Japanese Journal of Religious Studies* 41, no. 1 (2014): 51. I have simplified what is a winding road of Buddhist doctrinal disputes with far-reaching ramifications.

8. Waddell and Abe, *Heart of Dōgen's Shōbōgenzō*, 52.

9. Bielefeldt, *Treasury of the True Dharma Eye*, vol. 5, [63:17].

10. In running a search of a pdf file of Shōbōgenzō, I was only able to find the characters/phrase *jū hōi* ten times.

11. Bielefeldt, *Treasury of the True Dharma Eye*, vol. 7, [S8:4].

12. Bielefeldt, *Treasury of the True Dharma Eye*, vol. 7, [S8:4], n3.

13. This list arises from my study of SBGZ "Uji," which I discuss at length in my commentary *Being-Time: A Practitioner's Guide to Dōgen's Shōbōgenzō Uji* (Somerville, MA: Wisdom Publications, 2018).

14. Okumura, *Realizing Genjokoan*, 93.

15. Okumura, *Realizing Genjokoan*, 284n6.

16. Waddell and Abe, *Heart of Dōgen Shōbōgenzō*, 55. This author added bracketed comments.

17. Bielefeldt, *Treasury of the True Dharma Eye*, vol. 7, [S8:4].

18. Bielefeldt, *Treasury of the True Dharma Eye*, vol. 7, [V1:11].

19. Bielefeldt, *Treasury of the True Dharma Eye*, vol. 7, [V1:11].

20. In Buddhism, rebirth is like a rope made up of numerous individual strands. Since these strands (one lifetime) are woven together, the resulting rope's beginning strands are not the strands that are at the end of the rope. In this way, one's lifetime is one strand. It is affected by the strands adjacent to it, but numerous lifetimes, make up the rope. Therefore, one should not mistake rebirth as rebirth of an eternal soul or personal entity that does not die.

21. Kazuaki Tanahashi, ed., *Treasury of the True Dharma Eye: Zen Master Dōgen's Shobo Genzo* (Boston: Shambhala Publications, 2010), vol. 2, 862.

22. Waddell and Abe, *Heart of Dōgen's Shōbōgenzō*, 49. Italicization added by this author.

23. See the end of chapter 4 of this book for a discussion of mutual identity and mutual inter-being. An example of inter-being (more technically called mutual penetration) is being in a closed room with others and we breathe in one another's exhalations. Their "outside" cells become "inside," incorporating as part of our own bodies. We breathe the exhalation of

trees (oxygen) and depend on the sun to deliver a certain spectrum of ultraviolet light that we absorb through our skin and use to make vitamin D. We become the tree and sun, and the tree and sun become us. All these factors, the ones we know and the ones we do not know, are the activity of sustaining our life and others' lives through incorporating each other on a cellular level.

24. Tanahashi, *Treasury of the True Dharma Eye*, vol. 1, 332–33. Brackets added by this author.

25. Waddell and Abe, *Heart of Dōgen's Shōbōgenzō*, 50.

26. Waddell and Abe, *Heart of Dōgen's Shōbōgenzō*, 53.

27. For other examples of passageless-passage, see chapter 15.

28. Masao Abe, *A Study of Dōgen: His Philosophy and Religion* (Albany: State University of New York Press, 1992), 135. A more usual translation of the Japanese *kyōryaku* is "passage"; see Sōtō Zen Text Project, *Shōbōgenzō*, [20:8], n119; Waddell and Abe, *Heart of Dōgen's Shōbōgenzō*, 51; Thomas Cleary, trans., *Shōbōgenzō: Zen Essays by Dōgen* (Honolulu: University of Hawai'i Press, 1986), 106; Hee-jin Kim, trans., *Flowers of Emptiness: Selections from Dōgen's Shōbōgenzō*, Studies in Asian Thought and Religion vol. 2 (Lewiston, NY: Edwin Mellen Press, 1985), 227.

29. Kim, *Flowers of Emptiness*, 231n15.

30. Kim, *Flowers of Emptiness*, 231n15. *Nikon* (而今) is translated as "now," "right now," and "the eternal now." "Intra-epochal" refers to transitions within a period of time denoting a new development (epoch).

31. Waddell and Abe, *Heart of Dōgen's Shōbōgenzō*, 57.

32. Waddell and Abe, *Heart of Dōgen's Shōbōgenzō*, 54.

33. Waddell and Abe, *Heart of Dōgen's Shōbōgenzō*, 50. This author added bracketed word.

34. Bielefeldt, *Treasury of the True Dharma Eye*, vol. 5, [63:14-15]. Italics in original quotation.

35. Waddell and Abe, *Heart of Dōgen's Shōbōgenzō*, 51.

36. Waddell and Abe, *Heart of Dōgen's Shōbōgenzō*, 51.

Appendix 2: Practice-Enlightenment or Practice-Verification?

1. Another variation is whether the written translation is hyphenated (practice-realization or practice-verification) or written using "and" between words (practice and realization or practice and verification). Over coffee in March 2024, I asked Carl Bielefeldt about this. He said that he translated *shushō* as "practice and verification" because that is the way it is written. When it is

translated with a hyphen, the translator is responding to Dōgen's teaching that practice and realization or verification are one thing. (See "Bendowa" [On the Endeavor of the Way], question 6, "In buddha-dharma, practice and enlightenment are one and the same.") From this I gather that, strictly speaking, if translating what is written, then it should be "practice and verification or realization." If the translator is responding to Dōgen's overall teachings, then they might translate the phrase with a hyphen.

2. These comments are based upon email correspondence with Shohaku Okumura in early 2023. Since I do not read Japanese, I have relied upon his help. Any mistakes are entirely my own.

3. Hee-Jin Kim, *Dōgen on Meditation and Thinking: A Reflection on His View of Zen* (Albany: State University of New York Press, 2007), 21.

4. Francis H. Cook, *Sounds of Valley Streams: Enlightenment in Dōgen's Zen* (Albany: State University of New York Press, 1989), 10.

5. Cook, *Sounds of Valley Streams*, 11. A conversation with Daijaku Kinst led me to Francis Cook's discussion of the meaning of *shushō*. She discusses this in *Trust, Realization, and the Self in Sōtō Zen Practice* (Honolulu: University of Hawai'i Press, 2015), 33-41.

6. William Bodiford and T. Griffith Foulk, contribs., *Treasury of the True Dharma Eye: Dōgen's Shōbōgenzō; An Annotated Translation by the Sōtō Zen Text Project* (Tokyo: Sōtōshu Shumachō, 2023), vol. 8, "Supplementary Notes to the Translation: Practice and Verification," 483. Japanese characters are omitted.

7. I am quoting an email correspondence between Shohaku Okumura and myself in March 2024. This quotation is from Okumura's revised translation of Menzan Zuihō's *Jijuyu-Zanmai*. Menzan Zuihō (1683-1689), while by no means a contemporary of Dōgen Zenji's, had a major impact on how Dōgen is understood. William Bodiford wrote of Menzan Zuihō that his understanding of Dōgen "has come to define the orthodox interpretation of Dōgen for modern Sōtō." See William Bodiford, *Sōtō Zen in Medieval Japan* (Honolulu: University of Hawai'i Press, 1993), 50.

8. Carl Bielefeldt, ed., *Treasury of the True Dharma Eye: Dōgen's Shōbōgenzō; An Annotated Translation by the Sōtō Zen Text Project* (Tokyo: Sōtōshu Shumachō, 2023), vol. 6, [T12:14]. The complete list of the eight understandings are: few desires, knowing contentment, enjoying quietude, diligent exertion, not neglecting mindfulness, practicing meditation, cultivating wisdom, and not engaging in frivolous discourse.

9. Bielefeldt, *Treasury of the True Dharma Eye*, vol. 1, [03:4], n27.

10. Kazuaki Tanahashi, ed., *Treasury of the True Dharma Eye: Zen Master*

Dogen's Shobo Genzo, vol. 1 (Boston: Shambhala Publications, 2010), 242. This is a slightly different translation of *ken mon kaku chi*.

11. There is some confusion about two fascicles: one titled "Hotsu Mujō Shin," and the other "Hotsu Bodai Shin." Tanahashi treats them as two separate texts with two different titles and writes that they were given on the same day but intended for different audiences. Tanahashi, *Treasury of the True Dharma Eye*, vol. 1, xxxiv. But the more recent Sōtōshu translation identifies both fascicles as having the same name while acknowledging that they have different content. In the Sōtō Zen Text Project translation, one version appears as "Hotsu Bodai Shin" in the Seventy-Five-Chapter Compilation of the SBGZ and the other (with the same name) in the Twelve-Chapter Compilation. Bielefeldt, *Treasury of the True Dharma Eye*, vol. 5, introduction to fascicle 63, SBGZ Seventy-Five-Chapter Compilation, "Hotsu Bodai Shin"; and vol. 6, introduction to fascicle T4, SBGZ Twelve-Chapter Compilation, "Hotsu Bodai Shin." Consequently, you may find this quotation under either of these names, depending upon the translator's source material.

12. Tanahashi, *Treasury of the True Dharma Eye*, vol. 2, 650. Italics and brackets added by Tanahashi.

13. Gudo Nishijima and Chodo Cross, trans., *Master Dogen's Shobogenzo* (London: Windbell Publications, 1994), bk. 3, 158.

14. Shohaku Okumura, *The Mountains and Waters Sūtra: A Practitioner's Guide to Dōgen's "Sansuikyō"* (Somerville, MA: Wisdom Publications, 2018), 105.

15. Cook, *Sounds of Valley Streams*, 66. This author has added "verify" in brackets.

16. Tanahashi, *Treasury of the True Dharma Eye*, vol. 1, 29.

17. Cook, *Sounds of Valley Streams*, 66.

18. Taigen Dan Leighton and Shohaku Okumura, *Dōgen's Extensive Record: A Translation of the Eihei Kōroku* (Boston: Wisdom Publications, 2004), 521-22.

19. Bielefeldt, *Treasury of the True Dharma Eye*, vol. 1, [1:15]. Brackets and italicized text are in the original quotation.

20. Cook, *Sounds of Valley Streams*, 11.

21. Cook, *Sounds of Valley Streams*, 10-11.

Appendix 3: Introduction to *Okikigakishō* (御聴書抄) by Zuiko Redding

1. William M. Bodiford, *Soto Zen in Medieval Japan* (Honolulu: University of Hawai'i Press, 2022), 45.

2. Unpublished notes from Shohaku Okumura.

3. Bodiford, *Soto Zen in Medieval Japan*, 46.

4. Steven Heine, "'When Mountains Can No Longer be Seen': A Critical History of Interpretations of an Ambiguous *Shōbōgenzō* Sentence," *Journal of Chan Buddhism* 2, nos. 1-2 (2020): 6-7, 21-22.

Bibliography

Abe, Masao. *A Study of Dōgen: His Philosophy and Religion.* Albany: State University of New York Press, 1992.

Bielefeldt, Carl, ed. *Treasury of the True Dharma Eye: Dōgen's Shōbōgenzō; An Annotated Translation by the Sōtō Zen Text Project.* 8 vols. Tokyo: Sōtōshū Shūmuchō, 2023.

Bodiford, William M. "Rewriting Dogen." *International Zen Studies* 12, no. 4 (2019).

———. *Sōtō Zen in Medieval Japan.* Honolulu: University of Hawai'i Press, 1993.

Brooks, David. *How to Know a Person: The Art of Seeing Others Deeply and Being Deeply Seen.* New York: Penguin Random House, 2023.

Buswell, Robert E. Jr., and Donald S. Lopez, Jr. *The Princeton Dictionary of Buddhism.* Princeton, NJ: Princeton University Press, 2014.

Chang, Garma C. C. *The Buddhist Teaching of Totality: The Philosophy of Hwa Yen Buddhism.* University Park: Pennsylvania State University Press, 1977.

Cleary, Thomas, trans. *Shōbōgenzō: Zen Essays by Dōgen.* Honolulu: University of Hawai'i Press, 1986.

Conze, Edward. *Buddhist Thought in India: Three Phases of Buddhist Philosophy.* Ann Arbor: University of Michigan Press, 1967.

Cook, Francis H., trans. *How to Raise an Ox: Zen Practice as Taught in Zen Master Dogen's Shobogenzo.* Boston: Wisdom Publications, 2011.

———. *Hua-Yen Buddhism: The Jewel Net of Indra.* University Park: Pennsylvania State University Press, 1977.

———. *Sounds of the Valley Streams: Enlightenment in Dōgen's Zen.* Albany: State University of New York Press, 1989.

Dōgen, Eihei, Kōshō Uchiyama, and Thomas Wright, trans. *How to Cook Your Life: From the Zen Kitchen to Enlightenment.* Boston: Shambhala Publications, 2013.

Endō, Asia. "The *Lotus Sūtra* as the Core of Japanese Buddhism: Shifts in Representations of Its Fundamental Principle." *Japanese Journal of Religious Studies* 41, no. 1 (2014): 45–64.

Gard, Richard, and Stanley Weinstein, eds. *Japanese-English Buddhist Dictionary: Revised Edition.* Tokyo: Daitō Shuppansha, 1991.

Hall, Michele, producer. *Nature.* PBS. Season 41, episode 6, "Soul of the Ocean." Aired January 5, 2023.

Harvey, Peter. *An Introduction to Buddhism: Teaching, History, and Practices.* Cambridge: Cambridge University Press, 1990.

Heine, Steven. *Did Dōgen Go to China? What He Wrote and When He Wrote It.* New York: Oxford University Press, 2006.

———. *Dogen: Japan's Original Zen Teacher.* Boulder, CO: Shambhala Publications, 2021.

———, ed. *Dōgen: Textual and Historical Studies.* New York: Oxford University Press, 2012.

———. *Flowers Blooming on a Withered Tree: Giun's Verse Comments on Dōgen's Treasury of the True Dharma Eye.* New York: Oxford University Press, 2020.

———. *Readings of Dōgen's Treasury of the True Dharma Eye.* New York: Columbia University Press, 2020.

———. "What Is on the Other Side? Delusion and Realization in Dōgen's 'Genjōkōan.'" In *Dōgen: Textual and Historical Studies.* Oxford: Oxford University Press, 2012.

———. "'When Mountains Can No Longer be Seen': A Critical History of Interpretations of an Ambiguous *Shōbōgenzō* Sentence." *Journal of Chan Buddhism* 2, nos. 1–2 (2020): 1–38.

Inoue, Gien. *A Blueprint of Enlightenment: A Contemporary Commentary on Dōgen Zenji's Gakudō Yōjinshū Guidelines for Studying the Way.* Olympia, WA: Temple Ground Press, 2020.

Japanese-English Buddhist Dictionary. Rev. ed. Tokyo: Daitō Shuppansha, 1991.

Kasulis, Thomas P. *Engaging Japanese Philosophy: A Short History.* Honolulu: University of Hawai'i Press, 2018.

———. *Zen Action Zen Person.* Honolulu: University of Hawai'i Press, 1981.

Katō, Bunnō, Yoshirō Tamura, and Kōjirō Miyasaka, trans. *The Threefold Lotus Sutra: The Sutra of Innumerable Meanings, The Sutra of the Lotus Flower of* the Wonderful Law, and The Sutra of Meditation on the Bodhisattva Universal Virtue. Tokyo: Kosei, 1988.

Kato, Kazumitsu Wako. *Sky Flowers on the Day Before: My Life Guided by Zen Buddhism.* Self-published, 2019.

Kim, Hee-Jin. *Dōgen on Meditation and Thinking: A Reflection on his View of Zen.* Albany: State University of New York Press, 2007.

——. *Eihei Dōgen: Mystical Realist.* Boston: Wisdom Publications, 2004.

——, trans. *Flowers of Emptiness: Selections from Dōgen's Shōbōgenzō.* Lewiston, NY: Edwin Mellen Press, 1985.

Kinst, Daijaku. *Trust, Realization, and the Self in Sōtō Zen Practice.* Moraga, CA: Institute of Buddhist Studies and BDK America, 2015.

Kodera, Takashi James, trans. *Dogen's Formative Years in China: An Historical Study and Annotated Translation of the Hōkyō-ki.* Boulder, CO: Prajñā Press, 1980.

LaFleur, William R. *Dōgen Studies.* Studies in East Asian Buddhism 2. Honolulu: University of Hawai'i Press, 1985.

Leighton, Taigen Dan, and Shohaku Okumura, trans. *Dōgen's Extensive Record: A Translation of the Eihei Kōroku.* Somerville, MA: Wisdom Publications, 2004.

——. *Dōgen's Pure Standards for the Zen Community: A Translation of Eihei Shingi.* Albany: State University of New York Press, 1996.

Loori, John Daido. *The True Dharma Eye: Zen Master Dōgen's Three Hundred Koans.* Boston: Shambhala Publications, 2005.

Low, Albert William. *Genjokoan by Zen Master Dogen.* Self-published, 2014.

Nishijima, Gudo, and Chodo Cross, trans. *Master Dogen's Shobogenzo.* 4 vols. London: Windbell Publications, 1994.

Nishijima, Gudo Wafu. *Master Dogen's Shinji Shobogenzo: 301 Kōan Stories.* Guilford, UK: Windbell Publications, 2003.

Okumura, Shohaku, trans. *Dōgen's Shōbōgenzō Zuimonki: The New Annotated Edition.* Somerville, MA: Wisdom Publications, 2022.

——. *Realizing Genjokoan: The Key to Dogen's Shobogenzo.* Boston: Wisdom Publications, 2010.

Okumura, Shohaku, and Taigen Daniel Leighton, trans. *The Wholehearted Way: A Translation of Eihei Dōgen's Bendōwa with Commentary by Kōshō Uchiyama Roshi.* Boston: Tuttle Publishing, 1997.

Padmakara Translation Group. *The Way of the Bodhisattva.* Rev. ed. Boulder, CO: Shambhala Publications, 2006.

Roberts, Shinshu. *Being-Time: A Practitioner's Guide to Dōgen's Shōbōgenzō.* Somerville, MA: Wisdom Publications, 2018.

San Francisco Zen Center. *Shōbōgenzō Genjō Kōan: An Analytic Study.* San Francisco: San Francisco Zen Center, n.d. This text is available online at https://brightwayzen.org/wp-content/uploads/2022/09/Genjo-Koan-Study -from-San-Francisco-Zen-Center.pdf.

Sasaki, Ruth Fuller, trans. *The Record of Linji.* Honolulu: University of Hawai'i Press, 2009.

Stone, Jacqueline I. *Original Enlightenment and the Transformation of Medieval Japanese Buddhism.* Honolulu: University of Hawai'i Press, 1999.

Suzuki, Shunryu. *Suzuki Roshi Lecture Transcripts.* These transcripts are available online at http://shunryusuzuki2.com/Detail1?ID=104.

Tanahashi, Kazuaki, ed., trans. *Enlightenment Unfolds: The Essential Teachings of Zen Master Dogen.* Boston: Shambhala Publications, 1999.

——, trans. *Moon in a Dewdrop: Writings of Zen Master Dōgen.* San Francisco: North Point Press, 1985.

——, trans., ed. *Treasury of the True Dharma Eye: Zen Master Dogen's Shobo Genzo.* 2 vols. Boston: Shambhala Publications, 2010.

Uchiyama, Kosho. *How to Cook Your Life: From the Zen Kitchen to Enlightenment.* Somerville, MA: Wisdom Publications, 2005.

——. *Opening the Hand of Thought: Foundations of Zen Buddhist Practice.* Somerville, MA: Wisdom Publications, 2004.

Uchiyama, Kosho, and Thomas Wright, trans. *Refining Your Life: From the Zen Kitchen to Enlightenment.* New York: Weatherhill Press, 1983.

Waddell, Norman, and Masao Abe, trans. *The Heart of Dōgen's Shōbōgenzō.* Albany: State University of New York Press, 2002.

——. "Dōgen's *Shōbōgenzō Zenki* 'Total Dynamic Working' and *Shōji* 'Birth and Death.'" *Eastern Buddhist,* n.s., 5, no. 1 (May 1972).

Weitsman, Mel, Michael Wenger, and Shohaku Okumura, trans. *Dōgen's Genjo Koan: Three Commentaries.* Berkeley, CA: Counterpoint Press, 2011.

Whitfield, Randolph, trans. *Records of the Transmission of the Lamp.* 8 vols. Published by the author, 2015.

Winfield, Pamela. *Icons and Iconoclasm in Japanese Buddhism: Kūkai and Dōgen on the Art of Enlightenment.* Madison, NY: Oxford University Press, 2013.

Yasutani, Hakuun. *Flowers Fall: A Commentary on Zen Master Dōgen's Genjōkōan.* Boston: Shambhala Publications, 1996.

Yong, Ed. *An Immense World: How Animal Senses Reveal the Hidden Realms Around Us.* New York: Random House, 2022.

Ziporyn, Brook. *Beyond Oneness and Difference: Li and Coherence in Chinese Buddhist Thought and Its Antecedents.* Albany: State University of New York Press, 2013.

Credits

Shohaku Okumura, excerpts from *Realizing Genjokoan: The Key to Dogen's Shobogenzo.* Copyright © 2010 by Shohaku Okumura. Reprinted with the permission of The Permissions Company, LLC on behalf of Wisdom Publications, wisdompubs.org.

The translation of *Okikigakishō* of Genjo-koan, © by Sanshin Zen Community, translated by Shohaku Okumura, and edited by Zuiko Redding, is reprinted with permission of the Dogen Institute and Wisdom Publications.

Excerpts from *The Heart of Dōgen's Shōbōgenzō*, © 2002 by State University of New York, translated by Norman Waddell and Masao Abe, is reprinted with permission of SUNY Press.

Index

Abe, Masao, 24, 44, 112, 119, 177, 235n2
abundance, xv, 30, 37-40, 202, 235n8
activity-response, 116-18, 248n1
activity-unremitting, 101, 129, 159-61,
    246nn8-9
aging, 87, 120, 244n10
analogies and examples, 227
    arriving at other shore, 28, 29, 234n17
    boat in ocean, riding in, xvii, 79, 80,
        82, 83, 106, 108-9, 110, 211, 218-20,
        247n6
    Buddha-body, sixteen-foot, 12, 33,
        181, 235n7
    "carry water," 8-9
    driving car in traffic, 60-61
    fire, 201, 205
    firewood and ash, xvi, 18, 84, 85,
        87-89, 90, 92, 93, 166-67, 169, 170,
        172, 174, 212-15
    fish leaping from water, 24, 233n3
    flowers falling/weeds growing, xv, 15,
        16, 28, 29, 30, 31, 39, 41, 42, 203
    gold of earth, xviii, 163, 225, 227, 228,
        256n13
    hand, 27
    hiking, 147
    illumination and darkness, xv, 55, 57,
        59, 61, 63, 64-65, 132, 142-43, 245n1,
        247n4
    Indra's Net, 238n12

    "lugging wood," 8-9
    maps, 124, 158
    moon's reflection, xvi-xvii, 55, 57, 58,
        96, 97, 99-100, 105, 113, 117, 207-8,
        215-18, 245n1
    quilt, 34, 35
    river transformed to cream, xviii, 157,
        163, 225, 228
    rope's strands, 243n3, 257n20
    seed and plant, 170
    traveler in search of sword, 55, 237n4
    viewing shore from boat, 15, 18
    walking on crowded sidewalk,
        147-48, 149
    wind, xviii, 151, 152, 153, 154, 155, 157,
        158-59, 162, 225-28
anger/aversion, 39, 43-44
ango (extended practice period), 2
arhats, 214
aspiration, 127-28, 129, 137, 163
attachment, 31, 37, 39, 42-45, 60, 75,
    86, 171
Avalokiteśvara, 35
awakened response, 17, 59-60, 85, 184
awakening
    attraction to, 32
    beginningless original, 206-7
    being-time of, 180
    and delusion, relationship of, 100-102
    and reality, nonduality of, 34-36

awakening (*continued*)
  self's role in, 16, 51, 63, 237n15
  sequential being-time in, 173
  totality of, 188
Ayuwang, Mount, 5

Banjin Dōtan, 192
Baoche (a.k.a. Hotetsu of Mount
  Mayoku), xviii, 77, 151-53, 155-56,
  159, 162, 225-28, 254n1, 255n5
being-time, 19, 31, 231-32n34, 233n3
  dharma positions and, 85, 165-66,
  176
  eternal now in, 179
  exertion and, 13
  integration in, 70
  knowing and not knowing in, 142
  mutual identity and inter-being in, 175
  particularity in, 86
  passage of, 12, 177-78, 180, 181
  sequential, 173
  totality of, 141
  transitional, 144
"Bendōwa" (On the Endeavor of the
  Way), 2, 32, 130-31, 162-63, 172,
  241n1
benefiting all beings, 107, 133
Bielefeldt, Carl, 258n1
birth-and-death
  as Buddha's life, 33, 47-48
  as nirvana, 10, 230n19, 244n9, 250n8
  as not inherently existing, 31, 92-93
"Bodaisatta Shi Shōbō" (Bodhisattva's
  Four Methods of Guidance), 138
bodhi mind/buddha mind, 51, 77
  bringing forth, 121, 136, 180
  nature of, 12
  present body and mind as, 16
  responding from, 39, 49, 53, 95, 99
Bodhidharma, 196
bodhisattva ideal, 113-14
bodhisattva path, 9, 131-32, 175

bodhisattva practice, 1
  as altruistic response, 161-62
  in daily life, 19, 39-40
  goal of, 243n4
  in midst of fire, 45
  tools for, 117
bodhisattva vow, 9, 45, 121
body and mind, 102-3
  as buddha mind, 16
  confusion about, 81, 211-12
  Dharma filling, xvii, 106, 107, 115-16,
  142, 218-20, 224
  in enlightenment, 129
body-mind, 58, 59, 60, 61, 90, 91, 121,
  207-8. *See also* dropping off body
  and mind
Book of Serenity, 134
boundaries, xviii, 37, 139-42, 143, 149,
  159, 177, 221-24
Brooks, David; *How to Know a Person*,
  133-34
Buddha Dharma. *See* Dharma
buddha-nature, 155, 233n8, 256n6
  accessibility of, 12
  of all beings, 46-51, 75, 224
  all reality as, 115-16
  as altruistic state of world, 101
  of bodhisattvas, 113-14
  buddha realization and, 77-78
  buddhas and, 51-52
  enlightenment and, 99-100
  manifesting, 1, 10, 14, 61, 185
  original lot and, 74, 241n3
  as original realization, 131
  and practice, relationship of, 4, 8, 154,
  158-60
  of teachers, 152
  total dynamic function of, 160-61
buddha(s), 56-57, 68, 110, 198
  actions of, 69
  actualizing/verifying, xv, 41, 50-54,
  60-61, 206-7

anthropomorphizing, 77
as ever-present, 227
killing, 220, 247n4
and living beings, relationship of, xv,
    33-35, 41, 46-48, 202, 205-6, 228
practicing with all, 127-28, 250n11
Buddha's family/house of Buddha,
    xviii, 157, 159, 162-63, 225, 226
Buddhism, goal of, 230n19
Buddhist multiverse, 129
"Bukkyō" (Teachings of the Buddhas),
    28, 114
"Busshō" (Buddha-Nature), 46-47,
    77-79, 116, 185, 197, 256n6

Caoshan, 248n2
causality, 67, 81, 82, 87-88, 179,
    180. See also unambiguous
    cause-and-effect
causes and conditions, 42, 43-44, 61,
    160, 161, 173, 178
Changqing Huileng, 140
characteristics, inexhaustible, xvii, 106,
    108-13, 218, 220-21
Ch'eng-kuan, 238n9
Chikan, Kyōgen, 55, 56, 60
China, 3-6, 7, 110, 163, 247n6
Chinzei (Kyūshū), x
Chōka Dōrin, 228
climate change, 45
clinging, 39, 45, 82, 114, 176
    self-centered, 235-36n2
    self-conscious, 38
    self-delusional, 61
codependent arising, 128, 140, 155
comparisons, 104-5, 117-18, 126, 217-18
compassion, 77, 176-77
    actualizing, 146
    bodhisattvas' rebirth and, 243n4
    in kenshō, 61
    nondual inter-being as, 233n11
    responding with, 36

for self and others, 138
from wisdom, 89
conceptualization, 31, 67, 144, 146,
    149, 212
conditioned arising, 160, 161
consciousness, mistaken
    understandings, 81
Cook, Francis H., 183-84, 189

Daichi Sokei, 192
"Daigo" (Great Awakening), 98, 100
Dai-i-zan Mountain, 56
"Daowu's 'Alive or Dead,'" 92-93,
    244n7
Dayuan of Dawei, 55, 56
De (senior monastic), 248n2
death, xvi, 84, 87, 90, 243n1
    fear of, 82
    as final end, 91, 243n2
    manifesting total function, 200,
        213-14, 215
    as not inherently existing, 92-93
    total realization of, 118, 249n3
deeds, good and evil, 72, 209, 228
deficiency, xv, 30, 37-40, 202, 235n8
delusion, 40, 107, 171, 173, 219
    accepting, 48
    and awakening, relationship of,
        100-102
    awareness of, 87
    deconstructing, 43
    delusion within, xv, 41, 46-54, 205-6,
        236nn10-11
    desiring to end, 32
    examining, 16
    interconnection and, 36
    labeling experience as, 71
    and reality, nonduality of, 34-36
    and realization, relationship of,
        53-54, 98, 143, 181, 202, 203-5,
        206, 228
    total, 204-5

Dharma, 30-31, 166, 187
  as always presencing, 155
  and Buddha, sameness of, 205
  deconstructing, 34
  and living beings, relationship of,
    208, 222-23
  partial and complete teachings of, 108
  preconceptions about, 76, 77
  reuniting with, 45
  seeking, initial, xvi, 74, 78, 209-11
  and self, relationship of, 44
  unfolding of, 111, 139
Dharma gates, 7, 17, 59, 64, 67, 126, 138
dharma positions, 25-27, 88-89, 182
  abiding in, 84, 95, 165, 167-69
  arising, 94-95, 103, 128
  before and after of, xvi, 84-85,
    166-67, 169, 172-73, 212-14
  being-time and, 141
  body and, 93
  enlightenment in, 99
  independent aspects of, 86, 92,
    166-67, 170-71
  multiplicity of, 167
  passage of, 177-79
  reflections in, 97
  reifying, avoiding, 176-77
  as sacred space, 134
  seven primary aspects, 169-70
  time-being as simultaneously
    presencing, 173-75
  as unique and universal,
    simultaneously, 109
Dharma practice, 28
  with all beings, 188
  continuous, 101, 113, 137, 160-62, 166,
    174-75
  Dōgen's view of, 8
  duality and, 39
  investigating, 19
  learning, 43
  necessity of, 158

  purpose, 161
  sanzen, meanings of, 70
  stopping, 118-19
  viewing one's own as small, 104-5
Dharma wheel
  limitless (mutan), 145-47, 253n1
  turning, xvi, 91, 205, 213
dharma-body of Buddha, 117, 248n2
dharmas
  all as Buddha Dharma, xv, 30, 32,
    199-200, 201, 202, 203
  buddha-ness of, 112
  co-causality of, 81
  integrating with, 70
  as neither good nor evil, 72, 73
  one, realizing, xviii, 130, 132-36, 140,
    141, 142, 221-24
  self and, 49, 66
  as true form, 80, 241n3
  as universal and particular, 174
discriminating mind, xvi, xviii, 79, 81,
  144, 145, 159, 222, 223
discrimination, two kinds, 14
Dōgen
  disciples, 190-91
  how to study, 17-21
  language use, 191, 192
  with tenzo in China, 3-6, 7, 9
  writings of, 2-3, 32, 158, 172
doubt, 16, 19, 101, 127, 129
dropping off body and mind, xvi, 63, 112
  actualizing/verifying, 123-24, 208-9
  definition, 235n2
  in everyday activities, 133
  fixed beliefs and, 83
  self and, 15, 238n1
  as skillful means, 232n38
  in zazen, 68-71

effort, 10, 30, 33, 116, 118-19
  collaborative, 36, 129, 136-37, 138
  continual/sustained, 8, 24, 120

delusion and, 74
fruit of, 147
hidden, 159
need for, 4, 12, 143, 158, 161-62
persevering in, 39, 45
See also total exertion
eight understandings of great persons,
184-85, 259n8
Eihei Kōroku (Dōgen's Extensive
Record), 69, 70, 107, 188, 191
Eihei Shingi (Pure Standards for the
Zen Community), 133
Eiheiji temple, 191
Ejō, 3, 190, 191
emptiness, 26, 38, 233n11
all dharmas marked by, 35
focusing on, 107
form and, 65-66
misunderstandings about, 98-99
Engo, 205
enlightenment, 137
actualizing, xviii, 145, 147, 166
aspiration for, 127-28, 129
meaning of, 131
misunderstanding, 107
personality and, 99
responding from, 50-51, 99-100
symbol, 97
translation of, 183-84, 186, 189
equalizing inequality, 25-27, 124, 198, 199
equanimity, 13, 39, 99, 124, 138
eternal now (nikon), 177, 179-81, 258n30
ever-presence, xviii, 157, 158, 225-26,
227-28
everyday life
attention in, 60
as Dharma gate, 7-8
Dharma incorporated into, 13, 21,
107-8, 114
enlightened responses in, 50-51,
99-100
experiential immersion in, 122-23

as field of awakening, 9
investigating, 143
motivation in, 9
practice actualized in, 5, 6, 8-9,
116-18, 125-26
practice-realization in, 10-11, 132-34
self, reifying in, 81-83
zazen and, 134
everydayness, state of, 8

faith, 36, 37, 66, 83, 129, 157, 187
Fazang, 168, 238n12
form realm, 243n3
four dhyana, 70, 239n14
four formless absorptions, 70, 239n14
"Fukanzazengi" (Recommending Zen
to All People), 2, 32
on human form, 128
on intellect, 157
on nonthinking, 135
on practice-realization, 4, 8, 154

"Gabyō" (A Painted Rice Cake), 61-62, 64
Gakudō Yōjinshū (Points to Watch in
Practicing the Way), 44
gender normativity, 255n5
genjōkōan
genjō, specific meanings, 1, 23-24
intimacy and, 149
kōan, specific meanings, 24-27, 124,
198-99, 233n8
meanings of term, 27-28, 123-25, 195,
197-98
"Genjōkōan," 11, 43, 163-64, 187, 188
audience for, 32, 154
on buddha mind, bringing forth, 16
composition, xix, 2-3, 32, 234n3
how to read, 18
opening lines, variant
interpretations, 32, 185, 234n4
placement in Shōbōgenzō, 1, 4, 9,
229n2, 229n8

"Genjōkōan" (continued)
    practice in everyday life in, 13–14
    purpose, 33
    on realization, 57
    on time, 172
    title, meaning of, 23–29, 196, 197–99
    on "to study the self," 15, 232n38
    and "Uji," relationship of, 165–66
    on verification, 70
Gensha, 205
Goshō (Okikigakishō "Genjōkōan")
    composition, 190
    on genjōkōan, meaning of term, 23,
        24–25
    history, 192
    importance of, 192–93
    on practice-verification and self,
        45–46
    purpose, 191
    shushō translation in, 183
    title, meaning of, 190
"Gyōji" (Continuous Practice), 101, 137,
    159–60, 174–75

"Hachi Dainin Gaku" (Eight
    Understandings of a Great Person),
    184–85, 259n8
Haku Kyoi, 228
harm, 37, 42–43, 73, 101
Heart Sutra, 2, 35, 65–66
Heine, Steven, 3, 4, 154
"Hotsu Bodai Shin" (Bringing Forth the
    Mind of Bodhi), 16, 136, 163, 169,
    180, 185, 260n11
Huayan Buddhism, 168
    mutual penetration and identity in,
        59, 65, 174, 257n23
    ten mysteries of, 238n9
human rebirth, 128–29, 161–62

ignorance, 75, 201
impermanence, 211

accepting, 39
    of dharma positions, 178
    of form world, 168–69
    inter-being and, 173
    mark of, 25, 233n7
    of self, 66, 79, 82, 87, 90, 91
intellect, 24, 43
    Dōgen and, 4, 6, 7
    and intuition, integrating, 66
    letting go of, 56
    limits of, 39, 95, 157
    practice and, 122
    in studying Dōgen, 17, 21
inter-being, 31, 50, 57, 89
    buddha-nature and, 77
    confusion about, 79
    dharma positions and, 86, 177
    dharmas and, 66, 232n38
    enacting, 175
    functioning process of, 93
    mutual, 257n23
    nonduality as, 233n11
    practice-realization and, 10, 52–53
    transmogrification and, 92
interconnection, 21, 28, 63, 88–89, 113
interdependence, 7, 12
intimacy
    with Dharma, 224
    Dōgen's understanding of, 143
    translations and meanings, 148–49,
        245n4
    viewing and, xviii, 145, 147

Jianyuan, 92–93, 244n7
"Jinzū" (Mystical Power), 8–9
"Jisho-zanmai" (Samadhi as
    Experience of the Self), 64
joy, 13, 28
judgment, 38, 52–53, 126, 148

"Kannon" (Avalokiteśvara), 20
karma, 40, 50, 81, 86, 87, 98, 171, 173

Kasulis, Thomas, 4, 6
"Kattō" (Twining Vines), 38, 235n9
"Keisei Sanshiki" (Sound of the Stream, Form of the Mountain), 55, 121
kenshō, 60-61
Kim, Hee-Jin, 57-58, 238n9
  on activity-unremitting, 160
  on daily life as practice, 125
  on discrimination, 14
  on exertion-and-verification and life-span, 119, 120
  on intimacy, 143, 148
  on passage, 177
  on shō, 183
Kinst, Daijaku, 131
knowing, 141, 142, 144, 149, 188
koans, 17
Kōshōshi temple, 2, 191
"Kūge" (Flowers of Emptiness), 45
Kyōgō, 23, 75, 208
  on all dharmas as Buddha Dharma, 199-200, 203
  on Baoche's fan, 225-26
  biographical information, 191
  on boat metaphor, 80, 211
  on body/mind, 207-8
  on buddhas, 206-7
  on buddhas and living beings, 206
  on delusion, 107
  on Dharma and living beings, relationship of, 222-23
  on Dharma filling body and mind, 219
  on firewood and ash, 213-14
  on life and death, 86
  on moon's reflection, 216
  on original person, 209-10
  on "person," 49
  on practice-verification, 204
  on rebirth, 91
  on self, 200-201
  on Shōbōgenzō title, 196
  on sutra titles, 195

  on time, 102-3
  on total immersion, 58-59
  on trace of realization, 71
  on verification, 51
  on wind metaphor, 158
  on zenki, 162
Kyoto, 191, 192
Kyushu, 3

labeling, 30-31, 71, 86, 104, 180
Layman Pang (a.k.a. Layman Ho-on), 8-9
Leighton, Daniel, 70
lineage, 129, 172
Lingyun Zhiqin, 140
Linji Yixuan, 247n4
listening and hearing, 111-12, 113-14, 208
Lotus Sutra, 167, 168, 195, 198, 202, 208

Magu, Mountain, 151
Mahākāśyapa, 196
Mahāparinirvāṇa Sutra, 226
Mahayana Buddhism, 161-62
  everyday life in, 38
  goal of, 230n19
  Heart Sutra's centrality in, 2
  rebirth in, 91, 243n4
"Maka Hannya Haramitsu" (Manifestation of Great Prajna), 2, 253n7
Manzan Dōhaku, 192
Mazu Daoyi, 254n1
"Menju" (Face-to-Face Conferral), 76, 185
Menzan Zuihō, 192, 259n7
merit field, 161
mind
  bringing forth, 163
  Dōgen's definition, 241-42n3
  as ground, 221
  ordinary, 14
  self-nature of, mistaken views, xvi, 79, 80, 83, 211-12

mind (*continued*)
  Triple World as one, 81, 220-21, 224, 226, 227
mindfulness, 135
"Mitsugo" (Secret Words), 148
motivation, 9, 72, 160, 161
"Muchū Setsumu" (Preaching a Dream in a Dream), 145, 146
"Mujō Seppō" (Insentient Beings Speak Dharma), 111-12
mutual identity, 59, 175, 238n12, 257n23
mutual penetration, 59, 238n12, 257n23

Nagarjuna, 250n1
nihilism, 46, 233n11
nirvana, 6, 33, 126, 137, 180
  as already available, 11-12
  birth-and-death as, 10, 230n19, 244n9, 250n8
  as fourth mark, 233n7
nirvana separate from rebirth, 230n19
Nishiari Bokusan, 48, 49, 113, 120, 193
no-arising, xvi, 90, 91-92, 93, 212-13, 215
no-inherent-existence, 26, 31, 35, 36-37
nonbeing (*mu*), 146, 149, 197, 200-201, 202, 220, 225, 250n1
nonduality, 51, 224, 233n11
  in being-time, 180
  of birth and death, 92
  of cause and effect, 87-88, 175
  dharmas as, 34
  duality and, 26, 58
  experiencing, 72
  of humans and the Way, 58
  and impermanence, relationship of, 173
  misunderstandings, 46
  of time and space, 128
nonobstruction, xvii, 57, 96, 100, 102-3, 175, 216, 218, 245n1
nonseparation mode, 56-57
no-perishing, xvi, 90, 91-92, 93, 212-13, 215

no-self, 14, 25, 28, 35, 53, 233n7
not knowing, 19, 140, 142, 144, 149, 188, 224
not-self, not-other, 56

oceanic beings, cooperative ecosystem of, 161
Okumura, Shohaku, xix, 70
  on *genjō*, 24, 253-54n3
  hand example, 27
  on *kōan*, 124
  on 100 percent, 170
  on *shushō*, 183, 184
  on study, 66-67, 187, 239n5
  on verification, 185
omnipresence, 227, 228
100 percent, 85-86, 94, 97, 170, 171, 179, 221, 244n10
one-flavor Zen, 7, 230-31n22
original face, 152, 155
original lot, 25, 26-27, 74-75, 199, 233n8
original person, 74, 77-78, 79, 209-11, 226, 240n1

Parinirvāṇa Sutra, 196
particularity, 57, 58, 61-62, 65, 86, 128
passageless passage, 128, 169, 177, 179
penetration, 159, 188
  of Dharma, xviii, 139, 140, 141, 143, 144, 149, 218-20
  of one dharma, 199-200, 221-24
people (*nin*), 74, 240n1
perception, xv, xvii, 14-17, 55, 207-8, 218, 220
  buddhas and, 206-7
  deceptive, 80, 83, 110
  Dharma and, 111
  immersion of, 57-59
  limited, 23-24, 108, 109
  nondual, 57-58
  nonperpetual, 65

shifts in, 109
without subject or object, 56
pivot-state, 118, 249n4
practice-enlightenment, 121
  carrying oneself toward, xv, 41-46,
    49, 53
  expressing, 144
  purpose, xviii, 130
  through self, xv, 15, 41-46, 49, 81,
    203-5, 235n2
  as way of living beings, xvii, 115, 119-21
  See also shushō
practice-realization, 7, 11, 29, 50, 258n1
  accommodation by, 116
  in action, 13
  actualizing, 123
  with all beings, 69, 137
  as basis of Way, 8
  commitment to, 118
  comparison and, 104
  continuous, 141, 143
  continuously verifying Dharma, 52
  dharma positions and, 85
  Dōgen's view of, 33, 130-31
  embodying, 151, 162
  expressing, 177
  fruition of, 147
  ground of, 121
  interdependence of, 12
  intimacy and, 16, 149
  oneness of, 107-8
  preconceptions about, 14
  problems-delusion and, 38
  simultaneity of, 185
  translation of, 10, 230n21, 231n28
  See also shushō
practice-verification, 10, 29, 258n1
  conveying oneself toward, 203-5
  ground of, 121
  in presencing moment, 11-12
  simultaneity of, 185
  as way of living beings, 221-25

See also shushō
Prajñāpāramitā Sutra, 195
precepts, 233-34n11
  bodhisattva, 150
  three pure, 72, 126, 250n9
presencing, 11-12, 67, 81, 93, 132, 166,
  175, 180-81
  of buddha-nature, 155
  as codependent and cooperative, 16
  of Dharma, 75, 155
  of dharma positions, 103, 171
  entering, 58-59
  in genjō, 24
  nonthinking and, 135
  and practice, simultaneity of, 159
  unique being-time in, 109

reality, 95
  actualization and actualized, xviii,
    122-26, 221
  altruism of, 113
  as community of all beings, 155
  foundational manifestation of, 160,
    255n5
  functioning of, 71, 141, 146
realization, 16, 186
  actualizing, 131
  attaining, xvi-xvii, 96, 102, 103,
    215-18
  as attentive response, 97, 98, 99
  beyond realization, xv, 41, 48-54, 56,
    60, 205-6
  boundaries and, 75
  as collaborative/relational, 36, 51
  enacting, 171
  and everyday life, relationship of, 33
  original, 71, 131, 208
  preconception about, 71-72
  as suchness, 47
  total, 24, 204-5, 233n3
  as ungraspable, 15, 63, 71-73, 208-9
  See also under delusion

realized response, 24, 47, 57, 85, 97-98, 100-101, 111, 116
rebirth, 90, 93, 120, 121, 244n9, 257n20
　continuity in, 243n3
　karma and, 173
　non-Buddhist views of, 91, 213, 214
Record of Kenzei, 4, 8
Reiun Shigon, 55-56, 60
relationships, vertical and horizontal, 25-26
Rujing, 2, 69, 152, 253n7

sahā world, 101, 121, 224, 246n7
Saichō, 168
samsara, 16-17, 19, 120, 244n9
San Francisco Zen Center, 6
"Sangai-yuishin" (Three Worlds are Inseparable from Mind), 81, 241n3
sangha, 76-77, 78, 125, 158
"Sansui Kyō" (Sutra of Mountains and Water), 112-13, 187
Śāriputra, 35
satori, 183-84
self, 20-21, 203-5
　attachment to erroneous views of, 75
　attachment to itself, 79
　in delusion, 42-44
　as dharma position, 166-67, 180, 181, 182
　fixed, absence of, xv, xvi, 18, 30, 34-37, 50, 65, 67, 79, 80, 166, 200-201, 212
　forgetting, xvi, 63, 67-68, 117, 166, 208-9, 235n2
　getting rid of, 64, 238n1
　as life, 33, 235n7
　limited view of, going beyond, 44-46
　and living beings, as synonymous, 204
　metaphor for, 97
　misperception of, 80, 175
　as not inherently existing, 36-37, 92, 167
　as particular and universal, 141

　as permanent, 80, 81, 83, 84, 86, 91
　personal experience of, 85-88
　in practice-realization, role of, xv, 15, 41-46, 49, 81, 203-5, 235n2
　and realization, cofunctioning of, 96-97, 100-102
　reifying, 171
　studying, xvi, 63, 64-67, 208-9
self and other, 14
　actualization and, 186
　body and mind of, 232n38
　boundary between, transitional, 140
　integrating, 117
　intimacy with, 149
　nondual perception of, 57-58
　permeability of, 139
　universal view of, 28
self-centeredness, 12
self-stability, 42
self-sufficiency, 174
Senika theory, 241n1
Senne, Yōkō, 1, 209
　on all dharmas as Buddha Dharma, 200
　on Baoche, 226-28
　biographical information, 191
　on bird's life, 121, 123
　on boat metaphor, 80, 212, 219-20
　on body and mind, 211-12
　on buddha, 207
　on Buddha Dharma, all things as, 103
　on comparisons, 104, 217-18
　on delusion and realization, relationship of, 203, 204-5
　on Dharma, seeking, 75
　on Dharma filling body and mind, 141-42, 224-25
　on Dharma transmission, 210-11
　on firewood and ash, 214-15
　on fixed as not fixed, 149-50
　on forgetting, 68
　on *genjōkōan*, 28, 123, 197-99, 250n1
　on good and evil, 72, 73

on inequality and equality, 26
on life and death, 92
on moon's reflection, 208, 218
on ocean, 109
on permanence, 83
on practice-verification, 223
on school's name, 196–97
on total immersion, 58
on Triple World, 81, 247n10
on wind metaphor, 158–59
on zazen, 134
on *zenki*, 162
sentiency, 143
sentient beings
    and buddhas, relationship of, xv,
        33–35, 41, 46–48, 202, 205–6, 228
    as ever-present, 227
    three marks in, 25, 233n7
Seppō, 205
Shākyamuni Buddha, 180, 224
Shantideva; *Guide to the Bodhisattva
    Way of Life*, 43
shikantaza (just sitting), 69
"Shizen Biku" (Monk of the Fourth-
    Stage Meditation), 173
"Shoaku-makusa" (Not Doing Evil
    Deeds), 72, 132, 209, 227–28
Shōbōgenzō, 3
    ancestors' sayings in, 227–28
    complications of, 1, 229n2, 229n8
    dharma positions in, 169, 257n10
    modern study of, 192, 193
    time in, 172
    title, meaning of, 196
    titles of fascicles, 23
Shōbōgenzō Zuimonki, 78, 112
"Shohō Jissō" (The Reality of All
    Things), 94
"Shōji" (Birth and Death), 10, 32–33,
    47–48, 169, 172, 243n1
"Shukke Kudoku" (Merit of Leaving
    Home), 128

shushō
    fluidity of, 189
    as practice-verification, 186–88
    translations of, variant, 183–85
sickness, 87
simultaneous establishment of
    concealment and disclosure
    principle, 58, 238n9
six senses, 111
six tastes, 133, 251n7
skandhas (aggregate), 100, 243n3
skillful means, 12, 89, 202, 232n38
Small Vehicle, 214, 223
Sōtō Zen (C. Caodong), 191
    enlightenment in, 186
    formal training in, 6
    "Genjōkōan," role of, 1
    in Japan, introduction of, 2
    name of, 196–97
    rituals, purpose of, 38
    in United States, 9, 231n27
Sōtō Zen Text Project, 20, 74, 119, 120,
    184, 253n3
soul, permanent, 80, 81, 83, 241n1,
    257n20
"Soul of the Ocean" (PBS), 161
spiritual journey, 127, 180–81
Śrīmālādevī Siṃhanāda Sutra, 195
Stone, Jacqueline, 167
student-teacher relationship, 151–53
    importance of, 76–77
    practice-verification in, 185–86, 187
    questions and answers in, 153–54
    transmission in, 155–56, 157
study and learning, 65, 67, 141, 172–73,
    187, 239n5
suchness, 8, 12, 47, 72–73, 155, 185
    abiding in, 166, 167, 174
    according with conditions, 168–69,
        256n6
    as basic nature, 161
    conceptual markers and, 146

suchness (*continued*)
  dharma positions and, 85, 95
  in *genjō*, 24
  marks of, 16
  synonyms, 256n5
suffering, 28, 38
  alleviating, 175
  bodhisattvas and, 45
  causing, 146, 176
  from delusion, 44
  emptiness and, 26
  liberation from, 16
  mark of, 25, 233n7
  of others, awareness of, 43–44
  precepts and, 233–34n11
  relationship with, transforming, 39,
    99, 131
sutras, 114, 195–96
Suzuki, D. T., 183
Suzuki, Shunryu, 39, 97, 98

Tanahashi, Kazuaki, 48, 119, 120, 139
Tassajara Zen Mountain Center, 43
teachers
  importance of, 112, 125, 185
  role of, 21, 64, 154, 158
  teaching devices, use of, 159, 226
  See also student-teacher relationship
Tendai school, 6, 167–68, 191
Tenpuku era, xix
"Tenzo Kyōkun" (Instructions for the
    Cook), 3
  on Dharma in all activities, 13
  on meeting *tenzo*, 4–5
  on one dharma, practicing, 133
tetralemma (fourfold negation), 250n1
Theravada tradition, 91, 230n19
The Thinker (Rodin), 60
thoughts, 76, 81–83, 135
three marks of existence, 233n7
Three Treasures, 125, 157
three virtues, 133, 251n7

thusness, 148–49
time(s), 34–35, 47, 77–78, 83, 177, 215
  awakening and, 98
  Buddha Dharma and, 30–31
  day, hours in, 235n7
  investigating, xvii, 96, 102–4, 216, 217
  life and death in, xvi, 90, 243n1
  as neither good nor evil, 72, 73
  past and future cut off, xvi, 84, 86, 92,
    166–67, 212, 214
  sequential, 128, 172, 180
total engagement, 59, 61, 118, 179, 247n4
total exertion, 13, 125, 231n34
  of all beings, 252n18
  of one dharma, 58, 61–62
  in practice, 12–13
total function principle, 26
  in life and death, 86, 92, 200, 213, 215,
    242n4
  virtue in, 113
  See also *zenki* (total dynamic
    function)
transmission, xviii, 209–11, 225
  oral, 213
  person-to-person, 76–77, 134
  in student-teacher relationship,
    155–56, 157
  warm-hand-to-warm-hand, 155
Triple World, 80, 81, 89, 212, 220–21,
    224, 226–27, 241n3
true form, 80, 202, 212, 256n5
true nature, 78, 233n8
  of all beings, 24, 25, 64, 78
  awakening to, 75
  of Dharma, 12
  of one thing, realizing, 130
  of self, 63, 66, 80
"Tsuki" (The Moon), 117, 248n2
two sides of one action, 27–28

Uchiyama, Kōshō, 135, 253–54n3
"Uji" (Being Time), 10, 12, 85

on dharma positions, seven primary aspects, 169-70
on dharma stages/positions, 168, 176
on donkey and horse, 140
on doubt, 19
on encountering, 67, 68
on entire being or entire world, 17
on exist over, exist as, 174
on immediate now, 179, 181
on ordinary views and Dharma, 75
on passage, 171, 177-78, 179, 244n10
on practice and attainment, 125
on practicing with all beings, 136, 252n18
on realization and delusion, 33
on time, 103
use of language in, 20
unambiguous cause-and-effect, 145, 147
universals and particulars
  body and person as, 50
  in dharma positions, 173-74, 175-76
  holding both, 36
  integrating, 37-38
  intersection of, 24-25

Vairocana Buddha, 224
verification, xvi, 51, 63, 136, 162-63, 239n2
  actualizing, 222
  Dōgen's definition, 68-69
  and exertion, oneness of, 120
  misunderstanding, 186-87
  translations, 52, 107, 184, 185
views
  fixed, 37, 88, 142
  holding on to, 82-83
  honoring different, 109-10
  mistaken, 201, 211, 212, 214
  not fixed, xviii, 140, 145, 147, 149, 222, 224, 253n3
  ordinary, 75, 103
  reifying one's own, 42-46

of universal inter-being, 89
virtue, 112, 113, 114, 161, 176, 248n13. See also three virtues
vows, 129. See also bodhisattva vow

Waddell, Norrman, 24, 44, 112, 119
water, four appearances, xvii, 106, 109, 218, 219, 247n9
wheel of birth and death, 91, 243n4
wisdom, 25, 36, 89, 144, 146, 184-85
words and phrases, 5, 6, 7
Wu, Emperor, 226

Xuansha Shibei (Zongyi), 94-95

Yasutani Roshi, Hakuun, 152
Yō Kōshū, xix, 2-3, 32
Yōkōji temple, 191, 192
Yuanwu Keqin, 92, 242n4
Yuehshan Hungtao, 252n14
"Yuibutsu Yobutsu" (Only a Buddha and a Buddha), 11, 69, 71, 72, 127, 129

zazen, 112, 143-44, 162-63
  as becoming buddha, 223
  Dōgen's belief in, 5-6
  dropping body and mind in, 69-71
  importance of, 9, 231n27
  inclusiveness in, 70-71
  one dharma penetrated in, 134
  preconceptions about, 76
  in Shōbōgenzō, 231n26
  "Think of not thinking" instruction, 135, 252n14
  time and, 172
"Zazengi" (Principles of Seated Meditation), 134
Zen Master of Mt. Magu. See Baoche (a.k.a. Hotetsu of Mount Mayoku)
zenki (total dynamic function), 26, 155, 160-62, 199, 255n5
"Zenki" (The Whole Works), 92, 118